To: Rev

Thank you

Truths that has

Such A Love For the u

Thereby Causing Me To Search

the Scriptures Leading To the Truths

Found in this Book. I Pray it

Greatly Blesses you

Love in Christ Jesus

Jim E Cosgrove

MW01601485

Mysteries of the Kingdom Revealed

Luis E. Caquias

BECAUSE IT IS GIVEN UNTO YOU TO KNOW THE MYSTERIES OF THE KINGDOM. . .
(Matthew 13:11)

ISBN 0-7414-4393-7

All scriptures referenced are taken from the King James Version (KJV) of the Bible. (Cambridge: Cambridge) 1769.

All definitions given from the original Hebrew and Greek words are taken from *The Strong's Exhaustive Concordance of the Bible*. Copyright 1980 by Abingdon Press Nashville, Tennessee

All definitions given are taken from *Webster's New Collegiate Dictionary* Copyright 1979 by G. & C. Merriam Company. Springfield, Massachusetts

Portions of the book *A Divine Revelation of Hell*, authored by Mary K. Baxter, copyright year 1993 and published by Whitaker House, (www.whitakerhouse.com) (pp. 191-193). Used with permission of Whitaker house.

All other references are as noted.

All capitalizations and underlined emphasis in the passages of scriptures quoted are added by the author.

Published by:

PUBLISHING.COM

1094 New DeHaven Street, Suite 100
West Conshohocken, PA 19428-2713
Info@buybooksontheweb.com
www.buybooksontheweb.com
Toll-free (877) BUY BOOK
Local Phone (610) 941-9999
Fax (610) 941-9959

Printed in the United States of America
Printed on Recycled Paper
Published August 2008

FOREWORD

by Dr. Jesus A. Caquias

The Christian Bible, comprised of various translations of the Hebrew Old Testament and the Greek New Testament, is the premiere religious book of the entire world. Hebrew and Greek are languages that do not have separate characters for numbers; each letter of these languages represents a specific enunciation and number, each having a value different from the others. Ivan Panin, a Russian mathematician in the early 1900s, demonstrated that the Bible was composed of supernatural books containing thousands of mathematical relationships, which are so intricately related that they could not have been written by mere men but had to have been supernaturally designed through the thousands of years that these books were written.[1]

Unlike all other religious books, the Christian Bible, comprised of the Hebrew Old Testament and the Greek New Testament, also contains thousands of prophesies that have, against all odds, come to pass, odds that would stagger the imagination, demonstrating that these things could not have been known had there not been supernatural revelation. Computers have revealed that not only does the text reveal ancient prophesy; there are also modern day prophesies revealed in the sequence of letters of various books. This revelation of modern day prophesies have become known as Bible codes.

---

[1] Ivan Panin, Bible Chronology, 1950, The Association of The Covenant People

iii

The Old Testament reveals the character of God and man's depravity, and the New Testament reveals God's love and His Salvation through His son, Jesus. In fact, the name *Jesus* in standard Hebrew, "יהשצ" (read from right to left), is pronounced "yahshua," meaning "salvation." While some argue that God does not have a son, the Old Testament in Proverbs 30 verse 4 declares:

[4]*Who hath ascended up into Heaven, or descended? who hath gathered the wind in his fists? who hath bound the waters in a garment? who hath established all the ends of the earth? what is his name, and what is his son's name, if thou canst tell? (KJV)* [2]

That it was commonly accepted that God must, therefore, have a son must be accepted as fact if we accept what history has to teach us.

This Jesus, called "the Christ," or "the Messiah," and in standard Hebrew, "Moshiac" (משיח), meaning the anointed one, is accepted as the one spoken of in the book of Daniel 9:25, where it states, "from the going forth of the commandment to restore and to build Jerusalem unto the Messiah the Prince...."[3] Moshiac is also the name of Moses, Exodus 2:10, in this instance also meaning to draw out, or to deliver, or preserve, or save. Moses himself prophesied that the day would come when God would raise up, from within the nation of Israel, a prophet who would be like Him. This coming prophet would speak divine words, and those who

[2] Proverbs 30:4, The King James Version, (Cambridge: Cambridge)1769, The Ultimate Bible Reference Library, Thomas Nelson, Inc.,1998,2001, Logos Research Systems, Inc., 1995-1997.

[3] Daniel 9:25, The King James Version, (Cambridge: Cambridge) 1769, The Ultimate Bible Reference Library, Thomas Nelson, Inc.,1998,2001, Logos Research Systems, Inc., 1995-1997.

refused to hear His words would give account for such refusal (Deuteronomy 18:15–19). This accountability aspect of the Messiah is reiterated in Proverbs 8:35-36: "For whoso findeth me finds life, and shall obtain favor of the Lord. But he that sinneth against me wrongeth his own soul: all that hate me love death" (KJV).[4] Proverbs 8:30 in the original Hebrew states that this Messiah was an "amora" (אמון): an artist, faithful workman, confidant, or craftsman, co-creator with God. John 1:1-3 states it more bluntly.

"In the beginning was the Word, and the Word was with God and the Word was God. The same was in the beginning with God. All things were made by him, and without him was not any thing made that was made" (KJV).[5]

This Jesus, also called the Christ, the son of God and co-creator with the Father, was sent by the Father to be sacrificed as a ransom for the sins of the world. God, being perfect, a divine judge, has a greater duty than any judge would on Earth; as such, He is obligated to punish our sins. No right judge on Earth, after finding an individual guilty, would let that individual go without some punishment. Violators of God's standard are punished with death. If God were not to be so authoritarian, He could not be God, but because He is God, He is obligated to punish those who violate His standard. Being a loving and merciful God, He has given us grace and leniency through His son, Jesus, by permitting Him to take our punishment

---

[4] Proverbs 835-36, The King James Version, (Cambridge: Cambridge) 1769, The Ultimate Bible Reference Library, Thomas Nelson, Inc.,1998,2001, Logos Research Systems, Inc., 1995-1997.

[5] John 1:1, The King James Version, (Cambridge: Cambridge) 1769, The Ultimate Bible Reference Library, Thomas Nelson, Inc.,1998,2001, Logos Research Systems, Inc., 1995-1997.

by dying, being punished for the sins that all of us have committed.

Through Jesus, God not only demonstrates His love to us, but also makes Himself tangible, a real being rather than a vague God somewhere out there with whom we have no tangible way to interact. God, through Jesus, made our relationship with Him tangible; a personal relationship with Him is now not only possible but mandated. Jesus came to show us how to have this special relationship with God through us becoming like Him. By taking Jesus into our being, becoming one with Him in our thoughts, actions and deeds, becoming a true likeness of Him, we can have a special relationship with God the father. The true followers of Christ's teachings are known as Christians. While many call themselves Christians, few are truly "Christ like."

No other person that ever lived acquired the status that Jesus acquired. Jesus was perfect before God. He had to be perfect to serve as the unblemished sacrifice for our sins. All other so-called gods were imperfect. Even Mary, the mother of Jesus, who is worshiped by some as if she were a deity, is imperfect; if she were a perpetual virgin and thus considered sinless, she failed because she did not consummate her marriage to Joseph, a mandate of all married women.

Anyone who reads about the life of Jesus in the Bible can only conclude that His life was consistently the purest of anyone in recorded history. None of His challengers were able to bring any valid charge against Him with respect to the laws of God. As written in Dr. Ravi Zacharias's book, *Jesus Among Other Gods*, all of the great religious leaders in history, leaders such as Buddha, Krishna, Mohammed, and the great prophets, struggled with staying free of the perceived wrongs of their day at some point or another in their lives. The Koran documents Moses asking for forgiveness after slaying the Egyptian (Surah 28,16), and Abraham asking for forgiveness on the Day of Judgment (Surah 26,82). Mohammad was told to ask for forgiveness for his faults in Surah 47 and 48. Mohammed was married to eleven wives, clearly an indication that he had failed on multiple occasions and dealt with lust at different times in his life, something that no one could accuse Jesus of. Krishna is recorded in the Bhagavad-Gita as having encounters with the milkmaids, and Buddha's multiple incarnations implied having lived imperfect lives. [6]

Jesus did not come seeking the truth; He claimed He was the truth. This one claim puts Jesus above all others. "I am the way, the truth, and the life. No one comes to the Father except through Me" (John 14:6). In fact, He said He was more than just the way; He said, "I and the Father are one." Regardless of how you interpret this, Jesus could not have said these things unless these words had some profound meaning, and this places Him in a category far above any would-be prophet or religious leader in history. It is recorded that Jesus could still the wind, heal the sick, make fine wine from water, miraculously multiply bread loaves, raise the dead, and walk on water. He was either who He said He was or He was the greatest imposter to have ever walked the Earth. Yet, He claimed He came to die for our sins.

When the governor of Judea, Pontius Pilate, asked Him, "Do You not know that I have authority

[6] JESUS Among Other Gods, Author: Ravi Zacharias, Copyright 2000 Publish by Word Publishing Nashville Tenn. A Thomas Nelson Company (pp. 40-42)

to release You, and I have authority to crucify You?" Jesus answered, "You would have no authority over Me, unless it had been given from above" (John 19:10, 11). When Jesus was arrested and one of His disciples tried to defend Him, drawing his sword and striking the servant of the high priest, cutting off his ear, Jesus stopped him, saying, "Put your sword away, for those who take the sword will perish by the sword. Do you not think that I cannot now pray to my Father, and He will provide me with more than twelve legions of angels?" (Matthew 26:52, 53). The Gospel account of the arrest, trial, and crucifixion of Jesus indicates that He made no attempt to defend Himself or to escape His situation. As written in Isaiah, "He was oppressed and He was afflicted, yet He opened not His mouth; He was led as a lamb to the slaughter, And as a sheep before its shearers is silent, So He opened not His mouth" (53:7).

There have been innumerable attacks on the biblical account, most of which involve perceived discrepancies with findings in science or history. These are perceptions because no one can truly know what happened; many facts are unknown or are biased in the mind of the claimant. One of the strongest attacks is the belief in evolution. In fact, many believers accept evolution as the method that God used to bring mankind about. Yet, for nearly a hundred years, geneticists in thousands of universities worldwide have been exposing the tiny fruit fly, a species of fly called the drosophila, to multiple mutagens, agents that cause mutations), such as radiation, ultraviolet rays, and various chemicals, effects comparable to tens of millions of years of evolution, and yet have failed to produce a different species of fly. Taken together, this has been the longest-running experiment dealing with evolution, an experiment that has demonstrated that mutations serve for adaptation but have no effect in producing new species.

Others argue that long before the Bible account, mankind existed in various parts of the world. The fact is that we do not really know how long Adam spent in the Garden of Eden or after Eve came onto the scene or where Cain went when he was sent away after killing Abel. Cain was cursed with a visible sign and left to establish another society in some other part of the world. We do not know what that sign was, but could it have been one of the signs that mark a different race today?

The Chinese are said to have existed long before the Bible account, but have they? Are they Adam's descendents through one of his sons, or the result of the great scattering after God caused mass confusion at the building of the Tower of Babel? Genesis 11:19 discusses how God scattered the people by confusing their languages 500 years before the Chinese language came into existence. This is said to have occurred about 2500 BC.

During the first three dynasties discovered in China, the Hsia dynasty, the Shang dynasty, and the Chou dynasty, the Chinese people worshiped the creator God Shang Di. The biblical account of creation and the ancient Chinese characters derived from a primitive understanding of creation are so much aligned that one would have to conclude that the ancient Chinese were familiar with the biblical account of creation early on. A website called Ancient Chinese Language of God, (at www. wbschool.org/chinesecharacters.htm), illustrates how the Chinese characters depict the biblical story and thus support the biblical account.[7]

---

[7] www.wbschool.org/chinesecharacters (February 23, 2006)

The revelation that all present day humans came from one woman, who is identified as "Eve," as revealed by genetic studies of mitochondrial DNA, is another piece of evidence in support of the biblical account. Recent studies on the rate of mutations occurring among humans suggest that this individual may have lived a mere 6000 years ago, a finding that is in line with what is recorded in the Bible.[8]

In the end, it comes down to what individuals want to believe. You can accept that we came about by chance without a purpose or that we were created by a divine being for a special purpose. The call is our own, and each must decide of his own free will. We are the instruments of a great lesson for the heavenly bodies, for our God is building a Holy Kingdom, and all that will reside therein must be worthy of the standing for which they are called.

The Bible teaches us that if we ask God for forgiveness for our sins and ask Jesus to be Lord of our lives and commit to changing our lives to become like Him, He is faithful and forgives us our sins and grants us eternal life. Still, many commit but fail in making the change. This happens because so many fail to fully understand God's word. That is the purpose of this book, to help you understand what Jesus said so that you can truly become like Him. If you have not made a decision to follow Christ, our hopes and prayers are that you will choose to accept and follow Christ as your Lord and savior and that this book helps you in your walk as you are changed to become more like Him.

---

[8] Carl Wieland, A shrinking date for Eve, www.answersingenesis.org/tj/v12/il/eve.asp (February 28, 2006)

Dedications

This book is dedicated first and foremost to God for the privilege, the honor, the opportunity, the pleasure, and the time that He has given me to see these precious truths in His Word and now share them with all those who are hungry for more of the Word of God.

I also wish to acknowledge my lovely wife, Mary, who has stood alongside me faithfully through all these years while God was working His will in my life. She never failed to pray for me at the times I was not able to pray for myself. I thank God for her faithfulness and unwavering devotion to Him.

I want to dedicate this book to my precious daughter, Catherine, as well. I pray that this book will help her to follow in the footsteps of Jesus Christ.

This book is also dedicated to my parents. While I was still a child, they saw the need to repent and turn to God, endeavoring to lead my siblings and me in the way that we should go.

Last but not least, I wish to dedicate this book to every man, woman, boy, and girl upon the face of the earth who truly want to know God and His Son in a more intimate way. May this book bring you into a closer relationship with God and give you a greater love for His blessed Word.

Acknowledgments

The author wishes to acknowledge the following people who have helped make this book a reality:

My brother, Dr. Jesus Caquias, for his insights and help in introducing me to the people who have helped with proofreading and with the cover design;

Zito Kare, for designing the cover for this book and the illustrations used in this book;

Mrs. Mary Shute, for the time devoted to proof-reading and making the necessary corrections;

Infinity Publishing, whose concept of publishing has opened the doors for authors like me, who would otherwise not have a platform with which to express ourselves to the world.

A Message to the Nation of Israel

My Dream

I dreamed a dream. In this dream, I was watching over a few children. There were four to six of them, (I cannot remember or see clearly), ranging in ages from one to thirteen. All at once, in the living room of this dwelling, (which seemed to resemble a cave in the side of a mountain, and the windows were just big openings overlooking the seashore), the room began to fill with Jewish children ranging from small children, ages four to six, to older ones, ages fourteen to seventeen or eighteen. They were all children; there were no adults. After they had piled in, hundreds of them, some standing and others sitting, I put on a shirt that one of them gave me. It looked just like the shirts that they were all wearing. They were all dressed in some kind of uniform that resembled the uniforms that parochial schoolchildren wear to school.

Every child's attention was focused on the center of the room, as if this event was something that happened on a regular basis. They were sort of waiting for the teacher to enter in and begin to teach. Out of somewhere, this rabbi appeared, an old man clothed in typical rabbi attire: black suit, yarmulke on his head, long sideburns, beard and hair.

He began to move his hand with an outstretched arm and finger, as if writing in the air. All the motions he made with his finger were performed in the water on the seashore. As he made a circle in the air, the circle was duplicated in the water, as if a large, unseen finger was doing the same motion in the water. Because the water was a light-brown murkiness, as the circle was made in the water, it stayed there because the difference in the shade of murkiness acted as a background to highlight the circle. The rabbi then proceeded to plunge his finger up from underneath the make-believe circle in the air through the center of the circle, and as he did, the unseen finger burst through the middle of the circle in the water, bursting up and back down, resembling the motions of the rabbi with his finger. As the water splashed back down, in the middle of the circle was an imprint of the seal of the rabbi, which was also the seal of the nation of Israel, the Star of David.

Both the children and I were looking back and forth at the rabbi and through the opening of the windows down to the seashore. I learned later that all this was done to serve as a witness that he was a true rabbi and that what he was going to say was truth and they should listen and believe him. This was done, (the motion with the finger and the mimicking in the water), as a sign that everything to follow was from the one that they needed to listen to.

The rabbi began to speak, and he said, "Our forefathers have always wanted to serve the gods of other nations. If the Egyptians had a god, we took that god for our own selves. If, while wandering through the wilderness, another nation had or served a god other than the true and living God, we would forsake our God and start serving their gods. If they offered their children to their gods by making them pass through the fire, we would do the same".

"There has always been a desire to serve the gods of other nations, and our God, the true and living God, told our forefathers that He destroyed those other nations because they served other gods and not Him. He told our forefathers, "Go and serve their gods, and when you get in trouble, call on them and see if they will deliver you in your time of trouble. In times of famine, call on them and see if they will send you rain for your crops and grass for your cattle. I bless, I protect, I keep, I give rain and food to those who serve Me."

The rabbi continued, "We are not blessed. We depend on others to protect us, we depend on others to send us help, food, aid. We are supposed to be a blessing to others, not others a blessing to us. The gentiles have the blessing, the food, the protection. For years, their God has protected them, given them rain in its season. All this has happened for years without number, and if they are serving a false god, then why has God let them go so long and not destroyed them? Why, because they are serving the true and living God and we must recognize it! We must recognize this fact and get on the same page. We must stand behind them, and we must become like dogs and eat of the crumbs that fall from the table of these children of God while there is still hope for us." The rabbi finished speaking, and because I was the only other adult there and because I was a gentile, out of respect towards me, he invited me to say a few words.

I began to speak, but it was not I who spoke but the Spirit of the Lord that spoke through me. I told them, "As gentiles, everything we have from God was given to us through the nation of Israel. If we have anything, a God, a hope, the Word of God, His law, a blessing, it is only because of the nation of Israel. Our God is the God of the nation of Israel. God has not forsaken you or cast you aside; rather, God has used the gentiles to make Israel jealous so that you come back to Him and serve Him according to His Word. You cannot get behind us. You must get in front of us, to guide us and lead us. God forbid that you should become as dogs to eat the crumbs that fall from our Father's table. We must sit together as brothers and feast from our Father's table. We must sit together and eat from the manna that comes from the Word of God".

End of Dream

It is the desire of God to bring the nation of Israel back to its rightful place among the nations of the world, but this will only happen when the nation of Israel returns to God and serves Him according to the knowledge of His Word.

What do you think nation of Israel? *28But what think ye? A certain man had two sons; and he came to the first, and said, Son, go work to day in my vineyard. 29He answered and said, I will not: <u>but afterward he repented,</u> and went. 30And he came to the second, and said likewise. And he answered and said, I go, sir: and went not. 31Whether of them twain did the will of his father? They say unto him, The first. Jesus saith unto them, Verily I say unto you, That the publicans and the harlots go into the kingdom of God before you. 32For John came unto you in the way of righteousness, and ye believed him not: but the publicans and the harlots believed him: and ye, when ye had seen it, <u>repented not afterward,</u> that ye might believe him (Matthew 21:28-32).*

Know for sure Oh nation of Israel, that you are that first son, because the Word of God was preached to you first and you said no to God. However, now you must repent <u>afterward</u> and go work in the Father's vineyard!

I pray that this book will be read by Jewish people all over the world and that their eyes, their ears, and their hearts will be open to the understanding of God's complete Word.

From the Author

It is the sincerest desire of the author to write this book for the purpose of educating those who profess to be Christians, but are not able to get the victory in their lives. There are many Christians who are fighting desires of the flesh and dealing with struggles in their everyday walk with the Lord who may or may not know that their hope is in the Word of God. Furthermore, if they knew His Word with a greater understanding, they would have the knowledge necessary to overcome and be victorious over those things in their lives that keep them from becoming the vessels of honor that God ordained them to be.

Many may or may not realize that the secrets to overcoming adversities, no matter what they are, is hidden in the Word of God, but they are helpless to change their situations because of their lack of knowledge of God's Word. Many of God's people are tired of being tossed to and fro by every wind of doctrine, while many others are unsure if they are even saved. The number of Christians who suffer from the trauma of not knowing who they are in Christ is staggering.

Others fight silent battles of uncertainty of whether God is really with them. Even though the scriptures assure us that He will never leave us or forsake us, many cannot bring themselves to the place where they know, beyond a shadow of a doubt, that God is always with them and in complete control, no matter what the situation or circumstance is in which they may find themselves.

The author believes that there are numerous people throughout the earth, who truly love God but are tired of the superficial preaching that comes from the pulpits, that fails to give them the hope and the understanding, that will bring them to the place in God for which their souls long.

God's people are hungry for a Word from God that will give them a sure foundation that they can stand on. For this reason, the author writes this book. It is by understanding God's Word that a person can know that he is being led of the Spirit of Christ, thereby being the reason for why Jesus, who is the incarnated Word of God, can say, "I am the way, the truth and the life, no man comes to the Father but by me."

Not only is the Bible the Word of God, but it is the very essence of who the Son of God is, the very Spirit, the very hope, as well as the very life that we take on when we read, study, and try to emulate God's Word. The Bible is not just a book with commandments, stories, and events in it that if you understand and follow its instructions you will one day obtain eternal life — and if you consider it that, that is all it is to you — but the Bible is the written form of who Jesus Christ is. He is the spoken Word of God that was made flesh, because God prepared a body for it, to fulfill all of God's requirements, to lead us to Him, to show us the Father, to reveal to us His thoughts, His intentions, and all that we need to know of God and His kingdom. Furthermore, that same spoken Word, which then became the liven Word, is still doing that today in the form of His Written Word. With all the power to save, to heal, to deliver, and to set free, as we endeavor to know Him, seek Him, desire Him, and become like Him, through the very life and power that emanates from the Word of God, His Son, the Lord Jesus Christ.

The author is not saying that the Bible that you may be holding in your hand or have gathering dust on your book shelf is Jesus Christ. However, until you come to the place where you realize that the Bible is the closest that you will ever come to knowing who Jesus is; you will never come to the place where all you live for is for God and His Word. When you understand this, God's Word will stand with you, comfort you, guide you, fight your battles, and do for you all that He promised He would do when He walked the face of the earth.

If you want to know Jesus, to walk with Him, to keep Him ever before you, to see His face, just close your eyes and look at His face; however, do not imagine a face like the one that you see in pictures. Instead, bring His Word before your eyes, meditate upon His Word, speak His Word to yourself, and by all means fall in love with it, for by so doing you will be falling in love with Him.

How can you pray, "Lord, I'm desperate for you, Lord, I hunger for you, Lord, I need more of you" when you are trying to know Him and follow Him apart from His Word?

How can you sing something like "Open my eyes, Lord, I want to see you" when your Bible sits where you put it the last time you went to church, and you only look at it when you are back in church and the minister asks you to open your Bible to a specific scripture?

How can you sing something like "Lord, Lover of my soul" if your life is consumed with the cares of this world, the deceitfulness of riches, and the lust of other things, while, (supposedly), the true lover of your soul is last, (if that), on your list? Jesus said, "Do not labor for the bread that is temporal but for that bread that will last for all eternity," the bread of life, the Word of God, our Lord and savior Jesus Christ.

When you sing a song like, "Lord, you are more precious than silver. Lord, you are more costly than gold. Lord, you are more beautiful than diamonds, and nothing I desire compares to you", do you ever stop to think that these are the same words that King David said when he said, "Thy Word is more to be desired than gold, yea, than much fine gold". Moreover, that he meditated upon His Word in the morning, at noontime, in the evening, and even while he laid upon his bed at night. This is why God said King David was "A man after my own heart."

This book is not intended to entertain, but rather to teach the reader of the hidden mysteries that are found in the Word of God. The mysteries hidden for ages, that are now, in these last of the last days being revealed to His people to know how to come to, and live for God.

No survey has been done to prove the validity of the information contained in this book or whether the information contained in this book will actually help the reader to become the man or woman of God that He has ordained them to be. However, many lives have been transformed and testimonies given of the impact that these revelations have had on the lives of those that have applied the principles contained in this book. The greatest evidence that the author can attest to is to that which has transpired in his own life. This has proven to him that if these truths have worked for him, then these same truths will work in the lives of anyone who knows these truths and applies them to their lives, for the Word of God does not lie. The Word of God neither was nor is sent for one individual, but for all mankind. The Word of God was written to teach, to instruct, and to guide all of us in the kind of life that a person should live in order to live the kind of life that is pleasing to God.

This book should not be read as if the reader is in a speed reading contest. Every line should be savored as if the reader has sat down to enjoy a gourmet meal, which can only be enjoyed by eating it slowly. It has been with great difficulty that the author has endeavored to transfer his thoughts as the Lord has revealed them to him, which has not been an easy task because many of these truths have been easy to see and understand in the spirit realm, but not easy to relate to another in spoken or written form. For this reason, it is of vital importance that the reader do all within his or her power to grasp the true meaning of the revelations given, to see clearly the mysteries explained in this book, even if it means reading the book more than once.

The author takes no credit whatsoever for the revelations contained in this book, nor has the author done anything greater than anyone else who has walked the face of the earth to obtain more favor of the Lord so as to receive the revelations written in this book. The author is nothing more than an instrument in the hands of God. The revelations are from God and no one else. Therefore, all the praise, glory, and honor belong to God and His Son Jesus Christ. The author, however, wishes to express his gratitude to God for the revelations that He has so graciously given to him, by writing this book. Because these revelations have changed his life in a profound way, so much so that it has inspired him to share the revelations in this book with all who are hungry for the Word of God.

Table of Contents

Introduction

When we really begin to identify with God's Word, we begin to understand that God's Word is like a puzzle. However, not like a puzzle that we buy in the store where we have a picture on the front of the box of all the pieces put together. Because with a store bought puzzle the picture aids us so that we can use it as a guide to pilot us along in interlocking one piece with another, until at the end we have a completed puzzle like that pictured on the box.

Now without this picture of the puzzle, we have to shuffle through the pieces trying to find a clue or a scene of some kind that will match another scene, to see if the pieces interlock; not knowing what to expect because we do not have a picture of the end result of that puzzle. However, as we find more pieces that fit perfectly together, we begin to grasp more or less what the completed puzzle will look like. Moreover, the further along we come to finishing the puzzle, the clearer the picture becomes in our minds, thereby it becomes easer and faster to find and identify the pieces and complete the puzzle.

God's Word operates under the same principles. As God gives you a revelation, that truth in and of itself is a piece of a bigger revelation. We understand it, we see the piece, we understand its meaning and what it is saying, but we are not able to see where this revelation is taking us or the end result of what God is trying to teach us. However, when God gives us another revelation, the truth of this second revelation now interlocks with the first revelation, so that we are able to see a major truth in the Word of God. As God in His infinite mercy and goodness reveals to us more truths, it becomes more evident to us what God desires out of His people.

We need to understand that that beautiful picture of a major truth in the Word of God — which was formed by smaller pieces of revelations interlocking with one another — now becomes nothing more than a large piece of an even bigger and greater revelation in the Word of God. What is transpiring before us is that this major revelation of truth, (made up of many small pieces of revelations), has become a large piece that will interlock with another large piece, which is also made up of still many other smaller revelations. These two major revelations, (separate from each other), that have been individually produced by many smaller revelations, (also separate from each other), interlock perfectly together by Gods infinite wisdom to form one bigger major truth in His Word.

As this process continues, the revelations grow and our desire to know His Word grows. The greater our desire for His Word grows, the less we desire the things and the pleasures of this world, until eventually; all that we live for is for God, His Word, His kingdom, and His people.

The more revelations you receive, the more pieces of this awesome puzzle of the Word of God you have. The more of this puzzle of God's Word that you put together, the more you realize that there is no end to the picture. The picture is as infinite as the universe itself. Furthermore, this is to be expected, because God and His Word are one; the two cannot be separated. God's Word is as infinite as God Himself, which is why the scripture warns us to "*Study to show thyself approved unto God, a workman that needeth not to be ashamed, rightly dividing the word of truth.*" II Timothy 2:15

The scripture specifies "rightly," because God knows that there is not only a right way to divide the Word of truth, there is also a wrong way. And as workmen in the kingdom of God, if we are not careful, we can wrongly divide the Word of truth and end up being ashamed when the Lord shows us how much we missed it.

This is the reason for why wisdom in the book of Proverbs chapter 8 verse 8 says, *"All the words of my mouth are in righteousness; there is nothing froward or perverse in them."*

The Hebrew word *froward* is

פָּתַל

pâthal, *paw-thal'*; a prim. root; and this word means to *twine*, i.e. (lit.) to *struggle* or (fig.) *be* (morally) *tortuous:*— (shew self) froward, shew self unsavory, wrestle.

Also notice that the word *perverse* is the Hebrew word עִקֵּשׁ

ʿiqqêsh, *ik-kashe'*; this word means *distorted;* hence, *false:*— crooked, froward, perverse. This word comes from the root word עָקַשׁ

ʿâqash, *aw-kash';* a prim. root; and the definition of this word is to *knot* or *distort;* (fig.) to *pervert* (act or declare perverse):— make crooked, (prove, that is) perverse (-rt).

What we can understand in this verse and from the definitions given, is that wisdom is revealing to us that when you study God's Word, if you believe that you received a revelation from God, and if you have to twine or struggle with it; if it is tortuous, or if you have to wrestle with one scripture to interlock it with another to get your point across, then give it up because it is not of God. Moreover, you will be building on a wrong foundation, which will only lead to your shame.

Realizing this about the Word of God helps us to be more prudent in our study while being very cautious what we teach others. A greater understanding of God's Word also helps us to see the vastness of His Word and the awesomeness of God.

CHAPTER ONE

WHERE DO WE BEGIN

¹⁹ There was a certain rich man, which was clothed in purple and fine linen, and fared sumptuously every day: ²⁰And there was a certain beggar named Lazarus, which was laid at his gate, full of sores, ²¹And desiring to be fed with the crumbs which fell from the rich man's table: moreover the dogs came and licked his sores. ²²And it came to pass, that the beggar died, and was carried by the angels into Abraham's bosom: the rich man also died, and was buried; ²³And in Hell he lift up his eyes, being in torments, and seeth Abraham afar off, and Lazarus in his bosom. ²⁴And he cried and said, Father Abraham, have mercy on me, and send Lazarus, that he may dip the tip of his finger in water, and cool my tongue; for I am tormented in this flame. ²⁵But Abraham said, Son, remember that thou in thy lifetime receivedst thy good things, and likewise Lazarus evil things: but now he is comforted, and thou art tormented. ²⁶And beside all this, between us and you there is a great gulf fixed: so that they which would pass from hence to you cannot; neither can they pass to us, that would come from thence. ²⁷Then he said, I pray thee therefore, father, that thou wouldest send him to my father's house: ²⁸For I have five brethren; that he may testify unto them, lest they also come into this place of torment. ²⁹Abraham saith unto him, They have Moses and the prophets; let them hear them. ³⁰And he said, Nay, father Abraham: but if one went unto them from the dead, they will repent. ³¹And he said unto him, If they hear not Moses and the prophets, neither will they be persuaded, though one rose from the dead (Luke 16:19-31).

Many people in their desire to know God and in their search for understanding of the scriptures, (to be certain that they are on the right path to reach the kingdom of God and obtain eternal life), often are unsure if they are doing what is right, because so many teach very different things. Furthermore, with so many different religions and denominations in the world, and one believing and many times insinuating that the other is wrong, how can one be sure what the truth is?

If we study the teachings taught by many of these religions, we can understand that much of what they teach is derived from the Bible. The Bible is the right source; it is the written form of God's infallible Word. It has stood the test of time and millions can attest to its truth and power. The Bible is the only entity in human life that, when understood and applied, has the power to change an individual into a nature like God Himself, holy and righteous.

Therefore, if we are going to begin a journey to find the truth, or the reason for why we exist, what our purpose is in life, and answers to many of life's questions, there is no greater place to begin than with the book that has given meaning and brought more joy and fulfillment to the human race, the Bible.

Where then are we to embark on our search of the scriptures? Is there a starting point that will launch us out of the harbor and lead us into the vast sea of wisdom and knowledge that will guide us clearly into the port of God's kingdom and to the treasure of eternal life? I would have to say "the Law and the Prophets!"

Why the Law and the Prophets? Because in the story we read at the beginning of this chapter, we learned of a rich man who died and went to Hell, the very place that every one of us hopes to avoid someday. However, to do this we must know how to avoid it. In this story, the rich man in Hell, seeing Abraham and Lazarus in his bosom, pleaded with Abraham to send Lazarus to his household because he had

5

five brothers, and he wanted him to testify to them so that they could avoid going to the same place. What the rich man was asking Abraham was to send Lazarus back from the grave to his brothers, who were still living on earth and to teach them what they needed to know and do, in order to one day, when they also left this life, receive eternal life and avoid going to Hell. Translated into Christian verbiage, he was asking Abraham to send Lazarus to his brothers to teach them how they could be born again. However, Abraham responded by telling him, "They have Moses and the Prophets; let them hear them. Furthermore, if they will not listen to them, neither will they be persuaded even if one rose from the dead."

(If an individual is not persuaded to repent by Moses and the Prophets, neither will that person be persuaded by one that rose from the dead, even if that one is the only son of God, the Lord Jesus Christ, because Jesus is the personification of Moses and the Prophets.

This story was being told by Jesus. He knew that He would be the only person that would ever rise from the dead, prior to the resurrection. Even with this in mind, He chooses His words carefully when telling this story, in order to let those that were listening to Him know, that when people do not allow the Law and the Prophets to persuade them to repent, He Himself is helpless at convincing them to repent!

Beside Jesus being all, that we needed to fulfill all of God's requirements so He could purchase our salvation; Jesus is also the Law and the Prophets, (Word of God), that was made flesh. He cannot override Himself. Therefore, if He is unable to perform His duties at persuading us to repent in the form of the Law and the Prophets, how can He now after having risen from the dead?)

A careful study of the scriptures will teach us that Moses and the Prophets never lived together at the same time. Therefore, he could not have meant for them to hear what Moses and the Prophets were preaching in the streets.

What he was referring to were the five books that Moses wrote, (also known as the Law), and all the books of the Prophets, (which at the time that Jesus told this story were the books of Joshua through the book of Malachi), referred to in our modern language as the Old Testament.

What Abraham was telling the rich man was that if his brothers would listen to what the Old Testament has to say, then they would receive the knowledge needed to obtain eternal life, because that knowledge would persuade them to repent, (if they applied it), . . .

(Luke 13:3, 5)

3. I tell you, Nay: but, except ye repent, ye shall all likewise perish.

5. I tell you, Nay: but, except ye repent, ye shall all likewise perish.

(II Peter 3:9) The Lord is not slack concerning his promise, as some men count slackness; but is longsuffering to us-ward, NOT WILLING THAT ANY SHOULD PERISH, BUT THAT ALL SHOULD COME TO REPENTANCE.

. . . and avoid going to Hell. Moreover, they also would be assured a place in glory like Lazarus.

Therefore, I, like Jesus, would have to say that our journey should begin with the Law and the Prophets. If Jesus felt that this is where they needed to start in order to repent, otherwise He Himself could not persuade them to repent. Then wisdom and logic would tell us to start there as well! So that when our lives here on earth are finished, we also can obtain eternal life and avoid Hell. While on this journey, hopefully we will also discover the answers to some of life's other questions. It is in the Law and the Prophets that we can find the hidden mysteries that will guide us like a treasure map on our journey to eternal life.

If we study the Old Testament, we begin to realize that it is a series of books about a people that God tried to make a people unto Himself. It is about their origin, their struggles, their conquests, and their punishments for their disobediences to God's commandments. All this took place while God was trying to make them HIS PEOPLE and HE THEIR GOD. The Old Testament in itself is not an easy book to comprehend. However, we can condense the Law and the Prophets into a profile which we can understand, thereby seeing the main objective of God, in order to know what is pleasing to Him and satisfy His instruction so we can avoid Hell and obtain eternal life.

Now we can know what this profile is, because Jesus Himself revealed this very thing in His teachings to those around Him. We find that when Jesus was asked about how to obtain eternal life, He responded with this answer:

(Luke 10:25-28)

25. And behold, a certain lawyer stood up tempting him saying, Master, what shall I do to inherit eternal life.

26. He said unto him, what is written in the law? How readest thou?

27. And he answering said, thou shalt love the Lord thy God with all thy heart, and with all thy soul, and with all thy strength, and with all thy mind, and thy neighbor as thyself.

28. And he said unto him, thou has answered right, this do, and thou shalt live.

In this passage of scripture, we notice that a certain lawyer asks Jesus, "What it is that I must do in order to obtain eternal life?" Jesus answers by asking him, "What is written in the Law? What do the scriptures teach you that you need to do in order to inherit eternal life?"

There are five books that Moses wrote that make up what is known as the Law. There are many different commandments, laws, and rules that are found in those five books. Yet this lawyer is able to translate everything that is written in those five books into two phrases: "You shall love

8

the Lord your God with all your heart and with all your soul and with all your strength and with all your mind" and "You shall love your neighbor as yourself." To this answer, the Lord tells him that he had answered correctly; now all he needed was to do those things and he would obtain eternal life.

Let us look at another piece of scripture where a similar situation arose and we will notice that here also the results are the same.

(Mark 12:28-34)

28. And one of the scribes came and having heard them reasoning together, and perceiving that he had answered Them well, asked him, "Which is the first commandment of all?

29. And Jesus answered him, "The first of all the commandment Is, Hear, O Israel; the Lord our God is one Lord:

30. And thou shalt love the Lord thy God with all thy heart and With all thy soul, and with all thy mind, and with all thy Strength: this is the first commandment.

31. And the second is like this namely; Thou shalt love thy neighbor As thyself. There is none other commandment greater than these.

32. And the scribe said unto him, "Well, Master, thou hast said the truth, for there is one God; and there is none other But he.

33. And to love him with all the heart and with all the understanding and with all the soul, and with all the strength, and to love his neighbor as himself, is more than all whole burnt offerings and sacrifices.

34. And when Jesus saw that he answered discreetly, he said unto him, "Thou art not far from the kingdom of God..."

Here we can see that in this conversation Jesus had with this scribe, the scribe was in complete agreement with what the Lord had said. Furthermore, the scribe added that to do these two commandments, there was nothing greater, no, not even all the outward appearances of worship to God with sacrifices and burnt offerings. To this remark, the Lord tells him, "You are not far from the kingdom of God." In other words, the Lord was telling him that he was so very close to knowing and doing what is needed to receive eternal life.

It is apparent that all that God would have man understand of the Law can be summed up in two statements, to love God with all that is in you, and to love your neighbor as yourself. Nevertheless, what role does the books of the prophet's play in all this? We find that in the book of Matthew, there is another incident where a lawyer asks him a question.

(Matthew 22:35-40)

35. Then one of them, which was a lawyer, asked him a Question, tempting him, and saying,

36. Master, which is the great commandment in the law?

37. Jesus said unto him, Thou shalt love the Lord thy God with all thy heart and with all thy soul, and with all Thy mind.

38. This is the first and great commandment.

39. And the second is like unto it, thou shalt love thy neighbor as Thyself

40. On these two commandments hang all the Law and the Prophets.

In this encounter, the Lord not only mentions the Law, but this time also includes the Prophets, raising the question why the Prophets were not mentioned in the other passages of scriptures? Because it is apparent that in the Law reside the instructions given for man to obey in order to obtain eternal life, and in the Prophets those instructions are explicated for man to understand them. These instructions, however, are only explained through the experiences of the nation of Israel. As the errors of the nation of Israel are recognized, the reader can then comprehend how and why Israel failed God and thereby understand what God requires from each one of us. Without the books of the Prophet, we would not be able to understand their errors, so as to help us not make the same mistakes.

The Law and the Prophets give substance to the teachings of Christ, while the teachings of Jesus Christ expound on the Law and the Prophets. Even though many of those teachings are in parables, the Epistles decode the parables for us, giving us a greater understanding of both.

Buried deep in the Law and the Prophets is the secret formula to understanding what it is that an individual has to do in order to obtain eternal life, and a person who searches for it as for buried treasure will eventually uncover it. It is the sincere desire of the author that the reader embark with him on this journey, as together we seek to find the greatest treasures that have been hidden since the foundation of the earth!

CHAPTER TWO

THE COVENANT

¹In the third month, when the children of Israel were gone forth out of the land of Egypt, the same day came they into the wilderness of Sinai. ²For they were departed from Rephidim, and were come to the desert of Sinai, and had pitched in the wilderness; and there Israel camped before the mount. ³And Moses went up unto God, and the LORD called unto him out of the mountain, saying, Thus shalt thou say to the house of Jacob, and tell the children of Israel; ⁴Ye have seen what I did unto the Egyptians, and how I bare you on eagles' wings, and brought you unto myself. ⁵Now therefore, if ye will obey my voice indeed, and keep my covenant, then ye shall be a peculiar treasure unto me above all people: for all the earth is mine: ⁶And ye shall be unto me a kingdom of priests, and an holy nation. These are the words which thou shalt speak unto the children of Israel (Exodus 19:1-6).

It is difficult for someone to understand the Law and the Prophets without first understanding the covenant that God made with the nation of Israel. Knowledge of the covenant is the "central nervous system" of our understanding of the Old Testament. To understand the covenant allows the reader to comprehend where and how the nation of Israel failed God. Furthermore, this allows the reader to see why and how the nation of Israel brought down the wrath of God upon itself. Moreover, this information is essential to anyone desiring to know God and serve Him faithfully because God still makes this covenant today with anyone that desires to have God as the Lord <u>his</u> God! This information is also needed to avoid the same pitfalls that the nation of Israel made.

There are many hidden mysteries in the Old Testament, but understanding the covenant serves as the master key that unlocks those mysteries.

We first need to know that the word *covenant* in the Old Testament is the Hebrew word בְּרִית

b°rîyth, *ber-eeth'*; (in the sense of *cutting*); a *compact* (because made by passing between *pieces* of flesh):— confederacy, [con-]feder[-ate], covenant, league.

Webster's definition of the word *compact* is, "To make an agreement; an agreement or covenant between two or more parties". The word *confederacy* is defined as "a league or compact for mutual support or common action: an alliance". The definition of the word *covenant* as described by Webster is "a usually formal, solemn, and binding agreement: a compact." The word *league*, according to Webster, is the word that means "an association of persons or groups united by common interests or goals."

Based on the definitions given above, we can understand that the covenant that the Lord made with the nation of Israel was an agreement specifying that if Israel does such-and-such, then God will do such-and-such, culminating in the nation of Israel being established as the people of God and He their God.

It is not enough to be the people of God; God must also be your God. This implies that there are reciprocal responsibilities to each other. This evidence is seen all though the scriptures.

(Jeremiah 31:33) But this shall be the covenant that I will Make with the house of Israel; after those days, saith the Lord, I will put my law in their inward parts, and write it in their hearts; and will be their God, and they shall be my people.

(Jeremiah 7:21-23)

13

21. Thus saith the lord of hosts, the God of Israel; Put your burnt offerings unto your sacrifices And eat flesh.

22. For I spake not unto your fathers, nor commanded them in the day that I brought them out of the land of Egypt, concerning burnt offerings or sacrifices:

23. But this thing commanded I them, saying, Obey My voice, <u>and I will be your God, and ye shall be My people</u>: and walk ye in all the ways that I have commanded you, that it may be well unto you

(Deuteronomy 29:12,13)

12. That thou shouldst enter into covenant with the Lord thy God, and into his oath, which the Lord thy God maketh with thee this day:

13. <u>That he may establish thee today for a people unto himself, and that he may be unto thee a God,</u> as he hath said unto thy fathers, to Abraham, to Isaac, and to Jacob.

It is obvious from the above verses and numerous other scriptures that are found in the Bible that it was God's desire to make the nation of Israel a people unto Himself, thus making Himself their God. And for this to have come to pass an understanding or agreement had to be drafted up, which is where the covenant comes into the picture.

The covenant consisted of ten do's and don'ts for the nation of Israel, known as the Ten Commandments. The stipulations were simple: Obey and Keep His covenant. God made clear that the nation of Israel had to perform these requirements as evidence that they were keeping His covenant. The giving of the covenant was brought about in three stages. First was the instilling of His fear in them; second was the giving of the Law; and third was the writing down of the Law. Furthermore, all who profess to be the people of God must understand these three stages because God still makes His covenant with us in the same manner.

WE MUST UNDERSTAND THE THREE STAGES OF THE COVENANT

Because the scripture says in Jeremiah 32:33, *"But this shall be the covenant that I will Make with the house of Israel; after those days, saith the Lord, I will put my law in their inward parts, and write it in their hearts; and will be their God, and they shall be my people,"* as well as in Hebrews 8:10, *"For this is the covenant that I will make with the house of Israel after those days, saith the Lord, I will put my laws into their mind, and write them in their hearts: and I will be to them a God, and they shall be to me a people,"* many ministers believe and teach that the format that God uses in the covenant (old or new) is only the giving of the law and the writing down of the law. The first stage, which is the instilling of the fear of God in an individual, is not understood as being part of the covenant. What we need to realize is that God never changes; He is the same yesterday, today, and forever. For this reason, the same format that He used in the past is still in use today.

Let us look at the giving of the Ten Commandments to see the three stages God used to make His covenant with the nation of Israel. We can then discover the same format in the new covenant. Notice that at the beginning of this chapter, we read that God tells Moses that He will make a covenant with the nation of Israel. Now we read in Exodus 19:10,11:

10. And the Lord said unto Moses, go unto the people, and sanctify them today and tomorrow, and let them wash their clothes,

11. And be ready against the third day: for the third day the Lord will come down in the sight of all the people upon Mount Sinai.

We read here where God was to meet the nation of Israel at Mount Sinai to make with them His covenant, but notice the events that followed prior to Him giving them His Ten Commandments.

(Exodus 19:16-18)

16. And it came to pass on the third day in the morning, that there were thunders and lightnings, and a thick cloud upon the mount, and the voice of the trumpet exceeding loud; so that all the people that was in the camp tremble.

17. And Moses brought forth the people out of the camp to meet with God; and they stood at the nether part of the mount.

18. And Mount Sinai was altogether on a smoke, because the Lord descended upon it in fire: and the smoke thereof ascended as the smoke of a furnace, and the whole mount quaked greatly.

Now we must ask ourselves, why such an awesome show of power? Why was it so necessary for the people to see the lightning, the fire, and smoke? Why did they need to hear all the thundering, and feel the ground quake and shake? The reason is that He wanted them to know that even though He was a merciful and loving God, He was also a jealous God, even a consuming fire, and He would not tolerate disobedience. He wanted them to see that He was very serious about the covenant that He was going to make with them and that He wanted them to take it serous as well. That He says what He means and He means what He says. In other words, He was trying to place the FEAR OF GOD in them! Observe the actions of the nation of Israel while God was making His covenant with them.

(Exodus 20:18-19)

18. And all the people saw the thunderings, and the lightnings, and the noise of the trumpet, and the mountain smoking: and when the people saw it, they removed, and stood afar off.

19. And they said unto Moses, Speak thou with us, and we will hear: but let not God speak to us, lest we die.

What transpired here? Well, quite frankly, when the people saw the terrible sight, they were scared to death. The sight before them was so terrible that the fear of God came upon them. They were too frightened to approach the mountain. However, this was precisely what God was trying to accomplish. This is the very reason for the elaborate show of power, to put His fear in them. Why? Because when the fear of God is in a person, that individual will not sin against Him.

(Exodus 20:20) And Moses said unto the people, Fear not: For God is come to prove you, and that His fear may be before your faces, THAT YE SIN NOT.

The fear of God in a person is the restraining force that keeps that person from sinning against God, just as the fear of flying keeps a person from traveling by plane or the fear of snakes strikes panic in a person, preventing him from getting close to one or even looking at one.

God was making a covenant with them, and that covenant required that they not do certain things and that they do certain things. However, God knew that on their own they would not be able to accomplish this. They needed to have a motivating force that would aid them in keeping those Ten Commandments; this is where the fear of God comes in. A person not doing what the Lord tells them to do and doing what the Lord tells them not to do is sinning against God. Nevertheless, with the fear of God upon that person, that individual will do what is right because of the fear of having to face God's consuming fire.

IS THE FEAR OF GOD IN YOU?

Even though God had succeeded in putting His fear in them, God knew that this was only temporal; He knew that eventually they would forget the scene before them and would resort to breaking His commandments, thereby sinning against Him.

(Deuteronomy 5:23-29)

23. And it came to pass, when ye heard the voice out of the midst of the darkness, (for the mounting did burn with fire,) that ye came near unto me, even all your heads of your tribes, and your elders;

24. And ye said, behold, the Lord our God hath shewed us his glory and his greatness, and we have heard his voice out of the midst of the fire: we have seen this day that God doth talk with man, and he liveth.

25. Now therefore why should we die? for this great fire will consume us: if we hear the voice of the Lord our God any more, then we shall die.

26. For who is there of all flesh, that hath heard the voice of the living God speaking out of the midst of the fire, as we have and lived?

27. Go thou near, and hear all that the Lord our God shall say: and speak thou unto us all that the Lord our God shall speak unto thee; and we will hear it, and do it.

28. And the Lord heard the voice of your words, when ye spake unto me; and the Lord said unto me, I have heard the voice of the words of this people, which they have spoken unto thee: they have well said all that they have spoken.

29. <u>O that there were such an heart in them, that they would FEAR ME, and keep all my commandments always</u>, that it might be will with them, and with their children for ever!

Notice in verse 29 the tone of regret in the Lord's words for not having been successful in placing His fear into the hearts of the people. He mentions that, "they have spoken well," in demonstrating that they feared Him, but He knew that it was only superficial; His attempt at placing His fear in their hearts had not succeeded. This is why He tells Moses, in verse 29, (translated into the author's own words), "O Moses, I would that the nation of Israel had the kind of heart that feared Me, because then they would not sin against Me, thereby keeping My commandments."

We have seen from the events we have read that during the making of the covenant, the first phase of the covenant involved instilling the fear of God in the nation of Israel. We can now learn that after this transpired, the second stage was the giving of the law, which we can read was done in Exodus chapter 20:1-17 after the elaborate show of power in Exodus 19:16-25. After the giving of the law, God proceeded to write the commandments down on tablets of stone. This is the third stage of the making of the covenant. This is also verified in other scriptures; notice that in the following verses, the same format is used as proof that God made His covenant with Israel in three stages.

(Deuteronomy 4:10-13)

10. Specially the day that thou stoodest before the Lord thy God in Horeb, when the Lord said unto me, Gather me the people together, and I will make them hear my words, that they may learn to fear me all the days that they shall live upon the earth, and that they may teach their children.

Notice that in verses 10 and 11, (which follows), we see the bringing about of the first stage of the covenant, the instilling of the fear of God by the terrible sight that He's a consuming fire, *(that they may learn to fear Me)*, and teach their children what? To also fear the Lord!

11. And ye came near and stood under the mountain: and the mountain burned with fire unto the midst of Heaven, with darkness, clouds, and thick darkness,

12. And the Lord spake unto you out of the midst of the fire: ye heard the voice of the words, but saw no similitude; only ye heard a voice.

13. And he declared unto you his covenant, which he commanded you to perform, even Ten Commandments...

Here, now, in verse 12 and part of verse 13, we find the second stage of the covenant, the giving of the law.

13...and he wrote them upon two tables of stone.

Concluding with the third stage of the covenant; writing them down.

A careful study of Deuteronomy 5, verse 22, will also reveal the same format:

(Deuteronomy 5:22) These words the Lord spake into all your assembly in the mount out of the midst of the fire, of the cloud, and of the thick darkness, with a great voice: and he added no more. And he wrote them in two tables of stones, and delivered them unto me.

God by His very nature is a merciful, kind, loving, gentle, and patient God, who only desires the best for His children, but at the very presence of sin, His anger heats up, transforming Him into a consuming fire devouring everything in its path. God knows this; He knows that when His patience runs out because of disobedience to His commandments, all violators will be consumed. Which is the reason why, at the making of His covenant, He reveals that side of Himself first, so the people would see that side of Him and His fear would be placed in them, so as to never want to cross Him and bring about His wrath and their destruction.

(Zephaniah 1:2, 3, 18)

2. I will utterly consume all things from off the land, saith the Lord.

3. I will consume man and beast: I will consume the fowls of the Heaven, and the fishes of the sea, and the stumbling blocks with the wicked; and I will cut off man from off the land.

18. Neither their silver nor their gold shall be able to deliver them in the day of the Lord's wrath; but the whole land shall

be devoured by the fire of his jealousy: for he shall make
even a speedy riddance of all them that dwell in the land.

GOD'S NEW METHOD OF PLACING HIS FEAR IN HIS PEOPLE

What God did on Mount Sinai He has not, nor will He do again, as the method by which He places His fear in us. However, He still today tries to place His fear in His people. And the approach He uses is the same method He used in the books of the Prophets, where He continued to try to instill His fear in the nation of Israel because they refuse to stop sinning against Him.

What was the approach that God used in the books of the prophets to try to instill His fear in His people then, and how is that same technique used by God today, to instill His fear in those that claim to be God's people?

Every time God's people sinned against Him by breaking His commandments, God punished them, numerous times destroying many. When they would continue to sin, He would tell them by the Prophets how other nations sinned against Him and how He had to destroy them. Many times they knew of the destructions because it was their own people that were destroyed and the destruction was all around them. God would then proceed to tell them that they were in violation of His commandments, and if they did not repent and turn from their evil ways, they would also be destroyed. Afterwards, He would proceed to prophesy through His prophet of His wrath that was going to fall upon them because of the evil of their ways, hoping His fear would enter into them, that fear causing them to repent and turn His wrath away. Which God said would be turned away if they repented, because the last thing that God wants to do is pour out His wrath. However, if people do not repent, they leave Him no choice!

21

Notice in the following verses the evidence of how God used this format in the books of the Prophets to try to instill His fear in them so that fear would produce a lifestyle in them that would be pleasing to Him. Furthermore, notice that this format is also brought about in three stages, though not necessarily in the same order.

The first stage was telling them of the destruction that came to others because of their evil ways.

(Jeremiah 5:3) O Lord, are not thine eyes upon the truth? thou hast stricken them, but they have not grieved; thou hast consumed them, but they have refused to receive correction: they have made their faces harder than a rock; they have refused to return.

(Zephaniah 3:6) I have cut off the nations: their towers are desolate; I made their streets waste, that none passeth by: their cities are destroyed, so that there is no man, that there is none inhabitant.

The second stage was telling them of their evil ways before His eyes.

(Jeremiah 5:7, 8)

7. How shall I pardon thee for this? thy children have forsaken me, and sworn by them that are no gods: when I had fed them to the full, they then committed adultery, and assembled themselves by troops in the harlots houses,

8. They were as fed horses in the morning: every one neighed after his neighbor's wife.

(Zephaniah 3:1-4)

1. Woe to her that is filthy and polluted, to the oppressing city!

2. She obeyed not the voice; she received not correction; she trusted not in the Lord; she drew not near to her God.

3. Her princes within her are roaring lions; her judges are evening wolves; they gnaw not the bones till the morrow.

4. Her prophets are light and treacherous persons: her priests have polluted the sanctuary, they have done violence to the law.

Third was prophesying of the future to show them how they would also be destroyed, if they did not repent.

(Jeremiah 5:9-11, 14-19)

9. Shall I not visit for these things? saith the Lord: and shall not my soul be avenged on such a nation as this

10. Go ye up upon her walls, and destroy; but make not a full end: take away her battlements; for they are not the Lord's

11. For the house of Israel and the house of Judah have dealt very treacherously against me, saith the Lord.

14. Wherefore thus saith the Lord God of hosts, Because ye speak this word, behold, I will make my words in thy mouth fire, and this people wood, and it shall devour them.

15. Lo, I will bring a nation upon you from far, O house of Israel, saith the Lord; it is a mighty nation, it is an ancient nation, a nation whose language thou knowest not neither understandest what they say.

16. Their quiver is as an open sepulcher, they are all mighty men.

17. And they shall eat up thine harvest, and thine bread, which thy sons and thy daughters should eat: they shall eat up thy flocks and thine herds: they shall eat up thy vines and thy fig trees: they shall impoverish thy fenced cities, wherein thou trustedst, with the sword.

(Zephaniah 1:2, 3, 14-18)

2. I will utterly consume all things from off the land, saith the Lord.

3. I will consume man and beast: I will consume the fowls of the Heaven, and the fishes of the sea, and the stumbling blocks with the wicked; and I will cut off man from off the land.

14. The great day of the Lord is near, it is near, and hasteth greatly, even the voice of the day of the Lord: the mighty man shall cry there bitterly.

15. That day is a day of wrath, a day of trouble and distress, a day of wasteness and desolation, a day of darkness and gloominess, a day of clouds and thick darkness

16. A day of the trumpet and alarm against the fenced cities, and against the high towers.

17. And I will bring distress upon men, that they shall walk like blind men, because they have sinned against the Lord: and their blood shall be poured out as dust, and their flesh as the dung.

18. Neither their silver nor their gold shall be able to deliver them in the day of the Lord's wrath; but the whole land shall be devoured by the fire of his jealousy: for he shall make even a speedy riddance of all them that dwell in the land.

Notice that while this process is going on, God informs them that they should receive wisdom and fear Him. Why is that? Why is it that God is hoping that they will receive wisdom and fear Him? Because the fear of God in a person or a people causes them to repent and turn from their evil ways. The fear of God in an individual causes that person to realize that God does not play games; He is a merciful God, but if they continue to sin and not repent, they will experience the other side of Him, His consuming fire. God expecting them to wise up and realize He means business and that, if His patience runs out, they will be destroyed by the fire of His wrath.

(Jeremiah 5:20-24)

20. Declare this in the house of Jacob, and publish it in Judah, saying,

21. Hear now this, O foolish people, and without understanding; which have eyes, and see not; which have ears, and hear not:

22. FEAR YE NOT ME? saith the Lord: will ye not tremble at my presence, which have placed the sand for the bound of the sea by a perpetual decree, that it cannot pass it: and though the waves thereof toss themselves, yet can they not prevail; though they roar, yet can they not pass over it?

23. But this people hath a revolting and a rebellious heart; they are revolted and gone.

24. Neither say they in their heart, LET US NOW FEAR THE LORD OUR GOD, that giveth rain, both the former and the latter, in his season: he reserveth unto us the appointed weeks of the harvest.

(Zephaniah 3:6-8)

6. I have cut off the nations: their towers are desolate; I made their streets waste, that none passeth by: their cities are destroyed, so that there is no man, that there is none inhabitant.

7. I SAID, SURELY THOU WILT FEAR ME, thou wilt receive instruction; so their dwelling should not be cut off, howsoever I punished them: but they rose early, and corrupted all their doings.

8. Therefore wait ye upon me, saith the Lord, until the day that I rise up to the prey: for my determination is to gather the nations, that I may assemble the kingdoms, to pour upon them mine indignation, even all my fierce anger: For all the earth shall be devoured with the fire of my jealousy.

It is expedient that the fear of God be placed in a person, for without it men are left to their own ways. There is no sense of accountability; there is no restraint, nothing to stop a person, a people, a country, or even a world from doing and living the way it pleases. God is very well aware of this fact, which is why, upon making the covenant with the nation of Israel, the placing of His fear is first and foremost on His agenda. This is also true in the new covenant.

(Jeremiah 32:38-40)

38. And they shall be my people, and I will be their God:

39. And I will give them one heart, and one way, <u>THAT THEY MAY FEAR ME FOREVER</u>, for the good of them, and of their children after them:

40. And I will make an everlasting covenant with them, that I will not turn away from them, to do them good; <u>BUT I WILL PUT MY FEAR IN THEIR HEART</u>, that they shall not depart from me.

The fear of the Lord is nothing short of an awesome fear of knowing that if we cross God, we will one day stand before Him and face His wrath for our disobedience to His Word. This does not mean that we can never make a mistake, because we are humans with many weaknesses, clothed in carnal flesh, and our very nature is enmity toward God. To error and sin is not to say that we are now without hope, doomed to wait for that frightful day when we will face God's fearsome wrath. This is why Jesus died and rose again, to make atonement for our sins. However, the person who thinks that he can live sinfully and not have to give an account to God because we are not under the law but under grace is just as foolish as the nation of Israel when they kept living their own evil ways and refused to heed God's warnings. For that individual has neither allowed the fear of God to come into his heart, nor does he comprehend the Word of God.

(Hebrews 12:25, 28-29)

25. See that ye refuse not him that speaketh, For if they escaped not who refused him that spake on earth, much more shall not we escape, if we turn away from him that speaketh from Heaven:

28. Wherefore we receiving a kingdom which cannot be moved, let us have grace, whereby we may serve God acceptably with reverence and Godly FEAR:

29. FOR OUR GOD IS A CONSUMING FIRE.

The three stages that God used in the books of the Prophets to place His fear in the nation of Israel is the same method that He still uses today. It is the method that Jesus used during His time here on earth. It is what the apostles used when they took over where Christ left off.

Moreover, it is what many great men of God used throughout history. The method is as simple as the following: (though not necessarily in this same order).

1. Telling people of their sins before God.

2. Informing them of the wrath of God that is coming upon the entire world because of its evil ways.

3. Telling them God does not tolerate sin. He did not before from others, not even His people, (this is why many were destroyed, and their history has been recorded in the Bible), and He will not now or in the future. Furthermore, if an individual does not repent, and turn from his sins, he will eventually bring upon himself the wrath of God in this life and in the next.

As in the books of the prophets, this kind of preaching will cause the fear of God to be instilled in the heart of the hearer, thereby causing them to repent and want to live right before God. If this part of the covenant is taking away from the church, then eventually God's people will lose their fear of God and live in sin without any fear of accountability. Additionally, those coming to God will not come the way that God has provided, and though they may profess Jesus as their savior, they will continue to live a deceived life in sin because that restraining force, the fear of God, will not be there to keep them from sinning.

27

(Titus 1:16) They profess that they know God; but in works they deny him, being abominable, and disobedient, and unto every good work reprobate.

MINISTERS OF THE GOSPEL, PLEASE DO YOUR JOB

The new covenant that God makes with His people is made through His ministers. It is through His ministers that He gives the law, and through His ministers that He writes His law in their hearts.

(II Corinthians 3:2, 3, 6)

2. Ye are our Epistle written in our hearts, known and read of all man:

3. forasmuch as ye are manifestly declared to be the Epistle of Christ ministered by us, written not with ink, but with the spirit of the living God; not in tables of stone, but in fleshy tables of the heart.

6. Who also hath made us able ministers of the new testament; not of the letter, but of the spirit: for the letter killeth, but the spirit giveth life.

It is also through His ministers that He places His fear in His people! The preaching of such subjects as Hell, fire and brimstone, and an eternal place of torment for those that live ungodly, and eternal damnation for those that do not turn to God, plus the coming wrath of God, have always played a very important roll in the preaching of the gospel. It is the concrete wall before a speeding vehicle to get a person to evaluate his life and see his need for a savior. It is what God uses to place His fear in His people, to aid them in living a holy and righteous life; however, they are also subjects that are rarely preached today. Many ministers have shunned them, fearing they will offend people and drive their congregations away. Others do not believe in Hell or a place of torment, while still others cannot bring themselves to preach this way because they just cannot fathom a loving God punishing people in this way. Whatever the reason, it is a deception of the Devil to keep the fear of God out of people so they can live in sin without their consciences bothering them. It is also the reason why there is so much sin in the church today!

Author's word of caution to ministers: If you are not ministering all of God's word, you are doing a great injustice to God's people, and one day you will be held accountable to God for it!

In the next chapter, we will learn why the fear of the Lord is so vitally important in the life of a believer.

CHAPTER THREE

THE FEAR OF THE LORD

[2]To know wisdom and instruction; to perceive the words of understanding; [3]To receive the instruction of wisdom, justice, and judgment, and equity; [4]To give subtlety to the simple, to the young man knowledge and discretion. [5]A wise man will hear, and will increase learning; and a man of understanding shall attain unto wise counsels: [6]To understand a proverb, and the interpretation; the words of the wise, and their dark sayings. [7]The fear of the LORD is the beginning of knowledge: but fools despise wisdom and instruction.

[10]My son, if sinners entice thee, consent thou not. [11]If they say, Come with us, let us lay wait for blood, let us lurk privily for the innocent without cause: [12]Let us swallow them up alive as the grave; and whole, as those that go down into the pit: [13]We shall find all precious substance, we shall fill our houses with spoil: [14]Cast in thy lot among us; let us all have one purse: [15]My son, walk not thou in the way with them; refrain thy foot from their path: [16]For their feet run to evil, and make haste to shed blood. [17]Surely in vain the net is spread in the sight of any bird. [18]And they lay wait for their own blood; they lurk privily for their own lives. [19]So are the ways of every one that is greedy of gain; which taketh away the life of the owners thereof. [20]Wisdom crieth without; she uttereth her voice in the streets: [21]She crieth in the chief place of concourse, in the openings of the gates: in the city she uttereth her words, saying, [22]How long, ye simple ones, will ye love simplicity? and the scorners delight in their scorning, and fools hate knowledge? [23]Turn you at my reproof: behold, I will pour out my spirit unto you, I will make known my words unto you. [24]Because I have called,

and ye refused; I have stretched out my hand, and no man regarded; ²⁵But ye have set at nought all my counsel, and would none of my reproof: ²⁶I also will laugh at your calamity; I will mock when your fear cometh; ²⁷When your fear cometh as desolation, and your destruction cometh as a whirlwind; when distress and anguish cometh upon you. ²⁸Then shall they call upon me, but I will not answer; they shall seek me early, but they shall not find me: ²⁹For that they hated knowledge, and did not choose the fear of the LORD (Proverbs 1:2-7, 10-29).

As we study and allow the Spirit of God to give us understanding of these passages, we can understand what the scriptures are telling us. That for someone to know wisdom, understanding, and knowledge, (verses 2 through 3). Especially if that individual is to instruct others, (verse 4). That individual has to hear and listen very carefully, (verse 5), to know what wisdom is saying, (verse 6). With this in mind, notice what the next verse says: "The fear of the Lord is the beginning of knowledge: but fools despise wisdom and instruction."

Also notice that Wisdom — after trying to direct their attention towards her, (verses 20 through 23), so that they would have the knowledge necessary to avoid making the wrong choices, (verses 10 through 19). When they would not listen, goes on to say what she says from verse 24 through verse 28 and concludes with verse 29: "For that they hated knowledge, and did not choose the fear of the Lord."

There is a hidden mystery here that we need to understand, because we see that the scriptures are letting us know that there is a direct connection between the fear of the Lord and knowledge. There is definitely an insinuation that when you hate the wisdom, knowledge or understanding that God can give, it is because you do not fear God. Or that somehow when you do not fear God it leads you, or moves you to hate whatever wisdom, knowledge or understanding you could receive from God.

Why do the scriptures say in verse 7, *"The fear of the LORD is the beginning of knowledge: but fools despise wisdom and instruction,"* and in verse 29, *"For that they hated knowledge, and did not choose the fear of the LORD"?* Because what the scriptures are indirectly trying to get us to see is that people who do not fear God are unknowingly or knowingly depriving themselves of the knowledge that God would give them if they would be wise and choose to fear Him. For the reason that God only gives wisdom, knowledge, and understanding to those who fear Him!

Since the fear of the Lord is the beginning of wisdom and knowledge, and because it takes certain types of messages to place the fear of the Lord in an individual. Furthermore, because many people do not want to hear those types of messages that would place the fear of the Lord in them, because they convict them and scares them because of the consequences awaiting them if they do not repent. Many of those same people have let their ministers know that those types of messages offend them; therefore, they would rather do without them. Because of this many minister have resorted to teaching cunningly devised fables, motivational messages, and messages that tickles their ears, instead of ministering messages teaching them the truths that would give them the wisdom, knowledge and understanding that they need. This is one way that people are hating knowledge and not choosing the fear of the Lord.

HOW IS IT THAT THE FEAR OF THE LORD LEADS US TO, OR PRODUCES KNOWLEDGE?

Remember that we said in chapter two, that the fear of the Lord is an awesome fear of God, because we know that if we do not do what is right, we will have to stand before Him one day and face His all-consuming wrath, (page 26, first paragraph, lines 13-15). Understanding this, we can see how the fear of the Lord is the motivator that drives an individual to search the scriptures for the truths needed to know how to live a life that is pleasing to God. This way, we can acquire the knowledge needed, thereby knowing how to live right before God, so as to not have to face His wrath on judgment day. (*Study to shew thyself approved unto God, a workman that needeth not to be ashamed, rightly dividing the word of truth 2 Timothy 2:15.*)

(Concerning our born-again experience, the fear of the Lord is the motivator that causes a person to see his or her need of a savior. Thereby turning from whatever evil lifestyle he or she may be living, to Jesus, the Word of God, (the light that illuminates the road that takes us to the kingdom of God,) so we are able to see our way clearly.)

For this reason, the scriptures say in Proverbs 9:10, "The fear of the LORD is the beginning of wisdom: and the knowledge of the holy is understanding."

As the fear of the Lord leads us to study His Word, (The fear of the LORD is the beginning of wisdom,) to know how to live before Him, we begin to understand the truths that teach us how we need to walk, (live,) before Him. As we endeavor to walk in those truths so that our ways are pleasing to Him, so we do not have to face His all-consuming wrath, we begin to feel a sense of satisfaction that now our lifestyle will keep us from having to face His all-consuming fire. This satisfaction begins to build a love in us for His Word, as well as, a greater desire to know His Word more, so as to live a life that is even more pleasing to God. Our love for His Word grows because in it we find the truths that will make us the kind of people for which we know God is looking. This is the reason for why Jesus, who is the very Word of God, said, *I am the way, the truth, and the life: no man cometh unto the Father, but by me.*" (John 14:6).

We start seeing His Word as the only true meaningful treasure in this life.

It is only when we love His Word that we desire it so, that that desire compels us to study and meditate upon His Word, thereby giving us the wisdom, knowledge and understand that we need and desire.

(Psalms 119: 97-100)

97. O how love I thy law! it is my meditation all the day.

98. Thou through thy commandments hast made me wiser than mine enemies: for they are ever with me.

99. I have more understanding than all my teachers: for thy testimonies are my meditation.

100. I understand more than the ancients, because I keep thy precepts.

In Hebrews chapter 4, verse one, we see the writer to the Hebrews admonishing them, "To fear, lest a promise being left us of entering into His rest any of you should seem to fall short." Later on in verse's 11 and 12, he gives them the secret of what it is that they need to do to make sure that they enter into that rest, otherwise they could fall after the same example of unbelief, thereby not being able to enter into that rest. In chapter 8, of this book, "Obedience or Disobedience," we will learn what that example of unbelief is, as well as the secret to enter into that rest. This secret formula to enter into that rest, we will understand is to "STUDY THE WORD OF GOD." However, realize that it must begin first with the first part of Hebrews 4:1, "LET US THEREFORE FEAR!" The fear of the Lord must be in place so as to cause us to study His Word, therefore leading us to the truths spoken of in this chapter and thereby producing the results taught in chapter 8 pages 129 and 130.

When our love for God's Word grows to the point that it is the very reason for why we live, we begins to fulfill the scriptures of Proverbs, chapter 2, verses 1 through 5.

(Proverbs 2:1-5)

1. My son, if thou wilt receive my words, and hide my commandments with thee;

2. So that thou incline thine ear unto wisdom, and apply thine heart to understanding;

3. Yea, if thou criest after knowledge, and liftest up thy voice for understanding;

4. If thou seekest her as silver, and searchest for her as for hid treasures;

5. Then shalt thou understand the fear of the LORD, and find the knowledge of God.

The fulfilling of these scriptures brings us to the place where we now understand the fear of the Lord, the reason behind it, how it benefits us, and how it enables us to become the people of God that we are supposed to be, and, moreover, how this fear keeps us from sinning against God. This cycle continues to repeat itself: we fear Him; this fear drives us to search the scriptures; we learn His ways and endeavor to walk in them, resulting in a sense of satisfaction for having learned truths that enable us to live right before Him. We grow in love for His Word as a result of that satisfaction, thereby desiring more and more of His Word. While this cycle is going on in our lives, there is a transformation that is taking place in us that we are not even aware of... At lease not until now... as we become more like Christ.

The greatest thing that you can do in this life is to show God that His Word, (Jesus, His Son), means more to you than life itself. That His Word is more to you than all the earthly treasures of this world combined. That loving and knowing His Word means more to you than the very food you eat and the water you drink. That His Word is more needful to you than even the very air you breathe. When we begin to come to this place with God's Word, we begin to touch Him in a way that truly touches the very heart of God.

We begin to move the hand of God in our lives as nothing else can. God begins to bring us to the place where a transformation takes place in us that has eternal value. Read carefully what chapter 2, verses 6 through 21 of Proverbs tells us.

(Proverbs 2:6-21)

6. For the LORD giveth wisdom: out of his mouth cometh knowledge and understanding.

7. He layeth up sound wisdom for the righteous: he is a buckler to them that walk uprightly.

8. He keepeth the paths of judgment, and preserveth the way of his saints.

9. Then shalt thou understand righteousness, and judgment, and equity; yea, every good path.

10. When wisdom entereth into thine heart, and knowledge is pleasant unto thy soul;

11. Discretion shall preserve thee, understanding shall keep thee:

12. To deliver thee from the way of the evil man, from the man that speaketh froward things;

13. <u>Who leave the paths of uprightness</u>, to walk in the ways of darkness;

14. Who rejoice to do evil, and delight in the frowardness of the wicked;

15. Whose ways are crooked, and they froward in their paths:

16. To deliver thee from the strange woman, even from the stranger which flattereth with her words;

17. <u>Which forsaketh the guide of her youth, and forgetteth the covenant of her God.</u>

18. For her house inclineth unto death, and her paths unto the dead.

19. None that go unto her return again, neither take they hold of the paths of life.

20. That thou mayest walk in the way of good men, and keep the paths of the righteous.

21. For the upright shall dwell in the land, and the perfect shall remain in it.

Notice that as you show God how much you love His Word, (verses 2 through 4), the understanding of the fear of the Lord begins to be produced in you, (verse 5). This in turn produces knowledge, because it causes you to want to know more of the Word of God as discussed earlier. This releases the hand of God to give you more wisdom, knowledge, and understanding, (verse 6). By this He is building in you a sound foundation that will ultimately bring you to the place where the end result will be that you become perfect.

Observe that as you grow in more wisdom, knowledge, and understanding, (verses 10 and 11), you avoid the pitfalls that befall others, (verses 12 through 19). The shameful thing about these two examples is that at one time they both knew God and walked upright before Him, ("Who leave the paths of uprightness," "Which forsaketh the guide of her youth"); they were instructed in the ways of God, and even had some kind of relationship, (covenant), with God, ("and forgetteth the covenant of her God"). Now, however, they have gone backward instead of forward in the Lord. Why is that? Because they either never had or they lost the FEAR OF THE LORD!

The fear of the Lord sets in motion the process that we have been discussing where the end result is perfection in all of God's Word. The fear of the Lord is the springboard that propels you into wanting to know God's Word, which causes you to pay very close attention as you study or hear the Word of God. Furthermore, this should be of utmost importance to you and should be first and foremost on your agenda; to know and understand God's Word, because this is first and foremost on God's agenda for your life when He pours out His Spirit upon you.

(Proverbs 1:23) Turn you at my reproof: behold, I will pour out my spirit unto you, I will make known my words unto you.

Because if you want to, not only dwell in the land, but remain in it, you must be perfect.

(Proverbs 2:21) For the upright shall dwell in the land, and the perfect shall remain in it.

Many ministers have either forgotten, or never learned of the importance of the fear of the Lord residing in the heart of a person.

The fear of the Lord leads us to the Word of God and produces a love for more of the Word of God.

Observe how in Deuteronomy chapter 6, God through His servant Moses, helps us to see the importance of the fear of the Lord being in a person.

(Deuteronomy 6:1, 2)

1. Now these are the commandments, the statutes, and the judgments, which the LORD your God commanded to teach you, that ye might do them in the land whither ye go to possess it:

2. That thou mightest fear the LORD thy God, to keep all his statutes and his commandments, which I command thee, thou, and thy son, and thy son's son, all the days of thy life; and that thy days may be prolonged.

When we read from verse 1 to verse 2, we get the impression that the Lord is telling them that if they will do what verse 1 says, that they will fear the Lord; that somehow the keeping of verse one will instill the fear of God in them.

However, this is not what the Lord is insinuating here!

What Moses is saying in verse one is, (in the authors own words), "listen nation of Israel I am going to go over again what God commanded me to teach you, So that when you get to the promise land you will do them." In verse two he continues, "Therefore, the first thing you must do is FEAR THE LORD YOUR GOD!"

Moses is trying to get them to see in verse two, that they must do this first, so that the fear of God will help them to keep the second part of that verse, which is, "to keep His statutes and His commandments."

Because Moses is giving them, a history lesson of what God commanded him to teach the people, and given that in the original setting that included first the instilling of the fear of the Lord in them. He is letting them know that in this second teaching it still includes the instilling of the fear of God. This is first on Gods agenda now, as it was when He first gave them the Ten Commandments on mount Si'nai.

After he begins to remind them of the importance of keeping Gods Word in verse 1, in verse 2 he endeavors to get them to see that even more important then that is the need of having the fear of God in them, because they need that in order to be able to keep His word.

(Deuteronomy 5:29) O that there were such an heart in them, that they would fear me, and keep all my commandments always, that it might be well with them, and with their children for ever!

This is why when he gets to verse 3 he reiterates the importance of making sure that the fear of God is in them by telling them, *"Hear therefore, O Israel, observe to do it."* - Observe to do what? - What he just told them to do in verse 2, *"That thou mightest fear the LORD thy God,"*

3. Hear therefore, O Israel, and observe to do it; that it may be well with thee, and that ye may increase mightily, as the LORD God of thy fathers hath promised thee, in the land that floweth with milk and honey.

Observe how in verses 4 and 5 he says . . .

(Deuteronomy 6:4, 5)

4. Hear, O Israel: The LORD our God is one LORD:

5. And thou shalt love the LORD thy God with all thine heart, and with all thy soul, and with all thy might.

. . . How can He expect them to go from fearing Him, (in verse 2), to loving Him with everything that is in them, (in verse 5)?

Because if they apply the principles discussed in this chapter, the fear of the Lord will produce such a love in them for the Word of God, that, that love will encompass both God and His Word, because the two are one. This is why He continues saying . . .

(Deuteronomy 6:6-9)

6. And these words, which I command thee this day, shall be in thine heart:

7. And thou shalt teach them diligently unto thy children, and shalt talk of them when thou sittest in thine house, and when thou walkest by the way, and when thou liest down, and when thou risest up.

8. And thou shalt bind them for a sign upon thine hand, and they shall be as frontlets between thine eyes.

9. And thou shalt write them upon the posts of thy house, and on thy gates.

He says what He says in verses 6 through 9 to let them know the importance of making His Word their all-in-all. However, this will not happen and cannot happen unless the fear of the Lord is there first to produce the love for the Word that will make His Word their all-in-all.

Observe how the Lord keeps making statements such as "AND THOU SHALT" love the Lord thy God, in verse 5.

Or, and these words. . . "SHALL BE" in thine heart, in verse 6. As well as "AND THOU SHALT," in verses 7 through 9.

These phrases seem to suggest that the scriptures are commanding the individual to do these things. However, these phrases also seem to imply that the individual will somehow come to the place where that person will perform the doing of those phrases.

Which is it, commanding them to do them, or telling them that they will do them? It is both!

The scriptures are letting them know that when they make the necessary effort to do as they are told to do, they will grow so much in love for that word that they will come to the place where they will just automatically do it. For the reason, that it will become their nature to do it.

However, observe how when he gets to verses 10 through 12 he warns them of the danger of forgetting the Lord that performed the doing of all this.

(Deuteronomy 6:10-12)

10. And it shall be, when the LORD thy God shall have brought thee into the land which he sware unto thy fathers, to Abraham, to Isaac, and to Jacob, to give thee great and goodly cities, which thou buildedst not,

11. And houses full of all good things, which thou filledst not, and wells digged, which thou diggedst not, vineyards and olive trees, which thou plantedst not; when thou shalt have eaten and be full;

12. Then beware lest thou forget the LORD, which brought thee forth out of the land of Egypt, from the house of bondage

Therefore, for this reason he reiterates again, in verse 13, the importance of the fear of the Lord being in them, thereby letting them know that the way to keep from forgetting the Lord is by always having the fear of the Lord in them.

(Deuteronomy 6:13) Thou shalt fear the LORD thy God, and serve him, and shalt swear by his name.

When the nation of Israel says to Moses in . . .

(Deuteronomy 5:24-27)

24. And ye said, Behold, the LORD our God hath shewed us his glory and his greatness, and we have heard his voice out of the midst of the fire: we have seen this day that God doth talk with man, and he liveth.

25. Now therefore why should we die? for this great fire will consume us: if we hear the voice of the LORD our God any more, then we shall die.

26. For who is there of all flesh, that hath heard the voice of the living God speaking out of the midst of the fire, as we have, and lived?

27. Go thou near, and hear all that the LORD our God shall say: and speak thou unto us all that the LORD our God shall speak unto thee; and we will hear it, and do it.

. . . As an indication that they feared the Lord and would do as He said. God knew that it was superficial; the fear of God was not completely in them. This is why God reponse back with the statment . . .

(Deuteronomy 5:28, 29)

28. And the LORD heard the voice of your words, when ye spake unto me; and the LORD said unto me, I have heard the voice of the words of this people, which they have spoken unto thee: they have well said all that they have spoken.

29. O that there were such an heart in them, that they would fear me, and keep all my commandments always, that it might be well with them, and with their children for ever!

They needed to have the fear of God in them to aid, strengthen and motivate them to do as He said in order for them to live.

(Deuteronomy 5:32 and 33)

32. Ye shall observe to do therefore as the LORD your God hath commanded you: ye shall not turn aside to the right hand or to the left.

33. Ye shall walk in all the ways which the LORD your God hath commanded you, THAT YE MAY LIVE, and that it may be well with you, and that ye may prolong your days in the land which ye shall possess.

However, that was not the case. The fear of the Lord was not in them. God knew that, and as a result, He knew that they would eventually resort to breaking His commandments. Which is why through Moses, God keeps telling them of the importance of having the fear of the Lord in them.

God had swore to their fore fathers to give them the land of promise, However they needed to live long enough to get to the promise land. Furthermore, only people that are righteous will live to see and enter the promise land. This is why in Deuteronomy chapter six verses twenty through twenty-five Moses makes this known to the nation of Israel

(Deuteronomy 6:20-25)

20. And when thy son asketh thee in time to come, saying, What mean the testimonies, and the statutes, and the judgments, which the LORD our God hath commanded you?

21. Then thou shalt say unto thy son, We were Pharaoh's bondmen in Egypt; and the LORD brought us out of Egypt with a mighty hand:

22. And the LORD shewed signs and wonders, great and sore, upon Egypt, upon Pharaoh, and upon all his household, before our eyes:

23. And he brought us out from thence, that he might bring us in, to give us the land which he sware unto our fathers.

24. And the LORD commanded us to do all these statutes, to fear the LORD our God, for our good always, that he might preserve us alive, as it is at this day.

25. And it shall be our righteousness, if we observe to do all these commandments before the LORD our God, as he hath commanded us.

This is why in this chapter 6, God, through Moses, is endeavoring to get the nation of Israel to see their need of fearing the Lord, so that fear will cause them to keep His covenant thereby making them righteous and keeping them alive to enter the promises land.

In the next chapter, we will learn how, when ministers preach truths that will put the fear of God in the hearts of the hearer that fear will cause the hearer to evaluate his or her life and choose to turn from that lifestyle to God for salvation.

CHAPTER FOUR

YE MUST BE BORN AGAIN!

[1]There was a man of the Pharisees, named Nicodemus, a ruler of the Jews: [2]The same came to Jesus by night, and said unto him, Rabbi, we know that thou art a teacher come from God: for no man can do these miracles that thou doest, except God be with him. [3]Jesus answered and said unto him, Verily, verily, I say unto thee, Except a man be born again, he cannot see the kingdom of God. [4]Nicodemus saith unto him, How can a man be born when he is old? Can he enter the second time into his mother's womb, and be born? [5]Jesus answered, Verily, verily, I say unto thee, Except a man be born of water and of the Spirit, he cannot enter into the kingdom of God. [6]That which is born of the flesh is flesh; and that which is born of the Spirit is spirit. [7]Marvel not that I said unto thee, Ye must be born again (John 3:1-7).

Of all the subjects discussed in the Bible, the subject of the new birth is the one that must be best understood, so that a person can truly comprehend what our salvation entails. I cannot emphasize the importance of understanding this chapter enough. Read it more than once; read it slowly and pay very close attention to what is written in it. Do not let outside interferences distract you as you read this chapter.

There are many different teachings preached in the religious world, but only the Word of God can guide us to the truth. Furthermore, if an individual misses it the first time, there is no redoing it. It would be the saddest day in one's eternal life to stand before God on that great and terrible day thinking that one is going to receive eternal life, only to have the Lord say, "I never knew you."

It is the author's belief that there is great misunderstanding in the area of the new birth, and because of the misunderstanding of those scriptures, the same scriptures that will lead many to eternal life will mislead many into an eternal damnation.

DO NOT BE DECEIVED!

In this story — which is not a story at all, but an actual event that happened in the life of the author many years ago — we will see why it is so very important to be following what the Word of God says and not what we think it says. This even convinced the author to search the scriptures for indisputable proof that will bring a person to truly know if the way that he is living is in fact what God desires or what man thinks.

The event took place at a construction site when I was an electrician working on building new houses. As was my custom, I would sit and read the Bible during my break, and if an opportunity arose, I would witness to someone. Well, there was this young man who, every Monday, would tell those who were interested to hear of his escapades during the weekend. Usually those events consisted of partying, drug use, and the different girls he would spend his time. Now this man was a well-built, good-looking young man who was seen on occasion with different girls, so his stories were not hard to believe. During one of my opportunities to witness to someone, this same young man heard me and said to the person I was witnessing to, "You should listen to him because I know what he's talking about, and he is telling you the truth."

Afterwards, I approached this young man and asked, "How do you know about the Bible?" He proceeded to tell me that he was a born-again Christian. Being a little baffled, I asked him, "How could you be a Christian and live the lifestyle that you profess to live, with all the partying, girls, and drugs?" He went on to inform me that he had been raised in a Baptist church, and that when he was younger he had accepted Jesus Christ as his Lord and Savior. As a result of that experience, he had been born again. He continued to share with me that he had been taught that once a person was born again, he could never lose his salvation, that no one could pluck him out of the hands of God.

Many well-meaning preachers and pastors do not realize that Satan, as cunning as he is, can take the best of teachings and twist them to cause the hearer to believe that they can walk a certain way and still reach Heaven.

This experience shocked me, as I did not know of the teachings of "Once saved, always saved." I was brought up in a small Spanish Christian church that did not teach this but instead preached holiness. Now holiness was a lifestyle that, though I heard of it, I never lived. Therefore, when I did my ungodly acts, I really feared dying in that condition, knowing that if I did, I would meet my creator and have to face the torments of Hell's fire. Furthermore, I thank God that I was never taught this young man's beliefs, since I probably would have gone down the same destructive route, believing like this young man that I could live any old way and still be saved.

After meeting this young man, I encountered many other so-called Christians that used this same concept to justify their unholy lifestyles. Many had run off with another's spouse, believing that God would overlook their actions. Others lived sinful lifestyles that did not seem to bother them because of what they had been taught. They believe sin is no longer an issue because we are no longer under the law. The law has been done away with and so it is no longer a sin. Many people I have met are living a deceived life because they believe this concept or concepts similar to it. Though it is taught in different outlines under different scenarios, the principles are the same and the results are the same: *There is a way that seems right to a man but the end of that way is the way of death (Proverbs 14:12; 16:25).*

UNDERSTANDING OUR NEW BIRTH

Let us look at the revelation behind the teaching of the new birth that the Lord was trying to get Nicodemus to see. That also needs to be seen by God's people in this day and time.

In the verses that we read at the beginning of this chapter, we see Nicodemus coming to the Lord and affirming that he believed Jesus was a teacher from God, to which Jesus responds that "unless a man is born again, he cannot enter the kingdom of God." Nicodemus explains that he cannot understand what the Lord is saying, and asks how this could be possible.

In Jesus' efforts to teach Nicodemus about the born-again experience, He perceives that Nicodemus does not believe Him. This fact is made known when Jesus tells him, *"Verily, verily, I say unto thee, we speak that we do know, and testify that we have seen; and ye receive not our witness. If I have told you earthly things, and ye believe not, how shall ye believe, if I tell you of heavenly things?" (John 3:11, 12).*

Jesus goes on to tell him that He is the son of man that descended from Heaven. He then prophesies to him: *"And as Moses lifted up the serpent in the wilderness, even so must the Son of man be lifted up. That whosoever believeth in him should not perish, but have eternal life"* (John 3:14, 15).

Why did Jesus say this? What was the significance of comparing Himself with the serpent that Moses lifted up in the wilderness? The serpent was not for the purpose that the people believed in that serpent to receive their healing; the purpose was just so that the people, when they looked at that

48

serpent, would receive their healing. And leave it at that. However, what was the reason for Jesus to say this statement to Nicodemus? He was prophesying! He was telling Nicodemus what was going to happen, so that when it did happen, they would believe that He was who He said He was and do as He said to do. In other words, so that people would BELIEVE HIM.

(Deuteronomy 18:18, 19, 21, 22)

18. I will raise them up a Prophet from among their brethren, like unto thee, and will put my words in his mouth; and he shall speak unto them all that I shall command him.

19. And it shall come to pass, that whosoever will not hearken unto my words which he shall speak in my name, I will require it of him.

21. And if thou say in thine heart, How shall we know the word which the LORD hath not spoken?

22. When a prophet speaketh in the name of the LORD, if the thing follow not, nor come to pass, that is the thing which the LORD hath not spoken...

A person cannot say he believes in Jesus if he does not believe Jesus. This is why the scriptures say, *"And as Moses lifted up the serpent in the wilderness, even so must the Son of man be lifted up, That whosoever believeth in him should not perish, but have eternal life."* The reason for Jesus being lifted up, as was the serpent, was to serve as a witness that what He said would come to pass, and that after it came to pass, they could believe that He was who He said He was, and by this, they could believe Him and thereby follow Him by doing as He told them to do.

If the verse was to say, "That whosoever believeth Him should not perish but have everlasting life," people would understand it more clearly, because then they would see that the implications are to believe Him, to believe what He says, and to do what He says. However, because the verse says, "that whosoever believeth in Him," this gives the reader or the hearer the belief or the insinuation that all he has to do is just believe that He is who He says He is. While making no effort on the part of the reader or hearer to do what He says to do — *And why call ye me, Lord, Lord, and do not the things which I say?* (*Luke 6:46*) — No effort on the part of the hearer or reader to make any changes in his or her lifestyle. *"They profess that they know God; but in works they deny him, being abominable, and disobedient, and unto every good work reprobate" (Titus 1:16).*

Furthermore, this only puts the reader or the hearer in a position where that person will one day just come forward, say a meaningless prayer of acknowledgment of Jesus Christ, confess sins that that individual has not repented of, and believe in a God who will not judge him or her for the lifestyle that he or she will continue to live. Because there is no true knowledge, of who God is and what His requirements are. And the requirements are made known to us by His Son, and if we do not believe His son, then we do not believe in His Son. Let us explain this a little more in detail, while we study carefully the next few verses.

(John 3:15-21)

15. That whosoever believeth in him should not perish, but have eternal life.

16. For God so loved the world, that he gave his only begotten Son, that whosoever believeth in him should not perish, but have everlasting life.

17. For God sent not his Son into the world to condemn the world; but that the world through him might be saved.

18. He that believeth on him is not condemned: but he that believeth not is condemned already, because he hath not believed in the name of the only begotten Son of God.

19. And this is the condemnation, that light is come into the world, and men loved darkness rather than light, because their deeds were evil.

20. For every one that doeth evil hateth the light, neither cometh to the light, lest his deeds should be reproved.

21. But he that doeth truth cometh to the light, that his deeds may be made manifest, that they are wrought in God.

Understanding clearly what these verses say is crucial to understanding the new birth.

When Jesus makes the statements in verses 15 and 16, the line of thought is that whosoever believeth in Him will receive eternal life. However, notice that in verse 17 He goes on to say, *"For God sent not his Son into the world to condemn the world; but that the world through him might be saved."* Now why does Jesus say that? If up to this point the concept has been that all that we have to do is believe in Him, why does God have to let us know that He did not send His son into the world to condemn it? He was not asked by anyone about the Son condemning us. What is the significance of bringing up the subject of condemnation? He brings up the subject of condemnation because this is how He explains what belief in Jesus necessitates.

UNDERSTANDING THE CONDEMNATION

The whole idea is that a person will receive eternal life if he believes in Jesus Christ; moreover, only those who believe in Him will not be condemned. Those who do not believe in Him are already condemned. We need to understand why they are already condemned and how this explains their unbelief in Jesus Christ. Furthermore, if we can understand what constitutes them not believing, then the opposite of that would be what adds up to an individual believing in Jesus Christ.

To understand who it is that believes in Jesus and who does not, to determine who will receive eternal life and who will not; we need to understand the condemnation. Because it is in understanding the condemnation that we get an understanding of what believing in Jesus Christ really means. Thereby understanding that it is not a person coming forward and expressing his belief that Jesus Christ is the son of God who died for the sins of mankind and then going on his or her merry way, deceived into believing that now he or she is spared from the wrath to come.

Let us study the condemnation to understand clearly, who really believes in Jesus Christ and who does not. Notice that verse 19 above says, *"And this is the condemnation, that light is come into the world, and men loved darkness rather than light, because their deeds were evil."*

To truly understand the condemnation we need to understand this small demonstration, so carefully read the next few paragraphs.

Let us say you are an individual on the road of life. While on this road, you come to a fork, which goes in many directions. Not knowing which road to take, you find there is a sign that says, "Only one of these roads leads to the kingdom of God and eternal life. All the other roads lead to death." You wonder, "Which one of these roads is the one that leads to life eternal?" Then out of nowhere comes a wise old man who tells you that the road that leads to eternal life is the one that is illuminated. All the other roads are in darkness because they lead to death. So now, it is just a matter of stepping on that road and continuing with your journey…or is it?

Many religious teachings make you think that is all it takes. This is why they just tell you to come forward, pray a simple prayer, believe that Jesus Christ is the son of God and that He died for your sins, and presto; you are saved. The Word of God, however, is full of many scriptures that tell a different story.

God has left us a clear understanding of which road to take. It is the only road that is illuminated! Although this seems simple, there is a problem. You believe that you do not have to do anything, just step onto that road and start walking to the kingdom of God and receive eternal life. However, (here is where the problem comes in); the problem is this: the light is not sent to illuminate YOU, but to illuminate your PATH, (*Thy word is a lamp unto my feet, and a light unto my path.*), so you can see your way clearly to continue on your way to the kingdom of God. However, the moment you step onto that road, the same light that was sent to illuminate your path, now also illuminates YOU. You are in the spotlight. All your deeds, all your actions, all your works are exposed because you are in the light.

REPENTANCE IS THE FIRST STEP TO THE BORN-AGAIN EXPERIENCE

People that have not repented live in shame, so they live in darkness because they do not want people to see their evil deeds. AND YOU CANNOT STEP INTO THAT LIGHT IF YOU HAVE NOT FIRST REPENTED AND TURNED FROM YOUR EVIL WAYS. Furthermore, because of the verse that says, (and the scriptures cannot be broken), *"That man love darkness rather than light because their deeds are evil; For every one that doeth evil hateth the light, neither cometh to the light, lest his deeds should be reproved."* Your evils deeds — if you have not repented first — will keep you from ever stepping onto that lighted road.

You may want to go to Heaven. You may want to receive eternal life. You may think or believe that you are saved and on your way to Heaven. However, if you have not repented first, your evil deeds will stop you and keep you from ever stepping onto that road, the only road that takes you to the kingdom of God. You can say that you are on that road; you can dance and shout that you are on that road, but according to scripture, YOU ARE NOT!

(Jesus the Christ, is the Word of God. The Word of God is the light that illuminates our path, (gives us understanding of how to come to God, *no man cometh unto the Father, but by me.*). If we do not repent, His Spirit through His Word will convict us of our evil deeds because it is their ministry to get us to turn from our evil ways. (And he said unto him, If they hear not Moses and the prophets, neither will they be persuaded, though one rose from the dead. Luke 16:31). Because the light is convicting us to repent and we do not, because we do not want to give up our evil ways, this causes us to hate the light and do everything possible to get as far away from the light as we can. Furthermore, because the light is the Word of God, and that light convicts people of their sins, that is the reason for why ministers are preaching what their congregations want to here, and why there are few messages about hell, the coming wrath of God and repentance from sins. It is their way of moving further and further from the light.)

Ministers MUST return to that old but biblically correct teaching of repentance. This is why such messages of Hell, fire and brimstone, the coming wrath of God, and the judgment of God are necessary: to put the fear of God in a person. Thereby, causing individuals to see their need of a savior and repent from a fearful and sincere heart, thereby turning to that savior, (Jesus, the Word of God, (the light)).

(And he said, Nay, father Abraham: but if one went unto them from the dead, they will <u>repent</u>. And he said unto him, If they hear not Moses and the prophets, neither will they be <u>persuaded, though one rose from the dead</u> (Luke 16:30, 31).

The Law and the Prophets both point us in the direction of repentance; it is their ministry to cause us to repent. Moreover, if we do not understand them and permit them to persuade us to repent, neither will we be persuaded though one rose from the dead, even if that one is the son of

God. Because Jesus is the culmination of the Law and the Prophets.

Modern day ministers are trying to turn people to Jesus while by-passing the law and the Prophets, and Jesus Himself said, "You cannot do it, because, *If they hear not Moses and the prophets, neither will they be persuaded, though one,* (me, myself and I,) *rose from the dead* ".

Many deceived persons have come forward and have professed Jesus as their Lord and Savior with their mouths, but then turn around and deny Him with their actions because they have not been taught correctly. *"They profess that they know God; but in works they deny him, being abominable, and disobedient, and unto every good work reprobate" (Titus 1:16).*

This is why verse 17 sounds like an apology, because God sent His son, (the light), to illuminate our paths so that we can see our way clearly to get to Heaven, not so that His son, (the light), would keep us off the road that takes us to Heaven. However, if we do not truly repent, our very actions are condemning us already because our evil deeds serve as the barrier that is preventing us from ever stepping onto that lighted road.

I can almost see God in Heaven shaking His head, saying, "I'm sorry, but if you do not make it in, do not blame My Son, (the light). I did not send Him to keep you from getting on that road, but to guide you down that road. Blame yourself for not turning from your evil deeds, which prevented you from ever stepping onto that road that would have brought you to Me".

When on that day some people see that they failed to make it in because they were deceived to think that they were on that road when in fact they were not, they will say, "Man, if that light had not been there I could have walked that road to the kingdom of God. But because that light was shining brightly, I refused to enter in. It was the light's

55

fault." No, it was your own for not repenting of your evil ways so that you could walk in that light, in clear view, unashamed because you would not have had anything to hide!

There are many people that profess Jesus as their Lord and Savior with their mouths, but their actions profess something else. We can see the verse that says "he that believeth is not condemned." But what constitutes that a person is not condemned is to step in the light and walk unobstructed in clear view of the light that will guide that person to eternal life. This is that person that truly believeth in Jesus Christ. Many people would understand their new birth if they knew what the scriptures mean when it says "He that BELIEVETH in Him."

Let us look at the word *condemn,* according to the original writings; condemn as found in John 3:17 and condemned as found in John 3:18 mean the same thing because in the two verses the same word is used. It is the Greek word κρίνω krinō, *kree'-no;* and this word means prop. to distinguish, i.e. *decide* (mentally or judicially);. . .

Now notice that the word *condemnation,* as found in John 3:19 is κρίσις krisis, *kree'-sis;* meaning decision (subj. or obj., for or against); . . .

After doing that small demonstration above to try to show what the condemnation is from the view of verse 19, and upon seeing what the words *condemn* and *condemned* mean according to the original writings, we can start getting a clear picture of what it means to believe or not believe in Jesus Christ.

"Those that believe in Christ are not condemned," (remember that the word *condemned* means "to distinguish, that is to decide"), whereas, "Those that believe not are condemned already." Verse 19 says, "This is the condemnation", (also keep in mind that the word condemnation means a decision, for or against). We can see

56

now, through the demonstration and the definition given, that Christ's judging us has nothing to do with this subject of whether we believe in Him or not. What it does have to do with is whether we make a decision to turn from our evil deeds or not.

What we can see here is that those who believe in Him are the ones who decide not to stay in darkness, but instead chose to turn from their evil deeds so they could step onto that lighted road and go on to the kingdom of God. Those who believe not are those who decided to stay in darkness. They did not decide to stay in darkness because they did not want to go to Heaven, but because they did not repent of their evil deeds; their evil deeds decided for them.

What transpires here is that the light forces a person to make a decision, for or against the light. You cannot continue in your sins and still believe you are going to make it in. You can believe that if you want, but eternity will tell a different story. This is what repentance is all about, turning from our evil ways to live according to God's holy law. If repenting were not necessary, why then did Jesus have to die? If we were fine living in our sins, why did we need Christ? If a holy life is not needed, then why preach, "Repent and be baptized?"

God gave us His law so that man would know how to live before Him. This way, man would live righteously and be found just and thereby justified to enter into eternal life. God sent His Son so that He would be the propitiation for our sins, and to lead us down the road that will produce the fruition of God's plan of salvation for and in our lives as we hear Him, believe in Him, and do as He says.

As we proceed in this book, we will see how the pieces of the puzzle of God's Word interlock to give us a beautiful picture of God's plan for salvation.

CHAPTER FIVE

WHAT IS TRUE REPENTANCE?

¹In those days came John the Baptist, preaching in the wilderness of Judaea, ²And saying, Repent ye: for the kingdom of Heaven is at hand. ³For this is he that was spoken of by the prophet Esaias, saying, The voice of one crying in the wilderness, Prepare ye the way of the Lord, make his paths straight. ⁴And the same John had his raiment of camel's hair, and a leathern girdle about his loins; and his meat was locusts and wild honey. ⁵Then went out to him Jerusalem, and all Judaea, and all the region round about Jordan, ⁶And were baptized of him in Jordan, confessing their sins (Matthew 3:1-6).

Not much is said anymore about repentance. It seems that you can go for weeks watching Christian television and never even hear a message on it. Most ministers no longer admonish the hearers to repent; just come forward and say a simple prayer of acknowledgement of Jesus Christ, and that He died on the cross for their sins and that is it, ZAP, you are saved; but at what expense? At the expense that the hearer will believe that now, they are spared from the wrath to come only to find out otherwise in the end.

Repentance begins with realizing that the way you live is not right before God because your lifestyle is contrary to God's commandments. And as a result of that, one day you will stand before Him and give an account of that lifestyle and receive your just punishment for it. Therefore, because of that knowledge, you turn from that lifestyle and endeavor to live according to God's holy commandments.

(Luke 13:3) I tell you, Nay: but, <u>except ye repent, ye shall all likewise perish.</u>

(2 Peter 3:9) The Lord is not slack concerning his promise, as some men count slackness; but is longsuffering to us-ward, <u>not willing that any should perish, but that all should come to repentance.</u>

Because we are privileged with having God's complete Word, another area of repentance is also realizing that God has designed a plan for our forgiveness and cleansing from our sins through the shed blood of His Son. As well as a way of living that will produce a nature in us that is like unto that of God Himself, so that the impulses, desires, urges, or inclinations to sin are no longer there.

You must truly repent and there must be some kind of substantiation that proves that you have in fact repented.

(Matthew 3:7, 8)

7. But when he saw many of the Pharisees and Sadducees come to his baptism, he said unto them, O generation of vipers, who hath warned you to flee from the wrath to come?

8. Bring forth therefore fruits meet for repentance:

(Acts 26:20) But shewed first unto them of Damascus, and at Jerusalem, and throughout all the coasts of Judaea, and then to the Gentiles, that they should repent and turn to God, and do works meet for repentance.

This kind of repentance removes those evil deeds that keep you from ever stepping into that lighted road that takes you to the kingdom of God. This is why if you are one of those that truly believes in Jesus Christ you already have the good deeds that allow you to walk in unobstructed view of the light; the good deeds or fruit meet for repentance. Better worded, good deeds that are evident that you truly have repented.

(John 3:21) But he that doeth truth cometh to the light, that his deeds may be made manifest, that they are wrought in God.

Now this does not mean that you will not make a mistake. You are not perfect, you could fall, but there has got to be in you a sense of having done wrong when you fall, and a remorse for that wrong that causes you to cry out to God for forgiveness, and a sincere desire to live right and not fall again. This is the indication of a true repented heart.

This is where God's designed way of living comes into play; as you follow in the teachings of His Son, He leads you down that road that takes you through the process that produces the Christ-like nature in you so that you grow in perfection and in the Christ-like nature where you no longer sin.

REPENTANCE BRINGS US TO JESUS CHRIST, AND JESUS CHRIST TAKES US THE REST OF THE WAY.

For this reason, it says, "Repent and be baptized every one of you in the name of <u>Jesus Christ</u> for the remission of sins, and ye shall receive the gift of the Holy Ghost."

Let us break this down. The scriptures say

(Matthew 3:2, 5-11)

2. And saying, Repent ye: for the kingdom of Heaven is at hand.

5. Then went out to him Jerusalem, and all Judaea, and all the region round about Jordan,

6. And were baptized of him in Jordan, confessing their sins.

7. But when he saw many of the Pharisees and Sadducees come to his baptism, he said unto them, O generation of vipers, who hath warned you to flee from the wrath to come?

8. Bring forth therefore fruits meet for repentance:

9. And think not to say within yourselves, We have Abraham to our father: for I say unto you, that God is able of these stones to raise up children unto Abraham.

10. And now also the axe is laid unto the root of the trees: therefore every tree which bringeth not forth good fruit is hewn down, and cast into the fire.

11. I indeed baptize you with water unto repentance: but he that cometh after me is mightier than I, whose shoes I am not worthy to bear: he shall baptize you with the Holy Ghost, and with fire:

Why does it say what it says in verses 2 through 11? Because our salvation begins first with repentance, which incorporates baptism! However, baptism comes in a progression of stages: Water, Holy Ghost, and Fire. The first stage is up to us; we have to make the necessary effort. And that is to truly repent and have proof that we from a sincere heart have repented, and then seal that with the waters of baptism, for the remission or the freedom or the forgiveness or the removal or pardon of those sins.

This is all part of our born again experience.

(John 3:5) Jesus answered, Verily, verily, I say unto thee, Except a man be born of water and of the Spirit, he cannot enter into the kingdom of God.

Many minister believe and teach that being born of water and of the Spirit means that we are first born naturally, (born of water) and then, when we come to God, we are born spiritually, (born of the Spirit). However, that is not what the scriptures are saying here. What the scriptures are referring to in this verse, is, our born again experience of repentance and being baptize in water, (born of water), for the remission of our sins and then being baptized in the holy ghost, (born of the Spirit) and fire.

Observe how when the Pharisees and Sadducees came to John's baptism to be baptized, John told them, "*O generation of vipers, who hath warned you to flee from the wrath to come? Bring forth therefore fruits meet for repentance.*" In other words, he was telling them, "You want me to baptize you as a seal that you have repented, then show me some proof that you have in fact repented."

Understanding what he says between verses 9 and 11 is crucial to understanding this whole concept. Notice what he says in verses 9 and 10: "*9. And think not to say within yourselves, we have Abraham to our father: for I say unto you, that God is able of these stones to raise up children unto Abraham. 10. And now also the axe is laid unto the root of the trees: therefore every tree which bringeth not forth good fruit is hewn down, and cast into the fire.*"

Why did he say that? Because they thought that as the seed of Abraham, they could bypass God's ordained format! They thought that John would not notice that they from a true heart had not repented! And they were right, because John could not see into their hearts to know if in fact they had truly repented. However, John knew that He who was coming after him could, and He would know if they had in fact repented, and if they had not, they would not be baptized with His Holy Ghost and fire. For this reason, he responds as he does, saying in verse 11, "I indeed baptize you with water unto repentance." Why would he say this, as an indication that he would baptize them, if in verses 7 and 8 the implications are that he would not baptize them? Because what he was really saying to them from verse 9 to 11 was, in the author's own words; "Don't think that just because you're Abraham's seed that you can bypass God's format. I will baptize you with water, because I do not know if in fact you have repented. I do not see any fruit that indicate to me that you have repented, because I cannot look on the inside. I only see the outside, so perhaps you have repented. Nevertheless, there comes one after me who is greater than I, who knows all things and sees even into your heart. He is the one that baptizes with the Holy Ghost and Fire. You can fool me, but you will not be able to fool Him, and if you have not truly repented, He will know it and you will not be baptized by Him."

When we have done our part then that opens the door for the fulfilling of the scriptures of John 14:15-17 and Acts 2:38.

(John 14:15-17)

15. If ye love me, keep my commandments.

(The keeping of His commandments is the evidence of a true repented heart. This should cause us to see our need to seal it with the baptism of repentance for the remission of those sins, in water, in His name, this brings us to the place where we are then sealed with the holy Spirit of promise (Ephesians 1:13).)

16. And I will pray the Father, and he shall give you another Comforter, that he may abide with you for ever;

(This is the baptism of the Holy Ghost.)

17. Even the Spirit of truth; whom the world cannot receive, because it seeth him not, neither knoweth him: but ye know him; for he dwelleth with you, and shall be in you.

(Acts 2:38) Then Peter said unto them, Repent, and be baptized every one of you in the name of Jesus Christ for the remission of sins, and ye shall receive the gift of the Holy Ghost.

With the baptism, (gift), of His Holy Ghost, we are now empowered to go to the next stage of baptism — and that is FIRE — as we do as He says to deny ourselves and take up our cross and follow Him. Through the crucifying and dying process of the trials and tribulations that conforms us into His image, where we take on the nature of God.

Thereby no longer having a sinful nature, but rather a Holy and righteous nature.

(1 Peter 2:21) For even hereunto were ye called: because Christ also suffered for us, leaving us an example, that ye should follow his steps:

(1 Peter 4:1) Forasmuch then as Christ hath suffered for us in the flesh, arm yourselves likewise with the same mind: for he that hath suffered in the flesh hath ceased from sin;

(Isaiah 48:10) Behold, I have refined thee, but not with silver; I have chosen thee in the furnace of affliction.

For this reason, repentance is realizing that God has designed a plan for our forgiveness and cleansing from our sins through the finished work of Jesus Christ, His son, through baptism in water. As well as a way of living that will produce a nature in us, that is like unto that of God Himself through the baptism in the Holy Ghost and fire.

Repentance is not thinking that you can go all week living any old way, and then come Saturday, go to confession, confess to an individual, and think that if you do as he tells you, you are forgiven. THAT IS NOT REPENTANCE. THAT IS DECEPTION, AND WILL ONLY TAKE YOU TO HELL!

There must be a true sense of urgency to turn from your wicked lifestyle and live according to God's Holy Law. Not all those do's and don'ts, but His Holy Covenant, the Ten Commandments. This is why the Son of God said, "A new commandment I give you, that you LOVE ONE ANOTHER." He is that prophet Moses said would come after him and would tell us all that we need to do by speaking to us the Word of God, and that we need to hear Him.

(Deuteronomy 18:18, 19)

18. I will raise them up a Prophet from among their brethren, like unto thee, and will put my words in his mouth; and he shall speak unto them all that I shall command him.

19. And it shall come to pass, that whosoever will not hearken unto my words which he shall speak in my name, I will require it of him.

(This is why you cannot just say that you believe in Him, but must do as He says, (*whosoever will not hearken unto my words which he shall speak in my name, I will require it of him*).

Loving one another is the fulfillment of the whole law. Because of this, Jesus said, "He that has My commandments and keeps them, he it is that loves Me," and if we love Him, we love Him that sent Him. For this reason, we need to keep HIS COMMANDMENTS OF LOVING ONE ANOTHER, BECAUSE AS WE DO THIS WE SHOW GOD HOW MUCH WE LOVE HIM! We are actively, in our efforts of loving one another, fulfilling the greatest of all the commandments, and that is *"Hear, O Israel; the Lord our God is one Lord: And thou shalt love the Lord thy God with all thy heart and With all thy soul, and with all thy mind, and with all thy Strength."*

Love is an action. We must be performing actions of love to be showing love. For example, if I tell my wife and my daughter that I love them and I never get off my lazy backside and get a job to support them and keep a roof over their heads and food on the table, then I am a liar. I do not love them, I only say I do, but I do not love them because I never show it.

We have to show God how much we love Him. However, because love is an action and God is never in any situation or predicament where we can show Him our love, He has designed it so that we show Him how much we love Him by how much we love His creation. God is never hungry for us to have to feed Him. He is never naked for us to have to clothe Him, nor is He ever homeless for us to have to take Him in. God is never sick or in jail for us to have to visit Him. However, He has ordained it such that when we do these things to the least of these His creation, (man); we are doing it unto Him. Therefore, as we show our love to our fellow man, we are expressing it to Him.

THIS IS THE WHOLE LAW AND PROPHETS IN A NUTSHELL

This is why when He separates the sheep from the goats, to those that He says, *"Depart from me, ye cursed, into everlasting fire, prepared for the Devil and his angels."* He never tells them, "Because you did not believe in Me" or "Because you were never born again", or "Because you never called on My name, this is why you are being cast out." Instead, He says, "Because you did it not to the least of these My brethren you did it not to Me." They were not keeping the two most important commandments of all on which hang all the Law and the Prophets, and that is, "To love God with all their hearts, with all their souls, with all their strengths and with all their mind" and "To love their neighbor as themselves". This is the substantiation of a true repented heart and the evident token of a person who truly believes in Jesus Christ. This merits your receiving eternal life.

(Luke 16:27-31)

27. Then he said, I pray thee therefore, father, that thou wouldest send him to my father's house:

28. For I have five brethren; that he may testify unto them, lest they also come into this place of torment.

29. Abraham saith unto him, They have Moses... (Law)... and the prophets; let them hear them.

66

30. And he said, Nay, father Abraham: but if one went unto them from the dead, they will repent.

31. And he said unto him, If they hear not Moses and the prophets, neither will they be persuaded, though one rose from the dead.

All through the Old Testament, (the Law and the Prophets,) the Lord's anger is expressed to them because of their failure to see the main objective of keeping His covenant. That was to love Him above all that could be loved and to love one another, by expressing that love to each other by caring for each other, in particular those less fortunate, like the widows, orphan, strangers, and poor, by feeding, clothing, sheltering, and caring for them.

In Mary K. Baxter's book *A Divine Revelation of Hell*, (which the author strongly recommends that all those who call upon the name of the Lord read at least once a year), published by Whitaker House, she says in chapter 21, "False Religion":

> I heard Jesus say, "my people should love one another and help one another. They must hate sin and love the sinner...
>
> As Jesus spoke, the earth opened and we were back in Hell...
>
> I followed Jesus on a very crooked and dirty trail... As we drew nearer, I saw that the people were whole, but dead. They were composed of gray, dead flesh and they were bound together with a rope of bondage... I knew that this was a part of Hell... They were deeply engrossed in conversation.
>
> Jesus said, "Let's listen to what they're saying."

One man said, "Did you hear about this man Jesus who came to take away sin"?

Another responded, "I know Jesus. He washed my sins away. In fact, I don't know what I'm doing here."

"Nor do I", said the first.

Another said, "I tried to witness to my neighbor about Jesus, but he wouldn't listen. When his wife died, he came to me to borrow the money for her funeral... I turned him away. I knew he would spend the money for something else anyway. We have to be good stewards of our money.

The first man spoke again. "Yes brother, a boy at our church needed cloths and shoes, but his father drinks so I refused to buy anything for his son.

"Well", said another, "we must always teach others to live like Jesus. That man had no right to drink. Let him suffer."

Jesus said, "O foolish people and slow of heart, awaken to the truth, and love one another with fervent love. Help the helpless. Give to those in need without any thought of getting anything in return.

"If you will repent, O earth, I will bless you and not curse you. Awaken from your sleep and come unto Me."

A Divine Revelation of Hell is peppered with over two hundred references to the Son of God Himself or Mary Baxter pleading with the readers to repent.

There must be evidence that you have repented and are trying to produce those fruits as proof that you have in fact repented and believe in the Son of the living God, the Word of God.

Now all you need is to endeavor to live that lifestyle while you take up your cross and follow Jesus. As He leads you down that road called life, sometimes carrying you, sometimes walking next to you, as you go through those trials or troubles that produce in you His nature so that you become as it were like God Himself, holy and righteous in love, mercy, longsuffering kindness, peace, joy, gentleness, goodness, faith, meekness, and temperance.

The Four Gospels say it this way, "Thou shalt love the Lord thy God with all thy heart, and with all thy soul, and with all thy strength, and with all thy mind, and thou shalt love thy neighbor as thyself." However, you never see it that way again in the Epistles; what you do see is, "For all the law is fulfilled in one word, even in this; Thou shalt love thy neighbor as thyself."

What happen to the first one, "Thou shalt love the Lord thy God"? Why does it not say, "For all the law is fulfilled in two words, even in this; 'thou shalt love the Lord thy God with all thy heart, and thou shalt love thy neighbor as thyself'"?

Did He do away with the first part? Do we no longer have to love Him first and foremost? Does that mean that we put man ahead of God in our love and devotion? Does that mean that we embrace the teachings that man is God and the universe revolves around man — the new age teachings? NO, NEVER!

The scriptures are letting us know that this is how we show God how much we love Him when we express that love to His creation, (man).

Any teaching that teaches that man can hurt man, or any religion, law, government, people, or individual that hurts God's creation and does not make an effort to preserve it, save it, help it, keep it, care for it, feed it, clothe it, house it, and so forth is in direct violation of God's commandments. They are in sin, and will one day stand before God and give an account to Him for their wrong and will face the punishment of an eternal torment in Hell. There is no Purgatory. No place of rest. No water, no air, no comfort, no food, no friends, no family, no hope, no escape, no nothing, but an understanding that this is where you will be forever, along with your memories of how you could have repented when you had the opportunity, but you rejected God and His Holy Word, Jesus the only Son of God. You will know and understand then, like the rich man in hell, how vitally important it was to repent to avoid the torments of hell.

God has designed a way that we can keep His covenant without the worries of all the do's and don'ts, thereby making us righteous and justified to enter into eternal life. When God looks on us, He sees us righteous, not because we are righteous but because we are covered with the righteousness of His Son, while His Son takes us down that road that produces in us His righteousness.

If we take all the Word of God and pour it into a glass, stir it up, and pour it out, we get the gospel of Jesus Christ. It we take the gospel of Jesus Christ, (the teachings of the Son of God), pour it into a glass, stir it up, and pour it out, we get the Law and the Prophets. If we take the Law and the Prophets, pour them into a glass, stir them up, and pour them out, we get the Ten Commandments. If we take the Ten Commandments, pour them into a glass, stir them up, and pour them out, we get the two most important commandments of all, to love God with all that is in you and to love your neighbor as yourself. If we take those two most important commandments of all, pour them into a glass, stir them up, and pour them out, we get "for all the law is fulfilled in one word even in this 'you shall Love your neighbor as yourself.'" And if we leave this in the glass and let it settle to the bottom of the glass, when we look at it we see *"Hear, O Israel; the Lord our God is one Lord: And thou*

70

shalt love the Lord thy God with all thy heart and With all thy soul, and with all thy mind, and with all thy Strength."

Let me paint a picture for all those that have ears to hear and eyes to see. Think of the person in your life that you love the most. Keeping that person in your thoughts, follow carefully in this illustration while really putting yourself in this situation.

You have a son, a daughter, a brother, a sister, a grandson or granddaughter, or whomever. Let us say a son for illustration purposes. Your son is a drug addict, and he is tired of you nagging him to change, so one day he just ups and leaves. You do not know where he is, but he has been gone a long time. You have a dream with your son. Now, you cannot go to him, but you can see him and feel everything that he feels. Here is your son living on the gutter of some street. There are people walking all around him, but nobody notices or they choose not to notice and turn their eyes away.

You are looking at your son and he is dirty and smelly from not bathing. He has sores all over his body and you can actually feel the pain of those sores and the irritation and smell of having not taking a bath. Your tongue sticks to the top of your mouth, as you know it is sticking to the top of his, because of his thirst from not having had anything to drink, not even water. Your stomach hurts and is tight, because you feel his hunger. You cannot believe the desperation in his heart, the hopelessness that he is feeling at this time. The loneliness that he is feeling is so strong that even death to him would seem like a welcome friend. You can sense his anger at those who pimped him, used him, lied to and deceived him that ultimately led to his demise.

The tears stream down your face as you see him and feel all his hurt and pain, though his eyes are dry because there are no more tears in his from crying day and night for just one caring person. You see this and you feel it, but there is nothing you can do. You cry out, "Is there no one to help?

Can't anybody see him? Will somebody please help him? SOMBODY PLEASE HELP HIM." You wonder, "Is everybody blind? Can they not see?" When you see those who turn their heads in the other direction pretending that no one is there, and just walk right by him.

Your heart is rent from your chest to see your son there in that condition and no one to help; help is so close but yet so far away.

You could care less how he got there; you do not care that he sold his body to buy the drugs that put him there. You do not care that he is dirty or smelly, all you know is that he is your son and he needs help, and you, who care cannot help him, and there is not a soul in the whole world that will. "WON'T SOMEBODY PLEASE HELP HIM?" you cry.

God is looking down from Heaven and through His eyes, He sees His creation, created in His own image, His sons and daughters. He feels their pain and hurt, lying in the gutters of life, dirty and hurting, lonely and without hope or help, and He cries, "Won't somebody help? Doesn't anybody understand? Is there nobody who cares?"

He does not care that our own sins put us there. He just wants to help us, clean us up, and bring us back to Him. However, He does this through you and me, and if we do not do it, who will?

DO NOT BE DECEIVED YOU THAT ARE READING THIS CHAPTER!

Many people will read this chapter and be deceived! Why? Because they are living a wicked lifestyle that is neither hurting anybody nor affecting the lives of others in a bad way. (For example, two men or two women living together as if married — a homosexual lifestyle — or a man and a woman engaged in a sexual relationship who feel that

72

they are not hurting anybody because they do not have spouses.) These people will be deceived into thinking that now, they can go through all the motions of a Christian; attend church, read the Bible, pray, and so forth, and never have to repent of their lifestyle because they are fulfilling the law of loving one another. Thereby meeting God's requirement of being saved and so therefore think that they will escape the wrath of God to come.

Do not be deceived, you who are reading this book, especially this chapter. God ordained it this way because God is love and His whole kingdom revolves around all his creation, (in Heaven and on earth), loving one another. It is this simple because this is the Law and the Prophets. Therefore, the Almighty designed it this way because he does not want any to perish but that we all repent and be saved. This does not, however, in any way exclude us from being Holy as He is Holy. All those that are God's and all that pertain to God MUST BE HOLY!

CHAPTER SIX

HOW AND WHY TO TRULY REPENT

¹⁶The law and the prophets were until John: since that time the kingdom of God is preached, and every man presseth into it. ¹⁷And it is easier for heaven and earth to pass, than one tittle of the law to fail. ¹⁸Whosoever putteth away his wife, and marrieth another, committeth adultery: and whosoever marrieth her that is put away from her husband committeth adultery. (*Luke 16:16-18*)

Many people do not know the importance of repentance. In addition, many ministers have failed to see the need of the people to repent. Without repentance, there can be no salvation. Your failure to repent keeps you from going any further then the entrance to the road that leads you to the kingdom of God; you cannot cross the threshold, you cannot go in, you cannot walk in the light of Gods Word.

For people to understand the truth behind repentance and various scriptures surrounding it, people need to understand why Jesus said what He said in Luke 16: 16 thru 18 above. Let us look very closely at these scriptures to see the truths behind them.

The scripture says, *"The law and the prophets were until John: since that time the kingdom of God is preached, and every man presseth into it."* Notice that is says, "The law and the prophets were until John," from the time of John, (forward), up until the time that Jesus was making this statement; He said, "The kingdom of God is preached".

Now we know that the first part of this verse is referring to the Old Testament speaking up Until John the Baptist appeared on the scene. However, what does it mean when it says, "Since that time the kingdom of God is preached"? Moreover, how did this bring about every man pressing or endeavoring to press into it? Let us first learn what it is that was "preached".

IF THE SCRIPTURES SAYS,
"THE KINGDOM OF GOD IS PREACHED",
WHAT WAS BEING PREACHED?

Let us first look at what John the Baptist was preaching; since he was first on the scene and according to scriptures, it began with him, (*The law and the prophets were until John: "SINCE THAT TIME THE KINGDOM OF GOD IS PREACHED"*).

(Matthew 3:1, 2)

1. In those days came John the Baptist, preaching in the wilderness of Judaea,

2. And saying, Repent ye: for the kingdom of heaven is at hand.

The second on the scene was Jesus, let us look at what He came preaching.

(Matthew 4:17)

17. From that time Jesus began to preach, and to say, Repent: for the kingdom of heaven is at hand.

(Mark 1: 14, 15)

14. Now after that John was put in prison, Jesus came into Galilee, preaching the gospel of the kingdom of God,

15. And saying, The time is fulfilled, and the kingdom of God is at hand: repent ye, and believe the gospel.

Notice and keep in mind that there are two vital messages here and that they are linked together, and they are

"REPENT" and why repent, because "THE KINGDOM OF HEAVEN IS AT HAND"!

Let us now look at those that Jesus commissioned to preach the gospel. Let us see what they preached as they where instructed by Jesus. These were third and fourth on the list to preach the gospel of the kingdom.

First, let us look at the 12 disciples.

(Luke 9:1, 2 and 6)

1. Then he called his twelve disciples together, and gave them power and authority over all devils, and to cure diseases.

2. And he sent them to preach the kingdom of God, and to heal the sick.

6. And they departed, and went through the towns, preaching the gospel, and healing every where.

However, look closely at what they preached, as made evident in Matthew 10: 1 and 7 and Mark 6: 7 and 12.

(Matthew 10:1 and 7)

1. And when he had called unto him his twelve disciples, he gave them power against unclean spirits, to cast them out, and to heal all manner of sickness and all manner of disease.

7. And as ye go, preach, saying, The kingdom of heaven is at hand.

(Mark 6:7, 12)

7. And he called unto him the twelve, and began to send them forth by two and two...

12. And they went out, and preached that men should repent.

Now let us consider the 70 that he commissioned after the 12 disciples.

(Luke 10:1 and 9)

1. After these things the Lord appointed other seventy also, and sent them two and two before his face into every city and place, whither he himself would come.

9. And heal the sick that are therein, and say unto them, The kingdom of God is come nigh unto you.

Observe and take notice that in the preaching of the kingdom of God there are two vital messages to this preaching and these are, one, "Repent," and two, "For the kingdom of God is at hand."

(NOTE: Before we continue with this revelation, we need to understand why Jesus gave power to the twelfth disciples as well as the seventy He commissioned to heal the sick and cast our devils. The primary reason was to serve as a witness that they were sent from God and were preaching what God had told them to preach so that the people would stop, take notice and listen to them.

(John 3:1, 2)

1. There was a man of the Pharisees, named Nicodemus, a ruler of the Jews:

2. The same came to Jesus by night, and said unto him, Rabbi, we know that thou art a teacher come from God: for no man can do these miracles that thou doest, except God be with him.

(Hebrews 2:3-4)

3. How shall we escape, if we neglect so great salvation; which at the first began to be spoken by the Lord, and was confirmed unto us by them that heard him;

4. God also bearing them witness, both with signs and wonders, and with divers miracles, and gifts of the Holy Ghost, according to his own will?)

What does this mean? Why did they preach this and why did the Lord say about these statements, "The kingdom of God is preached, and every man presseth into it?" Furthermore, why is it that this kind of preaching caused

"EVERY MAN" to "PRESS" into the kingdom of God?

For us to understand the repentance part of the preaching, we must understand why they preached, "FOR THE KINGDOM OF GOD IS AT HAND." Understand that there were two parts to their message. One was to repent, and the second was, "BECAUSE" or "FOR" the kingdom of God is at hand. And without us understanding what was meant by, "for the kingdom of God is at hand", we cannot see why we must repent and the importance of repenting!

What did they mean by this? What is it that they were telling the people, that the people understood that made them do whatever possible to press into the kingdom? The answer is found in the law and the prophets!

Among other things, the law and the prophets had been prophesying for the longest time that God would one day set up a kingdom; His kingdom. A kingdom that would rule and reign for all eternity.

(Genesis 49:10) The sceptre shall not depart from Judah, nor a lawgiver from between his feet, until Shiloh come; and unto him shall the gathering of the people be.

(Daniel 2:44) And in the days of these kings shall the God of heaven set up a kingdom, which shall never be destroyed: and the kingdom shall not be left to other people, but it shall break in pieces and consume all these kingdoms, and it shall stand for ever.

(Daniel 7:9, 10, 13, 14, 27)

9. I beheld till the thrones were cast down, and the Ancient of days did sit, whose garment was white as snow, and the hair of his head like the pure wool: his throne was like the fiery flame, and his wheels as burning fire.

10. A fiery stream issued and came forth from before him: thousand thousands ministered unto him, and ten thousand times ten thousand stood before him: the judgment was set, and the books were opened.

13. I saw in the night visions, and, behold, one like the Son of man came with the clouds of heaven, and came to the Ancient of days, and they brought him near before him.

14. And there was given him dominion, and glory, and a kingdom, that all people, nations, and languages, should serve him: his dominion is an everlasting dominion, which shall not pass away, and his kingdom that which shall not be destroyed.

27. And the kingdom and dominion, and the greatness of the kingdom under the whole heaven, shall be given to the people of the saints of the most High, whose kingdom is an everlasting kingdom, and all dominions shall serve and obey him.

The scribes know this and so did the Pharisees and Sadducees. Furthermore, because they taught the people the law and the prophets, the people knew this as well.

EQUALLY, JUST AS IMPORTANT THE PEOPLE KNEW THAT GOD WOULD CLEAN UP THIS EARTH PRIOR TO SETTING UP HIS KINGDOM!

However, more then this, the people also knew that prior to God setting up His kingdom, He would do something first. And, that something was to clean up the earth. The rulers and the people knew that God would one day judge the earth and wipe out all unrighteousness first.

(Isaiah 13:5-11 and 13)

5. They come from a far country, from the end of heaven, even the LORD, and the weapons of his indignation, to destroy the whole land.

6. Howl ye; for the day of the LORD is at hand; it shall come as a destruction from the Almighty.

7. Therefore shall all hands be faint, and every man's heart shall melt:

8. And they shall be afraid: pangs and sorrows shall take hold of them; they shall be in pain as a woman that travaileth: they shall be amazed one at another; their faces shall be as flames.

9. Behold, the day of the LORD cometh, cruel both with wrath and fierce anger, to lay the land desolate: and he shall destroy the sinners thereof out of it.

10. For the stars of heaven and the constellations thereof shall not give their light: the sun shall be darkened in his going forth, and the moon shall not cause her light to shine.

11. And I will punish the world for their evil, and the wicked for their iniquity; and I will cause the arrogancy of the proud to cease, and will lay low the haughtiness of the terrible.

13. Therefore I will shake the heavens, and the earth shall remove out of her place, in the wrath of the LORD of hosts, and in the day of his fierce anger.

Malachi 4:1 For, behold, the day cometh, that shall burn as an oven; and all the proud, yea, and all that do wickedly, shall be stubble: and the day that cometh shall burn them up, saith the LORD of hosts, that it shall leave them neither root nor branch.

(Zephaniah 1:2, 3 and 14-18)

2. I will utterly consume all things from off the land, saith the LORD.

3. I will consume man and beast; I will consume the fowls of the heaven, and the fishes of the sea, and the stumblingblocks with the wicked; and I will cut off man from off the land, saith the LORD.

14. The great day of the LORD is near, it is near, and hasteth greatly, even the voice of the day of the LORD: the mighty man shall cry there bitterly.

15. That day is a day of wrath, a day of trouble and distress, a day of wasteness and desolation, a day of darkness and gloominess, a day of clouds and thick darkness,

16. A day of the trumpet and alarm against the fenced cities, and against the high towers.

17. And I will bring distress upon men, that they shall walk like blind men, because they have sinned against the LORD: and their blood shall be poured out as dust, and their flesh as the dung.

18. Neither their silver nor their gold shall be able to deliver them in the day of the LORD'S wrath; but the whole land shall be devoured by the fire of his jealousy: for he shall make even a speedy riddance of all them that dwell in the land.

(Zephaniah 3:8) Therefore wait ye upon me, saith the LORD, until the day that I rise up to the prey: for my determination is to gather the nations, that I may assemble the kingdoms, to pour upon them mine indignation, even all my fierce anger: for all the earth shall be devoured with the fire of my jealousy.

(Joel 2:1-3, 10 and 11)

1. Blow ye the trumpet in Zion, and sound an alarm in my holy mountain: let all the inhabitants of the land tremble: for the day of the LORD cometh, for it is nigh at hand;

2. A day of darkness and of gloominess, a day of clouds and of thick darkness, as the morning spread upon the mountains: a great people and a strong; there hath not been ever the like, neither shall be any more after it, even to the years of many generations.

3. A fire devoureth before them; and behind them a flame burneth: the land is as the garden of Eden before them, and behind them a desolate wilderness; yea, and nothing shall escape them.

10. The earth shall quake before them; the heavens shall

tremble: the sun and the moon shall be dark, and the stars shall withdraw their shining:

11. And the LORD shall utter his voice before his army: for his camp is very great: for he is strong that executeth his word: for the day of the LORD is great and very terrible; and who can abide it?

For this reason when John came on the scene and started preaching, "Repent, For the kingdom of heaven is at hand", the people knew, that, "if the kingdom of heaven was at hand", then that meant that the coming wrath of God, (that the law and the prophets had been prophesying about), "was even closer". Because the wrath of God, according to scriptures, would fall prior to God setting up His kingdom.

(Zephaniah 3:8 and 9)

8. Therefore wait ye upon me, saith the LORD, until the day that I rise up to the prey: for my determination is to gather the nations, that I may assemble the kingdoms, to pour upon them mine indignation, even all my fierce anger: for all the earth shall be devoured with the fire of my jealousy.

9. For then will I turn to the people a pure language, that they may all call upon the name of the LORD, to serve him with one consent.

(Malachi 4:1-3)

1. For, behold, the day cometh, that shall burn as an oven; and all the proud, yea, and all that do wickedly, shall be stubble: and the day that cometh shall burn them up, saith the LORD of hosts, that it shall leave them neither root nor branch.

2. But unto you that fear my name shall the Sun of righteousness arise with healing in his wings; and ye shall go forth, and grow up as calves of the stall.

3. And ye shall tread down the wicked; for they shall be ashes under the soles of your feet in the day that I shall do this, saith the LORD of hosts.

(Daniel 7:7, 8, 11, 15, 16, 17, 23, 26, 27)

7. After this I saw in the night visions, and behold a fourth beast, dreadful and terrible, and strong exceedingly; and it had great iron teeth: it devoured and brake in pieces, and stamped the residue with the feet of it: and it was diverse from all the beasts that were before it; and it had ten horns.

8. I considered the horns, and, behold, there came up among them another little horn, before whom there were three of the first horns plucked up by the roots: and, behold, in this horn were eyes like the eyes of man, and a mouth speaking great things.

11. I beheld then because of the voice of the great words which the horn spake: I beheld even till the beast was slain, and his body destroyed, and given to the burning flame.

15. I Daniel was grieved in my spirit in the midst of my body, and the visions of my head troubled me.

16. I came near unto one of them that stood by, and asked him the truth of all this. So he told me, and made me know the interpretation of the things.

17. These great beasts, which are four, are four kings, which shall arise out of the earth.

23. Thus he said, The fourth beast shall be the fourth kingdom upon earth, which shall be diverse from all kingdoms, and shall devour the whole earth, and shall tread it down, and break it in pieces.

26. But the judgment shall sit, and they shall take away his dominion, to consume and to destroy it unto the end.

27. And the kingdom and dominion, and the greatness of the kingdom under the whole heaven, shall be given to the people of the saints of the most High, whose kingdom is an everlasting kingdom, and all dominions shall serve and obey him.

Therefore, because of this fact, the people, upon

hearing what John was preaching, "To repent and be baptize for the remission of sins"; Understanding that this was how they could escape the wrath to come, came to his baptism to be seal with the waters of baptism in order to escape the wrath to come.

However, the people were missing a vital link to this whole concept. And this was that they needed to repent first, otherwise the whole plan of Gods salvation for them, (as well as for us), would not and could not work.

...We have already learned to some degree, in the pass two chapters of this book, why this will not and cannot work...

This is why John, upon seeing not only the Pharisees and Sadducees...

(Matthew 3:7 and 8)

7. But when he saw many of the Pharisees and Sadducees come to his baptism, he said unto them, O generation of vipers, who hath warned you to flee from the wrath to come?

8. Bring forth therefore fruits meet for repentance:

...but the people as well...

(Luke 3:7 and 8)

7. Then said he to the multitude that came forth to be baptized of him, O generation of vipers, who hath warned you to flee from the wrath to come?

8. Bring forth therefore fruits worthy of repentance...

...come to his baptism to be baptize, he rebuked them saying, "Bring forth therefore fruit worthy or meet for repentance". In the authors own words, "Let me see some proof that you have repented, this whole plan that God design to allow you into His kingdom so you can escape the wrath to come will not work if you do not repent first".

Just as there are in our day, churches full of people

that claim to be saved because they profess to know the Lord but yet with their deeds they are denying Him, because they have never repented. There were people in those days that thought that they could escape the coming judgment of God by going through the motions without really repenting.

And it would not and could not work, because people trying to press into the kingdom by any other means then by the way that God had ordained; Jesus likened them to a man who divorces his wife and marries another, he commits adultery. And he that marries her that is divorced also commits adultery.

Ministers preach that people can come as they are; not to worry about it; Jesus accepts you as you are sin and all. Though this is somewhat true, this does not mean that there is no repentance involve. You still have to repent, you still have to, from a true sincere heart, repent and have fruit as proof that you have repented.

This does not mean that you are perfect and that you will not make a mistake. This means that you realize that the way that you live is not right before God and you are sorry for the way that you live and you truly are turning and want to turn from those sins to God through His Son, so He can empower you to become victorious over those sins.

This is how John prepared the way before Him, by telling the people to repent. Because he, (John), knew that the road that Jesus was going to walk on was the road of our life's. Moreover, our sins represented the rough places on that road. Our sins represented the crookedness of that highway. Our sins also represented the mountains and valley that the Lord would have to walk on.

Which is way when Malachi prophesies in chapter 3 verse 1 saying, *Behold, I will send my messenger, and he shall prepare the way before me: and the Lord, whom ye seek, shall suddenly come to his temple, even the messenger of the covenant, whom ye delight in: behold, he shall come, saith the LORD of hosts.*

This was in fact God the Father talking to God the Son and telling Him, *"As it is written in the prophets, Behold, I send my messenger before thy face, which shall prepare thy way before thee. (Mark 1:2)"*

Who was that messenger? John the Baptist! Furthermore, how was he to prepare the way before Him? By making straight in the desert a highway for our God! How? By exalting every valley and making low every mountain. As well as, by making the crooked straight and the rough places plain.

(Isaiah 40:3 and 4)

3. The voice of him that crieth in the wilderness, Prepare ye the way of the LORD, make straight in the desert a highway for our God.

4. Every valley shall be exalted, and every mountain and hill shall be made low: and the crooked shall be made straight, and the rough places plain:

Even though John was the one that was sent to prepare the way for the Lord, he himself was not the one that would actually be doing the roadwork. He was just the supervisor that supervised the road repairs. The actual work would be done by the ones that he was telling, or rather preaching, "Hey, you over there remove that boulder from the road". "You over there lower that mountain and raise that valley". "You over there need to straighten that highway and fill up those pot holes".

This is why it says of him, "The voice of one crying in the wilderness "PREPARE YE THE WAY OF THE LORD"". He was to tell them what to do to prepare the way and those that heard him were to do it.

HOW THEN WAS HE TELLING THEM TO PREPARE THE WAY?

However, you never find John in the four gospels preaching, "Prepare ye the way of the Lord". We cannot find that being his message. What we do see as his massage was "REPENT". And as the people heard him and repented they were preparing the way of their hearts for the messenger of the covenant to come.

(Malachi 3:1) Behold, I will send my messenger, and he shall prepare the way before me: and the Lord, whom ye seek, shall suddenly come to his temple, even the messenger of the covenant, whom ye delight in: behold, he shall come, saith the LORD of hosts.

The messenger of the covenant can come to His temple, (us), because through repentance and baptism for the remission of those sins that temple is now sanctified for the Lord to enter and dwell in. This is why if there is no true repentance, even though that individual may have been baptized, that person will not be baptized with the holy ghost, because the Spirit of God WILL NOT inhabit a defiled body.

This is why a person must repent, so as to remove those evil deeds that prevent him or her from ever stepping onto that lighted road...that lighted road being Jesus the Word... that can take that individual all the way to the kingdom of God. Also to sanctify that temple that the messenger of the covenant can come into.

(John 14:20) At that day ye shall know that I am in my Father, and ye in me, and I in you.

(John 8:12) Then spake Jesus again unto them, saying, I am the light of the world: he that followeth me shall not walk in darkness, but shall have the light of life

Moreover, while on this road, as Jesus reveals to that

person things that are not right before God, that person repents of them as well and tries to live according to that Word that Jesus revealed to him that he needs to be doing.

James 1:22. But be ye doers of the word, and not hearers only, deceiving your own selves.

This is why the scriptures say, *"The law and the prophets were until John: since that time the kingdom of God is preached, and every man presseth into it. And it is easier for heaven and earth to pass, than one tittle of the law to fail. Whosoever putteth away his wife, and marrieth another, committeth adultery: and whosoever marrieth her that is put away from her husband committeth adultery (Luke 16:16-18.)"* and why every man was pressing into it, AND COULD NOT!

Read carefully what the Lord is saying here and try to understand. "Since that time the kingdom of God is preached and every man presseth into it". Notice how He then says, "And it is easier for heaven and earth to pass, than one tittle of the law to fail". Why does He say this? What does verse 17 have to do with verse 16? How does it continue with Jesus' train of thought? Will one tittle or one jot of the law ever fail? No! On the other hand, will heaven and earth pass? NO! However, why then does He make this statement? He was letting them know that the most sound and sure thing in this whole universe is the soundness and sureness of the heavens and earth. They will never pass away. However, even with the sureness that they cannot fail the Word of God is so much surer, that if there were a possibility that anything could fail it would be the heavens and the earth but never the Word of God.

Nevertheless, why does He make this statement after telling them that all man presseth into the kingdom of God? Moreover, why after making that statement does He say, "Whosoever putteth away his wife, and marrieth another, committeth adultery: and whosoever marrieth her that is put away from her husband committeth adultery." Because He is trying to get them to see that, the law is the barrier that keeps them and will keep them from entering in. Furthermore, if even one tittle of the law is still standing they are hopeless and helpless at entering in. The law must be moved out of the way so they can enter in, otherwise they would be no different then a man who divorces his wife to marry another, he and she are both adulterous. It is as if the Lord is telling them, "If you try to marry me while the law is in place you commit adultery. Furthermore, you are trying to get me to commit adultery as well".

(Romans 7:1-4)

1. Know ye not, brethren, (for I speak to them that know the law,) how that the law hath dominion over a man as long as he liveth?

2. For the woman which hath an husband is bound by the law to her husband so long as he liveth; but if the husband be dead, she is loosed from the law of her husband.

3. So then if, while her husband liveth, she be married to another man, she shall be called an adulteress: but if her husband be dead, she is free from that law; so that she is no adulteress, though she be married to another man.

4. Wherefore, my brethren, ye also are become dead to the law by the body of Christ; that ye should be married to another, even to him who is raised from the dead, that we should bring forth fruit unto God.

We become dead to the law when we repent and are baptized into or in Jesus Christ, thereby removing that barrier that keeps us from entering in.

Let us look at the definitions of this word, "presseth", according to the original word.

Presseth βιάζω **biazō**, *bee-ad'-zo;* from *970;* to *force,* i.e. (refl.) to *crowd oneself* (into), or (pass.) to *be seized:*— press, suffer violence.

This word comes from the Greek word βία **bia**, *bee'-*

ah; (through the idea of *vital* activity); *force:*— violence.

Notice what the Lord is saying here. "You people are using force to get into the kingdom. You are pushing and shoving each other to crowd yourselves into the kingdom. You are using violence to get into the kingdom, AND YOU CANNOT DO IT! You are trying to buck the system and you cannot do it. Because the system is, "THE LAW"! Furthermore, as long as the law is there, the law itself keeps you from going in. The law will not fail; heaven and earth will pass away before one tittle of the law fails".

The law serves as the barrier that keeps us from entering in. This is why we need to repent and do works as proof that we have repented. Those works being summed up in one word, "LOVE", "CHARITY"!

Jesus said, *"For verily I say unto you, Till heaven and earth pass, one jot or one tittle shall in no wise pass from the law, till all be fulfilled." (Matthew 5:18)*

He was not saying that one jot or one tittle would never pass from the law, nor was He saying that heaven and earth would pass away, but rather that heaven and earth would pass away first, before one jot or one tittle would pass from the law; "TILL ALL BE FULFILLED". And when would all be fulfilled? Well, in your life and in mine as individuals, when we walk in love!

(Romans 13:8-10)

8. Owe no man any thing, but to love one another: for he that loveth another hath fulfilled the law.

9. For this, Thou shalt not commit adultery, Thou shalt not kill, Thou shalt not steal, Thou shalt not bear false witness, Thou shalt not covet; and if there be any other commandment, it is briefly comprehended in this saying, namely, Thou shalt love thy neighbour as thyself.

10. Love worketh no ill to his neighbour: therefore love is the fulfilling of the law.

When an individual has repented and is baptize in or into Jesus, he or she becomes dead to the law, therefore that removes that barrier, (THE LAW), that keeps him or her from entering into the kingdom of God, and now he or she is spared from the wrath to come. The works that proof that that individual has repented, (loving one another), that individual will endeavor to produce as a result of him or her having repented.

All through the scriptures; when the scriptures prophesied about the wrath of God that was to fall, it also warned the people to repent, (turn), to God so that they could be spared from that wrath that was going to fall.

(Joel 2:1 and 2, 10-13)

1. Blow ye the trumpet in Zion, and sound an alarm in my holy mountain: let all the inhabitants of the land tremble: for the day of the LORD cometh, for it is nigh at hand;

2. A day of darkness and of gloominess, a day of clouds and of thick darkness, as the morning spread upon the mountains:...

10. The earth shall quake before them; the heavens shall tremble: the sun and the moon shall be dark, and the stars shall withdraw their shining:

11. And the LORD shall utter his voice before his army: for his camp is very great: for he is strong that executeth his word: for the day of the LORD is great and very terrible; and who can abide it?

OBSERVE HOW HE NOW WARNS
THEM TO REPENT

12. Therefore also now, saith the LORD, turn ye even to me with all your heart, and with fasting, and with weeping, and with mourning:

13. And rend your heart, and not your garments, and turn unto the LORD your God: for he is gracious and merciful, slow to anger, and of great kindness, and repenteth him of the evil.

(Zephaniah 1:14-18 and 2:1-3)

14. The great day of the LORD is near, it is near, and hasteth greatly, even the voice of the day of the LORD: the mighty man shall cry there bitterly.

15. That day is a day of wrath, a day of trouble and distress, a day of wasteness and desolation, a day of darkness and gloominess, a day of clouds and thick darkness,

16. A day of the trumpet and alarm against the fenced cities, and against the high towers.

17. And I will bring distress upon men, that they shall walk like blind men, because they have sinned against the LORD: and their blood shall be poured out as dust, and their flesh as the dung.

18. Neither their silver nor their gold shall be able to deliver them in the day of the LORD'S wrath; but the whole land shall be devoured by the fire of his jealousy: for he shall make even a speedy riddance of all them that dwell in the land.

HERE AGAIN IS WHERE GOD WARNS THEM TO REPENT

(Zephaniah 2:1-3)

1. Gather yourselves together, yea, gather together, O nation not desired;

2. Before the decree bring forth, before the day pass as the chaff, before the fierce anger of the LORD come upon you, before the day of the LORD'S anger come upon you.

3. Seek ye the LORD, all ye meek of the earth, which have wrought his judgment; seek righteousness, seek meekness: it may be ye shall be hid in the day of the LORD'S anger.

TAKE NOTE AND UNDERSTAND THAT THE FEAR OF THE LORD IS THE MOTIVATOR NEEDED TO CAUSE A PERSON TO REPENT AND TURN TO GOD

Moreover, notice that it takes the fear of the Lord to cause an individual to turn, (depart), from evil, (repent).

(Proverbs 3:7) Be not wise in thine own eyes: fear the LORD, and depart from evil.

(Zephaniah 3:6 and 7)

6. I have cut off the nations: their towers are desolate; I made their streets waste, that none passeth by: their cities are destroyed, so that there is no man, that there is none inhabitant.

7. I said, Surely thou wilt fear me, thou wilt receive instruction; so their dwelling should not be cut off, howsoever I punished them:

(Jeremiah 5:22-24)

22. Fear ye not me? saith the LORD: will ye not tremble at my presence . . .

23. But this people hath a revolting and a rebellious heart; they are revolted and gone.

24. Neither say they in their heart, Let us now fear the LORD our God. . .

This is why, Jesus, after telling them what He said in verses 16 through 18, of Luke chapter 16; He goes into the story of the rich man in hell concluding with what He said in verses 27 through 31.

(Luke 16: 27-31)

27. Then he said, I pray thee therefore, father, that thou wouldest send him to my father's house:

28. For I have five brethren; that he may testify unto them, lest they also come into this place of torment.

29. Abraham saith unto him, They have Moses and the prophets; let them hear them.

30. And he said, Nay, father Abraham: but if one went unto them from the dead, "THEY WILL REPENT".

31. And he said unto him, If they hear not Moses and the prophets, neither will they be PERSUADED, (to repent) though one rose from the dead.

He, (Jesus), was emphasizing the importance of repentance so much so, that He has to bring a man in hell to warn people of the need to repent so as to avoid hell. This is why Jesus tell us, through the person of Abraham, in this story, that if the law and the prophets cannot persuade an individual to repent neither will He be able to when He rises from the dead.

Can you imagine, this man in hell has more wisdom of what it takes to make it in to the kingdom of God then most modern day preachers. Because he has enough understanding to know, that a person has to repent in order to make it in. While most minister of our day, do not. Moreover, how do we know that they do not? Because they fail so miserably to preach it!

HOW DOES THIS WHOLE CONCEPT OF REPENTANCE AND BAPTISM WORK AT BRINGING ABOUT GODS PLAN FOR OUR SALVATION

We said in chapter five, "What is true repentance", that our salvation begins with repentance, which includes baptism. However, that baptism is performed in a progression of stages, 1. "Water" 2. "Holy Ghost" and 3. "Fire". There is only one baptism, *One Lord, one faith, one baptism, Ephesians 4:5,* but there are three parts to that one baptism and a person that professes to be born again has to have all three parts in order to allow God to bring about all of His plan of salvation into his or her live.

Gods plan for our salvation is not only to save, heal and deliver us, but His ultimate goal for our lives are to conform us into the image of His son, (His Word).

(Romans 8:29) For whom he did foreknow, he also did predestinate to be conformed to the image of his Son...

This is how we are made into the image of God, (*Genesis 1:26 And God said, Let us make man in our image, after our likeness . . .*), where we no longer have the impulses, urges, desires, inclination, longings, and nature to sin.

However, we are saved, heal and delivered, when we from a true and sincere heart repent and are baptized for the freedom and forgiveness of those sins; (*Then Peter said unto them, Repent, and be baptized every one of you in the name of Jesus Christ for the remission of sins...Acts 2:38*). This in turn moves the hand of Christ to baptize us in the Holy Ghost; (*...and ye shall receive the gift of the Holy Ghost. Acts 2:38*), sealing us unto the day of redemption.

(Ephesians 1:13 and 14)

13. In whom ye also trusted, after that ye heard the word of truth, the gospel of your salvation: in whom also after that ye believed, ye were sealed with that holy Spirit of promise,

14. Which is the earnest of our inheritance until the redemption of the purchased possession, unto the praise of his glory.

However, those that have understanding of Gods Word realize that His plan does not stop here. There is still the third stage of that baptism, the fire, where Jesus by His Spirit, takes us down that crucifying road, (Spiritual Via Dolorosa), where we endure the trial and afflictions of life where we are transformed into the image of His son.

(Isaiah 48:10) Behold, I have refined thee, but not with silver; I have chosen thee in the furnace of affliction.

(Malachi 3:3) And he shall sit as a refiner and purifier of silver: and he shall purify the sons of Levi, and purge them as gold and silver, that they may offer unto the LORD an offering in righteousness.

This is why when Paul, teaching the Romans truths about baptism in Romans 6 verses 3-6, he says . . .

(Romans 6:3-6)

3. Know ye not, that so many of us as were baptized into Jesus Christ were baptized into his death?

4. Therefore we are buried with him by baptism into death: that like as Christ was raised up from the dead by the glory of the Father, even so we also should walk in newness of life.

5. For if we have been planted together in the likeness of his death, we shall be also in the likeness of his resurrection:

6. Knowing this, that our old man is crucified with him, that the body of sin might be destroyed, that henceforth we should not serve sin.

. . . Showing them that this is how this whole process works beginning first with repentance and baptism and ending with us walking in the likeness of His resurrection, (walking in newness of life). So that thereby we do not serve sin. However, notice that in between the two steps there must be the experience of being crucified with Him as well.

Observe and see that he does not say, "Know ye not, that so many of us as were baptized "IN WATER", into Jesus Christ were baptized into His death."

Neither does he say, "Know ye not, that so many of us as were baptized "IN THE HOLY GHOST", into Jesus Christ were baptized into His death."

Nor does he say, "Know ye not, that so many of us as were baptized "IN FIRE", into Jesus Christ were baptized into His death."

Furthermore, why does he not say these things? Because there is only one baptism, however, there are three stages to that baptism, 1. "Water", 2. "Holy Ghost", and 3. "Fire". And when he says, what he says from verses 3 through 6, he is referring to the total and complete process of baptism; "Water", "Holy Ghost", and "Fire".

There are many people that profess to be Christians, but are failing miserably in their walk with the Lord because of their lack of understanding of Gods Word. Additionally, because of their failure to honestly and truly repent and be baptize, "IN THE NAME OF JESUS CHRIST".

(Acts 19:1-6)

1. And it came to pass, that, while Apollos was at Corinth, Paul having passed through the upper coasts came to Ephesus: and finding certain disciples,

2. He said unto them, Have ye received the Holy Ghost since ye believed? And they said unto him, We have not so much as heard whether there be any Holy Ghost.

3. And he said unto them, Unto what then were ye baptized? And they said, Unto John's baptism.

4. Then said Paul, John verily baptized with the baptism of repentance, saying unto the people, that they should believe on him which should come after him, that is, on Christ Jesus.

5. When they heard this, they were baptized in the name of the Lord Jesus.

6. And when Paul had laid his hands upon them, the Holy Ghost came on them; and they spake with tongues, and prophesied.

Jesus never said, *"Go ye therefore, and teach all nations, baptizing them in the name of the Father, and of the Son, and of the Holy Ghost."* What He said was, *"Go ye therefore, and teach all nations, baptizing them IN THE NAME of the Father, and of the Son, and of the Holy Ghost."*

In the next chapter we will learn, how a love and desire for God's Word, (The Lord Jesus Christ), that was brought about as a result of the fear of the Lord, causing us to repent and turn to Jesus, (the Word of God). Not only aids us in obeying and keeping His commandments, but also moves the hand of God to circumcise our hearts, so that we perform what God is looking for in our lives; with the added twist of learning how to receive the blessings of God.

CHAPTER SEVEN

HEARKEN, OBSERVE, AND DO.

¹And it shall come to pass, if thou shalt hearken diligently unto the voice of the LORD thy God, to observe and to do all his commandments which I command thee this day, that the LORD thy God will set thee on high above all nations of the earth: ²And all these blessings shall come on thee, and overtake thee, if thou shalt hearken unto the voice of the LORD thy God. ¹³And the LORD shall make thee the head, and not the tail; and thou shalt be above only, and thou shalt not be beneath; if that thou hearken unto the commandments of the LORD thy God, which I command thee this day, to observe and to do them: ¹⁵But it shall come to pass, if thou wilt not hearken unto the voice of the LORD thy God, to observe to do all his commandments and his statutes which I command thee this day; that all these curses shall come upon thee, and overtake thee (Deuteronomy 28:1, 2, 13, 15).

As the people of God, it is unbelievable the numbers who do not understand the importance of making God's Word their all and all. Wanting to stress this point without having to repeat myself, I ask you to please read, "From the Author", again before we go into this next chapter.

To explain this next revelation so we can continue to build this puzzle of God's Word, I will explain it as if I were ministering it over the pulpit, as when I teach people how to receive their blessing God's way. In this manner, you can learn the importance of loving God's Word with all that is within you, while also learning how you, too, can receive your blessing God's way.

GOD DESIRES FOR HIS PEOPLE
TO BE BLESSED!

It is God's desire for His people to be blessed; we can see this throughout the scriptures. Many massages and teachings have been given and written on the subject. However, God Himself has provided a way for His people to be blessed, if they follow the format that He has designed.

In order for us to understand clearly how to receive our blessings the way that God has ordained, we need to first look at the way that man says we should receive our blessings.

Before we begin, the author wishes to say that he is in no way pointing fingers at any particular minister, denomination, or religious group. There are many great, godly men and women of God that are ministering the Gospel. It is not my intention to discredit them, nor am I saying that they are not teaching truth; however, until God has revealed to a minister what is truth, that minister can only preach or teach what he believes is of God, even if what he believes, is not of God.

(Acts 18:24-26, 28)

24. And a certain Jew named Apollos, born at Alexandria, an eloquent man, and mighty in the scriptures, came to Ephesus.

25. This man was instructed in the way of the Lord; and being fervent in the spirit, he spake and taught diligently the things of the Lord, <u>knowing only the baptism of John</u>.

26. And he began to speak boldly in the synagogue: whom when Aquila and Priscilla had heard, they took him unto them, <u>and expounded unto him the way of God more perfectly</u>.

28. For he mightily convinced the Jews, and that publicly, shewing by the scriptures that Jesus was Christ.

(Acts 19:1-5)

1. And it came to pass, that, while Apollos was at Corinth, Paul having passed through the upper coasts came to Ephesus: and finding certain disciples,

2. He said unto them, Have ye received the Holy Ghost since ye believed? And they said unto him, We have not so much as heard whether there be any Holy Ghost.

3. And he said unto them, <u>Unto what then were ye baptized? And they said, Unto John's baptism.</u>

4. Then said Paul, John verily baptized with the baptism of repentance, saying unto the people, that they should believe on him which should come after him, that is, on Christ Jesus.

5. When they heard this, <u>they were baptized in the name of the Lord Jesus.</u>

6. And when Paul had laid his hands upon them, the Holy Ghost came on them; and they spake with tongues, and prophesied.

As we read in the scriptures above, a certain minister of the gospel named Apollos, which the scriptures states was a man of God, had only known the baptism of John until Aquila and Priscilla expounded the scriptures to him more perfectly. He could not give what he did not have. As a result, the men at Ephesus could not receive what they needed from God until Paul showed up and corrected the matter. Well, in like manner, many ministers today are teaching only what they know, and if they are not correct, it does not mean that they are not of God.

Let us now continue with this revelation.

JUST BECAUSE SOMETHING SOUNDS GOOD
DOES NOT MEAN IT IS OF GOD!

As the Lord had me on an extensive study of what we are about to learn in this chapter, He woke me up one day about four in the morning and spoke to me. The Lord did not have me on a search of how I could be blessed, but rather on how I could know Him more intimately and desire Him more through His Word. (This is the main subject that I want you to grasp in this revelation).

He said, "Notice what many preachers are telling My people, and how many of their congregations are standing up and agreeing with them for things that I have not said. Consider how many of my people do not have enough understanding to know what is of God and what is of man. Many ministers will say things such as this: "If God has given you a dream, then you need to pursue your dream. You must run after it until you bring it into fulfillment. If God has put a seed in your womb, then you must cultivate that seed until you birth it forth. Do not let anything stop you from running after what you know God has set before you. Keep your eyes on your dream, on your seed, on your goal, on your blessing. Pursue it, run after it, and do not let anything stand in your way till you bring it to pass." Then God thundered in my mind and said, "MAN SAYS THESE THINGS! I DON'T!" He continued, "For Me to say that would be to tell My people to put another god before them, and I have said in My Word, 'THOU SHALT HAVE NO OTHER GODS BEFORE ME.'"

I could not help but feel the pain in the heart of God. A pain so deep and so moving, that we, God's ministers, could hurt our Lord and Savior so deeply, because of our ignorance of His Word. And the impact that what we say or teach has, not only on the lives of God's people, but on God as well, that all I could do was weep out of repentance for

God's ministers, for His people, and myself, asking Him to please forgive our sins and our ignorance.

This experience, however, turned into a light that illuminated God's Word, not only letting me see how we as God's people could receive His blessing His way and not man's way, but more importantly, what I needed to know in order to draw even closer to God by way of His Word.

Let us look at how man says you should receive your blessing, and then we can understand clearly, how to receive God's blessing His way.

HOW MAN SAYS YOU SHOULD RECEIVE YOUR BLESSING

In this next demonstration, I will be exaggerating, but I hope you will get the picture.

Imagine you are in church and some so-called prophet calls you out and says, "Brother So-and-so, God has shown me that He is going to bless you. He is going to bless you with your own business. You will prosper and be blessed."

(This may or may not be of God. That is not the issue. The issue is to get you to see the things that many times transpire and lead up to a person running after his or her blessings.)

Perhaps you are a good mechanic and you have been thinking about starting your own repair shop. Perhaps even your wife and friends have mentioned to you that you should. Consequently, because of this prophecy from this so-called prophet, you believe that this must be of God, (and still the issue is not if whether it is of God or not). Now you have all these thoughts in your mind. Then one day a well-known preacher comes to your church or you attend one of those services where you hear a message like the one stated previously. Where the minister preaches that if God has planted a dream in you; pursue it; go after it; do not let anything keep you from doing what you know God has placed in you to do. This is the icing on the cake; this was all you needed to run after your blessing.

Notice what happens. You begin to labor at starting your business. You do all the right things. You work hard at it, and maybe a year or two later, you are very successful. You are making money, going to church, paying your tithes; everything seems to be in order. Then one day you decide to close early and surprise your wife with an early day and some flowers. However, when you get home, you find your wife in bed with another man. (Do not think that things like this do not happen, because they do, and they happen to God's people).

Let us look at another scenario. You are at your place of business. As before, you are doing all you know to do; everything is fine, and then suddenly your wife calls. She is hysterical and says, "Our son has just been arrested. He robbed a store, and in the process a person has been killed." Now you are looking at your son being sent to prison for life or maybe even receiving a death sentence.

Let us look at still another scenario. You are at your place of business. Everything is fine. You are doing all you know to do and you get a pain in your stomach. You make an appointment with the doctor, and he informs you, "You have stomach cancer, and you have less then two years to live."

Wait! What is going on here? Why do things like this happen? We are supposed to be blessed, not cursed.

If you remember the first paragraph of this chapter, God has provided a way for us to receive our blessings, and if we obtain our blessing, (what we believe or think is our blessing), by any other way, our blessing becomes a curse.

(Deuteronomy 28:15) But it shall come to pass, if thou wilt not <u>hearken</u> unto the voice of the Lord thy God, to <u>observe</u> to <u>do</u> all his commandments and his statutes which I command thee this day; that all these curses shall come upon thee, and overtake thee:

PLEASE ALLOW THE SPIRIT OF GOD TO OPEN YOUR HEART TO UNDERSTAND

Notice what has transpired here. When ministers take scriptures such as Deuteronomy 30:19 — *I call Heaven and earth to record this day against you, that I have set before you life and death, blessing and cursing: <u>therefore choose life</u>, that both thou and thy seed may live* — and use them to tell you that God wants you to choose your blessing. Insinuating that God wants you to go after your blessing, because of the way they interpret that verse, those ministers use the Word of God to springboard you from the Word of God to your blessing. What they have done is send you out to your blessing. They are using, hopefully unknowingly, the Word of God to put another god before you. You are now going from the Word of God to your blessing. Your blessing has now become your god, because now the blessing is before you. It is now what you are running after. It is what you are pursuing, what you are now living for, and not the Word of God.

The only God that God has said we can have before us is His Word, which is the same as having God before us.

(Deuteronomy 6:4-9)

4. Hear, O Israel: The LORD our God is one LORD:

5. And thou shalt love the LORD thy God with all thine heart, and with all thy soul, and with all thy might.

6. And these words, which I command thee this day, shall be in thine heart:

7. And thou shalt teach them diligently unto thy children, and shalt talk of them when thou sittest in thine house, and when thou walkest by the way, and when thou liest down, and when thou risest up.

8. And thou shalt bind them for a sign upon thine hand, and they shall be as frontlets between thine eyes.

9. And thou shalt write them upon the posts of thy house, and on thy gates.

Even our Lord and Savior who is the very Word of God said:

(John 6:27) Labor not for the meat which perisheth, but for that meat which endureth unto everlasting life, which the Son of man shall give unto you: for him hath God the Father sealed.

Anytime we put anything before the Word of God, whatever it may be — our church, our ministry, our calling, our gifts, our family, friends, home, car, blessings, whatever — we put another god before the true and living God.

When we receive a blessing, (what we believe or think is our blessing), by any other means than by the way that God has ordained, our blessing becomes a curse. Let us look back at the first scenario, where you come home and find your spouse in bed with another. That is a curse!

(Deuteronomy 28:15, 30)

15. But it shall come to pass, if thou wilt not <u>hearken</u> unto the voice of the Lord thy God, to <u>observe</u> to <u>do</u> all his commandments and his statutes which I command thee this day; that all these curses shall come upon thee, and over take thee:

30. You shall betroth a wife, but another man shall lie with her.

Now, notice our second scenario, where you will have your son taken away from you and you have no power to stop it. That is also a curse!

(Deuteronomy 28:32) Your sons and your daughters shall be given to another people, and your eyes shall look and fail with longing for them all day long; and there shall be no strength in your hand.

And concluding with our third scenario, you went to the doctor and he gave you a bad report. Here again is a curse!

(Deuteronomy 28:27) The LORD will strike you with the boils of Egypt, with tumors, with the scab, and with the itch, from which you cannot be healed.

When we go after our blessing, (what we believe or think is our blessing), we receive our blessing another way than the way that God has provided, and when we do this, the curse overtakes us and our blessing becomes a curse.

(Deuteronomy 28:15) But it shall come to pass, if thou wilt not <u>hearken</u> unto the voice of the Lord thy God, to <u>observe</u> to <u>do</u> all his commandments and his statutes which I command thee this day; that all these curses shall come upon thee, and over take thee:

DO YOU HEARKEN, OBSERVE, AND DO?

By now, we should all be aware of what the format is that God has established for us to receive our blessing: HEARKEN, OBSERVE, and DO. At this point, we could close this chapter and go on to the next, but you would not have learned how to receive your blessing, because it is more than what meets the eye. There is a precious revelation hidden in these Scriptures that if we fail to see we have failed to discover a priceless diamond buried deep in God's Word. This precious truth will allow us to see not only how to receive our blessing, but more importantly, how much God longs for us to love, desire, and run after His Word. Furthermore, this is the main point that I want you to understand, because if you know this, and do it, undoubtedly blessings will come.

There is no doubt that God wants His people to be blessed, however, for this to happen, God has designed a pattern for His people to be blessed. We can say or we can preach and teach whatever we desire, but God's Word is the ultimate authority, and if we do not do it God's way, we will ultimately fail.

I believe that the pattern is found in Deuteronomy 28, because it is in this chapter that the Lord teaches us what it is that we need to do to be blessed, and if we do not follow that format, we are cursed instead.

Notice that the format does not change. However, you phrase it, it spells the same thing: hearken, observe, and do. Do this and you will be blessed. HOWEVER, we have a problem, and God knows that we have a problem, and the problem is this: as humans, we have the ability to hearken and we have the ability to observe; however, WE DO NOT HAVE THE ABILITY TO DO! If we really want to, we can as humans, hearken to God's Word. Moreover, we have the ability to observe God's Word, but no matter how hard we try, eventually we fail at doing God's Word. And this poses a problem because the stipulations for being blessed are to hearken, observe, and DO!

Now because God knows this and it is His desire for us to be blessed. God in His infinite wisdom and mercy made another covenant with His people, so that if we follow the format in this new covenant, it will produce the results needed to comply with His first covenant, and thereby bring to pass the blessings overtaking us and coming upon us.

Notice that after God shows them all the blessings and cursing in chapter 28 of Deuteronomy, with the format specified to be blessed or cursed. When He gets to chapter 29, knowing that they would not be able to comply with the requirements of the first covenant, (because they would not be able to do the "DOING" part of that covenant), He drafts another covenant knowing that this one they can fulfill.

(Deuteronomy 29:1, 10-15)

1. These are the words of the covenant, which the LORD commanded Moses to make with the children of Israel <u>in the land of Moab</u>, beside the <u>covenant</u> which he made with them in <u>Horeb</u>.

10. Ye stand this day all of you before the LORD your God; your captains of your tribes, your elders, and your officers, with all the men of Israel,

11. Your little ones, your wives, and thy stranger that is in thy camp, from the hewer of thy wood unto the drawer of thy water:

12. <u>That thou shouldst enter into covenant</u> with the LORD thy God, and into his oath, which the LORD thy God maketh with thee <u>this day</u>:

13. That he may establish thee to day for a people unto himself, and that he may be unto thee a God, as he hath said unto thee, and as he hath sworn unto thy fathers, to Abraham, to Isaac, and to Jacob.

14. Neither with you only do I make this covenant and this oath;

15. But with him that standeth here with us this day before the LORD our God, <u>and also with him that is not here with us this day</u>:

      Notice that God makes a second covenant with them in the land of Moab, which is separate from the one that He made with them in Horeb when they came out of Egypt. Understand also that according to verse 15, He not only makes this covenant with those that were there, but He also makes this covenant with us who were not present then, but are still part of the covenant of God as His people.

Carefully studying chapter 29, we can understand that God tells them of the covenant He is making with them, the reason for it, and with whom He is making this covenant. God, however, does not go into the stipulations of this covenant until He gets into chapter 30.

Now, keep in mind that a covenant is an agreement. One party does his part of the agreement, and because of his compliance, the other party fulfills his obligations.

Let us study those stipulations to get a clear understanding of what transpires here.

(Deuteronomy 30:1-10)

1. And it shall come to pass, when all these things are come upon thee, the blessing and the curse, which I have set before thee, and thou shalt call them to mind among all the nations, whither the LORD thy God hath driven thee,

2. And shalt <u>return</u> unto the LORD thy God, and shalt <u>obey</u> his voice according to all that I command thee this day, thou and thy children, with all thine heart, and with all thy soul;

3. That then the LORD thy God will turn thy captivity, and have compassion upon thee, and will return and gather thee from all the nations, whither the LORD thy God hath scattered thee.

4. If any of thine be driven out unto the outmost parts of Heaven, from thence will the LORD thy God gather thee, and from thence will he fetch thee:

5. And the LORD thy God will bring thee into the land which thy fathers possessed, and thou shalt possess it; and he will do thee good, and multiply thee above thy fathers.

6. And the LORD thy God will circumcise thine heart, and the heart of thy seed, to love the LORD thy God with all thine heart, and with all thy soul, that thou mayest live.

7. And the LORD thy God will put all these curses upon thine enemies, and on them that hate thee, which persecuted thee.

8. And thou shalt return and obey the voice of the LORD, and do all his commandments which I command thee this day.

9. And the LORD thy God will make thee plenteous in every work of thine hand, in the fruit of thy body, and in the fruit of thy cattle, and in the fruit of thy land, for good: for the LORD will again rejoice over thee for good, as he rejoiced over thy fathers:

10. If thou shalt <u>hearken</u> unto the voice of the LORD thy God, to <u>keep</u> his commandments and his statutes which are written in this book of the law, and if thou <u>turn</u> unto the LORD thy God with all thine heart, and with all thy soul.

Be aware that the requirements for this contract begin in verse 2. This is what Israel is required to do, and if they do this, then God will fulfill His part of the covenant, which goes from verse 3 all the way to verse 9. When we read verse 10, we see God reiterating what Israel's part of the covenant is. Notice carefully that the requirements for Israel to do in order to fulfill their part of the contract are:

1. Return or turn (verses 2 and 10).

2. Obey or hearken (verses 2 and 10).

3. Keep (verse 10).

At this point, we have to go into the original writings to find the definitions of *return* or *turn*, *obey* or *hearken*, and *keep*, so we can see clearly, what it is that we have to do to keep this covenant and to understand this revelation. Remember to keep in mind that this revelation is not to show how to be blessed, but rather to learn how to show God how much we love Him by way of His Word. The fact that we will be blessed because of being obedient to His Word is an added benefit.

Observe first that the word "obey" and the word "hearken" in verses 2 and 10 of chapter 30 and in verses 1, 13, and 15 of chapter 28 are the same word, although the translators used *obey* in one verse and *hearken* in the others. The words *obey* and *hearken* are the Hebrew word:

שָׁמַע

shâmaʿ, *shaw-mah';* a prim. root; to *hear* intelligently (often with impl. of attention, obedience, etc.; caus. to *tell*, etc.):— × attentively, call (gather) together, × carefully, × certainly, consent, consider, be content, declare, × diligently, discern, give ear, (cause to, let, make to) hear (-ken, tell), × indeed, listen, make (a) noise, (be) obedient, obey, perceive, (make a) proclaim (-ation), publish, regard, report, shew (forth), (make a) sound, × surely, tell, understand, whosoever [heareth], witness.

Notice that the words *obey* or *hearken* have everything to do with *listening and paying very close attention* to His Word and nothing at all to do with *doing* His Word. The same word *hearken* is also found in Isaiah 55:2 with the same implications.

(Isaiah 55:1-3, 6-11)

1. Ho, every one that thirsteth, come ye to the waters, and he that hath no money; come ye, buy, and eat; yea, come, buy wine and milk without money and without price.

2. Wherefore do ye spend money for that which is not bread? and your labor for that which satisfieth not? hearken diligently unto me, and eat ye that which is good, and let your soul delight itself in fatness.

3. Incline your ear, and come unto me: hear, and your soul shall live; and I will make an everlasting covenant with you, even the sure mercies of David...

6. Seek ye the LORD while he may be found, call ye upon him while he is near:

7. Let the wicked forsake his way, and the unrighteous man his thoughts: and let him return unto the LORD, and he will have mercy upon him; and to our God, for he will abundantly pardon.

8. For my thoughts are not your thoughts, neither are your ways my ways, saith the LORD.

9. For as the heavens are higher than the earth, so are my ways higher than your ways, and my thoughts than your thoughts.

10. For as the rain cometh down, and the snow from Heaven, and returneth not thither, but watereth the earth, and maketh it bring forth and bud, that it may give seed to the sower, and bread to the eater:

11. So shall my <u>word</u> be that goeth forth out of my mouth: it shall not return unto me void, but it shall accomplish that which I please, and it shall prosper in the thing whereto I sent it.

Notice that the word *incline*, (verse 3 "Incline your ear") is the Hebrew word נָטָה

nâṭâh, *naw-taw'; a prim. root; meaning to *stretch* or spread out;...

What is God trying to tell His people in these verses, as He is in chapter 30 of Deuteronomy verses 2 and 10? That when He speaks, His Word is going to drop down like rain, and because His Word is so precious, they should desire it so much that if they could they would stretch and spread their ears out like a blanket so as to not lose not even one drop of His Word.

We can see that the first requirement in this second covenant is to love His Word with all your heart and soul to the point that you want to listen very carefully to what God is saying so that you hear everything He has to say. Keep in mind as stated earlier that the words "Obey" or "Hearken" have nothing to do with doing His Word but rather with paying very close attention to His Word.

Now I want to direct your attention to the word "keep", which is the second requirement of the nation of Israel in order for them to fulfill this covenant and be blessed.

Once again you need to understand that the word "keep" in verse 10 of chapter 30 and the word "observe" in chapter 28 verses 1, 13 and 15 are also the same word as found in the original writings, but there worded differently by the translators. The word *keep* and the word *observe* are the Hebrew word שָׁמַר

 shâmar, *shaw-mar';* a prim. root; prop. to *hedge* about (as with thorns), i.e. *guard;* gen. to *protect, attend to,* etc.:— beware, be circumspect, take heed (to self), keep (-er, self), mark, look narrowly, observe, preserve, regard, reserve, save (self), sure, (that lay) wait (for), watch (-man).

Look closely and realize that here these two words *keep* and *observe* also have nothing at all to do with doing God's Word; however, they have all to do with protecting and guarding the Word that you get from God. Being real careful not to lose or allow anyone or anything to take or steal the Word that God has given to you.

Let us now study the last and final requirement for the nation of Israel so that they can be blessed, and that is for them to turn or return.

Here again we will see that the words *turn* and *return* are one and the same as before.

The word *turn* and the word *return*, according to the original writings, are the Hebrew word שׁוּב

shûwb, *shoob;* a prim. root; to *turn* back (hence, away) tran. or intr., lit. or fig. (not necessarily with the idea of *return* to the starting point);...

114

Upon studying the words *turn* or *return*, we see that the implications are to look away from whatever one has his eyes focused upon and look to God. It is not necessarily for them to return back to where they left off. Now, why are the words turn or return, (that means to turn back, hence away), used? Because God wants them to hear what He has to say and He wants their undivided attention. If God's Word is as important and precious to them as it is to God, then they will want to face Him as a gesture that He is all they want to listen. That His Word is that important to them, that they will give Him their undivided attention.

How many times have you gone to someone's house and had something you wanted to share with them but they had the television on? They may lower the volume, but as you were talking to them, their focus was more on the television. Every so often, they would glance at you and nod or say, "Really" or "Is that a fact," but you know they were not really paying attention because they were not really interested in what you had to say. They only pretended to be. God does not appreciate this. He wants your undivided attention. If you say you love God, then you should want to hear everything that He has to say.

Understanding all this helps us to see that in this new covenant, the objective of God is not for the people of God to do His Word, for He knows they do not have the ability. They can try, but they will fail miserably. Instead, it is for them to show Him how much they desire His Word. He wants them to show Him that His Word is more to them than anything else that they could receive. That they want to pay very close attention to His Word so as to not miss one drop of His Word that He pours down from Heaven to them. That His Word is so precious to them that they will guard it with their life so as to not lose it.

(Realize, people of God, that this revelation very much resembles the revelation in the parable of the sower, discussed in chapter nine of this book, and furthermore how, when we apply these truths, which are similar in both revelations, we get the results that God is looking for in our lives).

Observe that in this new covenant, their part of the contract is to love His Word with all their heart and with all their souls, (it does not say this, but this is the implication). It does not have anything to do with doing His Word. Nevertheless, notice what God will do for them if they will do their part of this covenant; because remember, to be blessed you have to hearken, observe, and do, as specified in chapter 28, and so far, all they have done up to this point is just the hearkening and observing part; the doing part has not yet been fulfilled.

Notice two of the seven things that God will do for them if they will do their part:

(Deuteronomy 30:6, 8)

6. And the LORD thy God will <u>circumcise thine heart</u>, and the heart of thy seed, to love the LORD thy God with all thine heart, and with all thy soul, that thou mayest live.

8. And thou shalt return and obey the voice of the LORD, and <u>DO</u> all his commandments which I command thee this day.

Notice what has transpired here. As you, do the things that you can do — to hearken and observe — showing God that you desire His Word, love His Word, and need His Word. Realizing also that His Word is more precious than all the earthly treasures combined, thereby causing you to guard and protect His Word to keep from losing it or from allowing the enemy of your soul to take it from you, God will do His part. One important thing He does is to circumcise your heart, an uncircumcised heart being the main reason why you cannot do the doing part. Once this happens, we are assured in verse 8, that we will be able to do the <u>DOING</u> part. *8. And thou shalt return and obey the voice of the LORD, and <u>DO</u> all his commandments which I command thee this day.* We are now hearkening, observing, and by God who has worked in us the do, the doing part as well.

GOD HAS WORKED IN US THE DOING, BECAUSE GOD HAS PUT US IN THE MOLDING PROCESS, (ALSO REFERRED TO HERE AS CIRCUMCISING OUR HEART), THAT PRODUCES IN US THE DOING PART.

When you run after God's Word because of your love for it, the entire second covenant is now fulfilled on your part and God's. You are now doing the hearkening, the observing, and by the grace and mercy of God, the doing. Therefore, you are now meeting the requirements of His first covenant, Hearken, Observe, and Do, thereby causing the blessing to come upon you and overtake you.

You do not have to run after your blessings, pursue them, or seek them. If you run after God's Word, the blessings will seek you, will find you, will come upon you and overtake you! Nevertheless, this will never happen until you fall in love with Gods Word, the Lord Jesus Christ

(Deuteronomy 28:1, 2)

1. And it shall come to pass, if thou shalt hearken diligently unto the voice of the Lord thy God, to observe and to do all his commandments which I command thee this day, that the Lord thy God will set thee on high above all nations of the earth:

2. And all these blessings shall come on thee, and overtake thee.

It is high time that God's people open their eyes to the beauty and value of His Word, while running after and seeking for it, thereby allowing God to bring all other things into its place.

When God first made His covenant with the nation of Israel, what He required of them was to obey and keep His covenant. And this evidence is made known in the following verse.

(Exodus 19:5) Now therefore, if ye will <u>obey</u> my voice indeed, and <u>keep</u> my covenant, then ye shall be a peculiar treasure unto me above all people: for all the earth is mine:

As we can see, the doing part was never specified in the original covenant. God knew of their inability to perform it, which is why He needed to place His fear in them to keep them from sinning against Him until He could work in them the doing of the commandments. If the fear of the Lord had been in them, (as explained in chapters two and three), that would have produced the love for His Word needed to bring about the principles discussed in this chapter.

In the next chapter, we will learn the importance of paying very close attention to God's Word and the importance of studying God's Word for yourself to make sure you are in the way that God has ordained for you.

CHAPTER EIGHT

OBEDIENCE OR DISOBEDIENCE

⁸Though he were a Son, yet learned he obedience by the things which he suffered; ⁹And being made perfect, he became the author of eternal salvation unto all them that obey him; ¹⁰Called of God an high priest after the order of Melchisedec. ... ¹Therefore we ought to give the more earnest heed to the things which we have heard, lest at any time we should let them slip. ²For if the word spoken by angels was steadfast, and every transgression and disobedience received a just recompense of reward; ³How shall we escape, if we neglect so great salvation; which at the first began to be spoken by the Lord, and was confirmed unto us by them that heard him (Hebrews 5:8-10; 2:1-3).

It seems almost ridiculous to title this chapter *Obedience or Disobedience*, because no one that claims to be a Christian would deliberately disobey the Word of God. However, if a person understood the definition of these words, according to the original writings, he would see how many of God's people fail in obeying His Word, and as a result are transgressing the Word of God.

Let us look at the definitions of the words *obedience* and *disobedience*; (according to the original writings), so we can get a clear understanding of what God is saying in the scriptures and how many of His people are missing it.

Obedience... ὑπακοή hupakŏē, *hoop-ak-o-ay´;* from *5219; attentive hearkening,* i.e. (by impl.) *compliance* or *submission:*— obedience, (make) obedient, obey (-ing).

Notice that the primary definition of the word *obedience* is "attentive hearkening," which literally means *to pay very close attention to what you are listening to.* Now notice that this word comes from the Greek word ὑπακούω hupakŏuō, *hoop-ak-oo´-o,* and this word means to *hear under* (as a *subordinate*), i.e. to *listen attentively;* by impl. to *heed* or *conform* to a command or authority:— hearken, be obedient to, obey.

Note carefully what we are seeing here. The scriptures are trying to get us to see that when we pay very close attention to what the Word of God is saying, we hear clearly, what He says; therefore, we know exactly what He is saying and that is what we do. Because we heard Him clearly, and do as we hear, then we are in obedience by heeding or conforming to His commandments.

Note: Do not confuse what you just read with what we spoke about in the previous chapter. We still do not have the ability to do something just because we heard Him clearly and understand what we are supposed to do. Listening to Him carefully just gives us the understanding of what we are suppose to do so that we can endeavor to do it, not the ability to do it. However, we still have an obligation before God to make an effort to do His Word. That effort is our evidence that we are serious with God and our proof that we believe in Jesus Christ, His Word, thereby moving the hand of God in our favor to bring about the end result of the power of God in our lives to be able to do it.

The biggest problem with most people is they do not have sufficient love for the Word of God, (Jesus), to listen carefully to what the Spirit of God is saying from the Word of God.

Look very closely at the definition of the word *disobedience.*

Disobedience... παρακοή parakŏē, *par-ak-o-ay´;* from 3878 *inattention,* i.e. (by impl.) *disobedience:—* disobedience.

Notice that this word is the direct opposite of the word *obedience*, the primary definition being to not pay very close attention.

Now notice that this word comes from the Greek word παρακούω parakŏuō, *par-ak-oo´-o;* to *mishear*, i.e. (by impl.) to *disobey:*— neglect to hear.

When we understand what these two words mean, we can see where most of our problems come from, not only as individuals but also as a people. The problem stems from the fact that we do not pay very close attention to what the Word of God is saying to make sure that we are doing exactly, (or trying to do exactly), what He tells us to do.

Let us look at the word *transgression*; then we can know why when we mishear God's Word, it leads us to transgressing His Word.

Transgression... παράβασις parabasis, *par-ab´-as-is;* from 3845 *violation:*— breaking, transgression.

Observe that this word comes from the Greek word παραβαίνω parabainō, *par-ab-ah´-ee-no;* to *go contrary* to, i.e. *violate* a command:— (by) transgress (-ion).

(Hebrews 2:2) For if the word spoken by angels was steadfast, and every transgression and disobedience received a just recompense of reward;

When we understand the meaning of these two words, *transgression* and *disobedience*, as they relate to verse two of chapter two of the book of Hebrews, we can see that all of our mistakes come from not listening carefully to what we are hearing in the Word of God. Because we do not listen carefully, we mishear, thereby doing that which we think we hear. However, because we heard wrong, we are now doing wrong. We may believe that we are doing right because we think that we heard right, but because we are doing wrong, (because we have heard wrong we are now in violation of God's commandments, thereby transgressing God's Word.

Many of God's people are in violation of the Word of God because they are in churches where the minister is mishearing the Word of God. He teaches what he believes he hears, but because he has heard wrong, (because he is not paying very close attention to what the Word of God is saying), he is teaching wrong, and consequently leading his congregation to do as he says. However, because he is wrong, now his people are doing wrong, and in so doing, they are all transgressing God's Word.

All of our success as the people of God comes from knowing that we need the understanding of God's Word, and then walking in exactly what the scriptures tell us to do. Nevertheless, this will not happen if we do not make a careful effort at fulfilling the scripture that says, *"Study to shew thyself approved unto God, a workman that needeth not to be ashamed, rightly dividing the word of truth" (2 Timothy 2:15)*. Furthermore, this will not happen if we do not have sufficient love for the Word of God that will cause us to run after, seek for, and desire more of the Word of God. (See the introduction section of this book).

IF YOU LOVE GOD'S WORD WITH ALL THAT IS IN YOU, HIS WORD WILL DO FOR YOU WHAT YOU CANNOT DO FOR YOURSELF!

Let us look at a powerful revelation in the Word of God so we can more clearly see one of the great roles of God's Word in our lives, revealing that apart from His Word, we can never make it, therefore, the more we love and seek His Word, the more our ability to do His Word increases. It is the Epistle approach of decoding the Old Testament's truth of hearken, observe, and do, found in Deuteronomy chapter 28 through 30 that we discussed previously.

(Hebrews 3:1) Wherefore, holy brethren, partakers of the Heavenly calling, consider the Apostle and <u>High Priest</u> of our profession, Christ Jesus;

(Hebrews 4:14) Seeing then that we have a <u>great high priest</u>, that is passed into the heavens, Jesus the Son of God, let us hold fast our profession.

Notice that as the writer of Hebrews is trying to get them to consider this apostle and high priest of their profession, he calls Him a high priest in verse 1 of chapter 3. But upon having made known to them who He is, when he gets to verse 14 of chapter 4, he no longer calls Him a high priest, but he now calls Him a *"GREAT"* high priest.

What is the truth that the writer feels that he has made known about Christ Jesus, to whom he is writing this letter? Why does he no longer call Him a high priest, but now has to refer to Him as a *great* high priest?

Follow along, as we understand the mystery he is telling them.

We cannot go into all the context of what the writer is teaching them for this would require a whole chapter or more in itself, so we will just study the heart of this revelation.

(Hebrews 3:7-19)

7. Wherefore as the Holy Ghost saith, To day if ye will hear his voice,

8. Harden not your hearts, as in the provocation, in the day of temptation in the wilderness:

9. When your fathers tempted me, proved me, and saw my works forty years.

10. Wherefore I was grieved with that generation, and said, They do always err in their heart; and they have not known my ways.

11. So I sware in my wrath, They shall not enter into my rest.

12. Take heed, brethren, lest there be in any of you an evil heart of unbelief, in departing from the living God.

13. But exhort one another daily, while it is called To day; lest any of you be hardened through the deceitfulness of sin.

14. For we are made partakers of Christ, if we hold the beginning of our confidence steadfast unto the end;

15. While it is said, To day if ye will hear his voice, harden not your hearts, as in the provocation.

16. For some, when they had heard, did provoke: howbeit not all that came out of Egypt by Moses.

17. But with whom was he grieved forty years? Was it not with them that had sinned, whose carcasses fell in the wilderness?

18. And to whom sware he that they should not enter into his rest, but to them that believed not?

19. So we see that they could not enter in because of unbelief.

(It is very needful for God's people to understand that for us to come to the place where God is trying to bring us, many times it requires for us to go through things that are very difficult for us to bear as a human being. This is why Jesus said, *"If anybody will come after Me let him deny himself and take up his cross and follow Me,"* the cross representing suffering, pain, and death. However, these trying times in our lives are necessary if we are to become the children of God that we are supposed to be.

Also understand that many times, there are those that God has chosen for a higher calling in life, (in this life and in the life to come,) and this higher calling requires that we go through things that are even harder to bear than what someone else may have to go through. Speaking metaphorically, someone else may only have to bear a trying load that weighs only 30 pounds, whereas the load that you have to bear may be 100 pounds. If you do not know the

Word of God, you will not understand the reason for this; you may think that God is unfair, not realizing that your higher calling makes it necessary that you go through the greater trial.

As a result of all this, if there is anything in our hearts that would draw us to return to the comfort and ease of a non-Christian life when the Spirit of God tries to produce the results that He is looking for in us, there will be a tendency in us to want to depart from the living God. This is due because in us there is an evil heart of unbelief. Moreover, if we do not know that we have this evil heart of unbelief in us, serious consequences will happen, which is why we need to know how to overcome in this area.)

DOUBT IS LIKE FAITH: IF THE CONDITIONS ARE RIGHT, IT WILL GROW INTO A MIGHTY TREE!

Let us study what an evil heart of unbelief is, what it can do to us as well as those we have fellowship with, (primarily members of our church), and how this can cause us and those around us to lose out with God, (as revealed in the example that these verses talk about). More importantly, we must learn the mysteries spoken of here to know if we have an evil heart of unbelief and the steps to rid ourselves of it.

(Hebrews 3:12) Take heed, brethren, lest there be in any of you an evil heart of unbelief, in departing from the living God.

An evil heart of unbelief is a small seed of doubt that you are not completely sure if God is who He says He is, and or whether He will or can do what He says He will do. You do not fully believe His Word. (Note that this evil heart of unbelief comes from not having a complete assurance of

125

hope, which we will study at a later time). Moreover, this small seed of doubt, like faith, if the conditions are right, can and will grow into a huge tree of unbelief if left unchecked.

Notice that the word *unbelief* in Hebrews 3:12 above is the Greek word ἀπιστία apistia, *ap-is-tee´-ah;* and this word means *faithlessness,* i.e. (neg.) *disbelief* (*want of* Chr. *faith*), or (pos.) *unfaithfulness* (*disobedience*):— unbelief.

Observe that in this kind of unbelief, there is a lack of Christian faith. This is the same kind of unbelief that the man who wanted his son delivered of an evil spirit had when he told Jesus, "Lord, I believe, help Thou my unbelief." He had faith, but not enough. He was lacking in Christian faith.

(Mark 9:23, 24)

23. Jesus said unto him, If thou canst believe, all things are possible to him that believeth.

24. And straightway the father of the child cried out, and said with tears, Lord, I believe; help thou mine unbelief.

It is the kind of unbelief where you want to believe, but you just do not have the faith needed or desired to believe.

(Hebrews 3:18) And to whom sware he that they should not enter into his rest, but to them that believed not?

Notice also that the words *believed not* in Hebrews 3:18 above is the Greek word ἀπειθέω apĕithĕō, *ap-i-theh´-o;* from 545; this word means to *disbelieve* (willfully and perversely):— not believe, disobedient, obey not, unbelieving.

This word comes from the Greek word ἀπειθής apĕithēs, *ap-i-thace´;* which means, *unpersuadable,* i.e. *contumacious:*— disobedient.

Observe that this second kind of unbelief, (believed not), is an unbelief where you refuse to believe. Your unbelief has grown from a lack of Christian faith to unbelief

126

where it is unpersuadable; no matter what happens, you refuse to believe. Here there is no turning back. You willfully and perversely refuse to believe. Nothing can help you at this stage; no, not even God.

This is the reason why God came to the place where He said, *"So I sware in my wrath, They shall not enter into my rest."* Their unbelief had grown from an evil heart of unbelief to the place where there was no hope for them.

Not only that, but follow along carefully to see how this evil heart of unbelief, (which was in the heart of only a small handful of them), infested the majority of them so that most lost out with God.

IF YOU THINK THAT THE WAY YOU THINK, SPEAK, OR ACT ONLY AFFECTS YOU, YOU HAD BETTER THINK AGAIN!

For this reason, the writer to the Hebrews warns them to take heed lest there be in any of them this type of unbelieving heart. He knew that, if left alone, this kind of unbelieving heart would grow into a heart of greater unbelief and destroy not only the person with this evil heart of unbelief but also all those that this type of heart infects.

(Hebrews 3:15, 16)

15. While it is said, Today if ye will hear his voice, harden not your hearts, as in the provocation.

16. For some, when they had heard, did provoke: howbeit not all that came out of Egypt by Moses.

Let us look at these two verses carefully and understand how an evil heart of unbelief causes others to also lose out with God. In the case of the nation of Israel, except for a small number all missed out.

Notice that it says above: *"For some when they had heard, did provoke: howbeit not all that came out of Egypt."*

Let us look at the definition of the word *provoke* according to the original writings to understand what the scriptures are trying to tell us.

Provoke... παραπικραίνω parapikrainō, *par-ap-ik-rah'-ee-no;* to *embitter alongside*, i.e. (fig.) to *exasperate:*— provoke.

Webster defines the word *embitter* as "to make bitter,". . . This word *provoke* has the same characteristics as leaven. If you have a small amount, it will spread and infect all those with whom it comes in contact.

(Matthew 13:33) Another parable spake he unto them; The kingdom of Heaven is like unto leaven, which a woman took, and hid in three measures of meal, till the whole was leavened.

(Understand that this leavening process works for both good and evil effects, as we will learn later on in this book. Furthermore, knowing these principles and applying them to our lives will enable us to become mighty man and women of God.)

Understanding this, we can see that it was just a small handful of people who came out of Egypt that were bitter, (because of that evil heart of unbelief), but that bitterness spread like leaven until all of the people were infected.

This is why the scriptures warn us to take a look inside our hearts to see if we are the ones who have the evil heart of unbelief so that we are not the ones to start this snowball effect of embittering the others. Furthermore, if we are not the one with the evil heart of unbelief, it gives us the secret to how not to allow the bitterness to get into us if someone else who has it tries to pass it on.

(Hebrews 3:12, 13)

128

12. Take heed, brethren, lest there be in any of you an evil heart of unbelief, in departing from the living God.

13. But exhort one another daily, while it is Called Today; lest any of you be hardened through the deceitfulness of sin.

Notice what verse 13 above says after warning us about looking to see if in us is an evil heart of unbelief. Why is it telling us to exhort one another daily "lest any of you be hardened"? It is telling us to do this because this is the means of repelling the bitterness from being transferred into us.

In other words, what the nation of Israel should have done if they had known these truth was that when one would come and start saying something like, "This Moses does not know what he is doing, we are out here starving to death. We have no water to drink. Our children are hungry and thirsty. We would have been better off staying in Egypt", they should have responded with something like, "Did you forget what God did in Egypt, the miracles we saw, His power and greatness? If God has to, He will rain bread from Heaven and cause the rocks to spew out water!" This is how they would have exhorted one another daily, thereby repelling the bitterness from coming on them, while causing the other, (with the evil heart of unbelief), to examine his or her heart.

Now this is good advice for the one who is trying not to allow the bitterness to rub off on him or her. But, what about the one that has an evil heart of unbelief? How can he or she know this? Moreover, how does he or she deal with it to rid him or herself of it?

He has to do what we have been saying all along in verse 12 of Hebrews 3: "*Take heed, brethren, lest there be in any of you an evil heart of unbelief, in departing from the living God.*" Nevertheless, how does he or she do this?

Notice the definition of the word *heed* according to the original writings.

Heed... βλέπω blĕpō, *blep´-o;* a primary verb; to *look* at (lit. or fig.):— behold, beware, lie, look (on, to), perceive, regard, see, sight, take heed.

Understanding the meaning of the word *heed*, we can see that all we need to do is to look inside ourselves to make sure there is no evil heart of unbelief in us. Right? Yes, if we had the power to do that, but the problem is we do not! However, God in His infinite wisdom and mercy has provided a way that we can have someone look into us to see if in us there is an evil heart of unbelief. And this someone is our GREAT HIGH PRIEST. Remember, one of the ministries of the high priest was to cut open the sacrifices and clean their insides; but how does this transpire in our lives?

(Hebrews 4:11-14)

11. Let us <u>labor</u> therefore to enter into that rest, lest any man fall after the same example of unbelief

12. For the word of God is quick, and powerful, and sharper than any two edged sword, piercing even to the dividing asunder of soul and spirit, and of the joints and marrow, and <u>is a discerner of the thoughts and intents of the heart</u>.

13. Neither is there any creature that is not manifest in his sight: but all things are naked and opened unto the eyes of him with whom we have to do.

14. Seeing then that we have a <u>great high priest</u>, that is passed into the heavens, Jesus the Son of God, let us hold fast our profession.

In verse 11 above, we see the scriptures telling us to "Labor to enter into that rest lest any fall after the same example of unbelief." We have already studied how an individual can fall into the same "example of unbelief" from verse 12 through verse 19 of chapter 3. However, what does he mean to labor to enter into that rest? How do we do this? Understand that the word *labor* found in Hebrews 4:11 is the same word *study* that we find in 2 Timothy 2:15: "<u>*Study* to</u>

shew thyself approved unto God, a workman that needeth not to be ashamed, rightly dividing the word of truth."

Without knowing this, we would be confused as to what the Lord is trying to tell us when the scriptures continue from verse 11 above to verse 12. It seems as though verses 12 forward do not continue in the same line of thought as the previous verses. However, understanding the revelation that God is trying to teach us we see how the scriptures fit together perfectly.

Knowing the meaning of the word *labor,* we can see how as we study God's Word, the Word Himself, the Lord Jesus Christ, our high priest, rises up as a mighty two-edged sword; and as we are laboring in His Word, His Word begins to, (spiritually speaking,) cut us open, and that sword of God's Word pierces past our joints and marrow, dividing asunder of our soul and spirit all the way to the core of our problem — our heart! Seeing and discerning if in our heart is an evil heart of unbelief, and if there is, our high priest will circumcise our heart and remove that evil portion of unbelief before it has a chance to grow and cause us to lose out with God. This is how we take heed that there is not in us an evil heart of unbelief. It is the spiritual equivalent of a surgeon cutting us open to remove a cancer before it can grow and kill us.

If you think that when you study God's Word all you get is some insight and information, you have yet to know this awesome Word of God.

The definitions of the words, "quick" and "labor/study" are: Quick: ζάω **zao,** *dzah´-o;* a primary verb; to *live* (lit. or fig.):— life (-time), (a-) live (-ly), quick.

Labor/Study: σπουδάζω **spŏudazō,** *spoo-dad´-zo;* to *use speed,* i.e. to *make effort, be prompt* or *earnest:*— do (give) diligence, be diligent (forward), endeavour, labour, study.

Moreover, notice the definition of the words *naked* and *opened* above, according to the original writings.

Naked... γυμνός gumnŏs, *goom-nos´;* of uncert. aff.; *nude* (absol. or rel., lit. or fig.):— naked.

Opened... τραχηλίζω trachēlizō, *trakh-ay-lid´-zo;;* to *seize* by *the throat* or *neck,* i.e. to *expose* the *gullet* of a victim for killing (gen. to *lay bare*):— opened.

Upon looking at the definition of these words, we get a clearer understanding of one of the major role of our high priest. As we labor in God's Word, God's liven Word labors in us, bringing into fruition God's will and plan for our lives.

This is why the psalmist loved Gods Word and said in verses 23 and 24 of Psalm 139, "Search me O God and know my heart: Try me, and know my thought: And see if there be any wicked way in me, and lead me in the way everlasting."

However, God's people must understand that this will never take place if we do not have enough love for the Word of God to read, study, and meditate upon His Word.

Looking carefully at the words "study" and "labor" and realizing their meanings we can see that what God looks for is do we love His Word enough to run to our study chamber because we cannot wait to get alone with His Word as if we were meeting with our lover. Do we make an effort to arrange our lives so that His Word is first and foremost in our lives. Are we prompt and earnest, and do we give diligence and are we diligent towards the Word of God as we are, or more then we are to the other loves of our lives? Do we endeavor and labor in His Word with a greater passion and longing then we do for the other things in our lives?

As we fall deeper in love with God's Word, (Jesus His Son), we devote more time to study His Word, and because of this, we find ourselves with a renewed sense of desire to go all the way with God. As a result, those wrong things that were in our hearts, somehow just seem to disappear. Accordingly, our desire is also growing for more of God, His Word, His kingdom, His people, and His house of prayer, assuring us that our great high priest is busy at fulfilling His ministry in our body, His temple.

Let us continue on our journey through God's Word to see the importance of getting it in our hearts. And how this Word, (as we apply it), will transform us into the children of God that we are supposed to be, while the leavening process takes effect, causing others to become what we have become: an offspring of the Lord Jesus Christ.

CHAPTER NINE

PARABLE OF THE SOWER

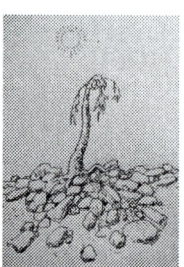

³And he spake many things unto them in parables, saying, Behold, a sower went forth to sow; ⁴And when he sowed, some seeds fell by the way side, and the fowls came and devoured them up: ⁵Some fell upon stony places, where they had not much earth: and forthwith they sprung up, because they had no deepness of earth: ⁶And when the sun was up, they were scorched; and because they had no root, they withered away. ⁷And some fell among thorns; and the thorns sprung up, and choked them: ⁸But other fell into good ground, and brought forth fruit, some an hundredfold, some sixtyfold, some thirtyfold. ⁹Who hath ears to hear, let him hear (Matthew 13:3-9).

Of all the parables that Jesus spoke about in the scriptures, the parable of the sower is the one with the greatest insight. Without understanding the mystery behind this parable, it is very hard to understand all the other parables. Reason being, the parable of the sower holds the master key that unlocks the mysteries to all the other parables.

(Mark 4:13) And he said unto them, Know ye not this parable? and how then will ye know all parables?

Now it is commonly taught that the parable of the sower is a parable about four different types of ground that represent four different types of people in the world. Furthermore, when the seed of God's Word is sown into their hearts, the type of ground that they have in their hearts, will determine whether they will continue with God or not.

Now we must understand that this parable is much more than that. Moreover, because of our lack of understanding of the revelations behind this parable, many of our other teachings have fallen very short of the mark of teaching God's people the truths in His Word.

This parable is more a teaching of spiritual growth. This parable is the Lord's way of teaching us the four steps of spiritual growth that we all go through as we endeavor to grow up in Christ. Which is why as we study this parable and compare it with the pictures shown, we can see that with every type of ground mentioned, there is not only a different type of ground, but there is a greater degree of growth associated with each type of ground.

Each one of these types of ground represents a type of person that went so far with God, but then went through something that made them give up and not make it. However, this does not mean that they could not have made it to the next level; this only means that they lacked the knowledge needed to overcome in that level and continue on to the next stage of growth. Therefore, that is what this parable is about, given us the insight as to why they failed, so we can use that knowledge to overcome, so we can climb to the next level until we reach full maturity.

We will all experience the difficulty of all these types of ground, as we endeavor to grow to the level of a full-grown tree that bears much fruit. For this reason, we need the understanding of God's Word to know what is needed to overcome those difficulties. Moreover, each type of ground also represents those areas of weakness in some Christians, which the enemy will use against them to stop that growth process and ultimately bring about their spiritual demise. For this reason, they need to beware of those vulnerabilities so as to take great care in overcoming in that area of their lives.

This parable the author would say is the circle of life, (Christian life), process that we, (who declare to be a child of God), have been birthed into, and continue to revolve around every time we climb into a higher level with Christ. Every time we grow from glory to glory, we do so upon the caravel of the sequences of events of this parable.

This parable is not saying, as many teach that there are four types of people on the earth and that they will never go beyond that ground in their life. If that were the case, then only one forth of the earth's populations that has ever existed, from the time of Christ until now would ever make it into the kingdom of God. On the contrary, we have living witnesses walking in the world today, that at one time or another failed in one of these levels, but learned from them and the next time they went around, overcame and climbed to the next level and are still climbing.

Let us closely look at this parable to see clearly, what the Lord has been trying to show us.

(Mark 4:14-20)

14. The sower soweth the word.

15. And these are they by the way side, where the word is sown; but when they have heard, Satan cometh immediately, and taketh away the word that was sown in their hearts.

16. And these are they likewise which are sown on stony ground; who, when they have heard the word, immediately receive it with gladness;

17. And have no root in themselves, and so endure but for a time: afterward, when affliction or persecution ariseth for the word's sake, immediately they are offended.

18. And these are they which are sown among thorns; such as hear the word,

19. And the cares of this world, and the deceitfulness of riches, and the lusts of other things entering in, choke the word, and it becometh unfruitful.

20. And these are they which are sown on good ground; such as hear the word, and receive it, and bring forth fruit, some thirtyfold, some sixty, and some a hundred.

We need to first notice that this parable begins with the Word being found in a seed form. As that word is sown, (or spoken about), in the four types of ground, there is growth with each type of ground that it is found in. In the first type of ground, all we see is the seed. When the seed is sown into the second type of ground, we see the seed grow from a seed, in the wayside ground, to a sapling in the rocky ground.

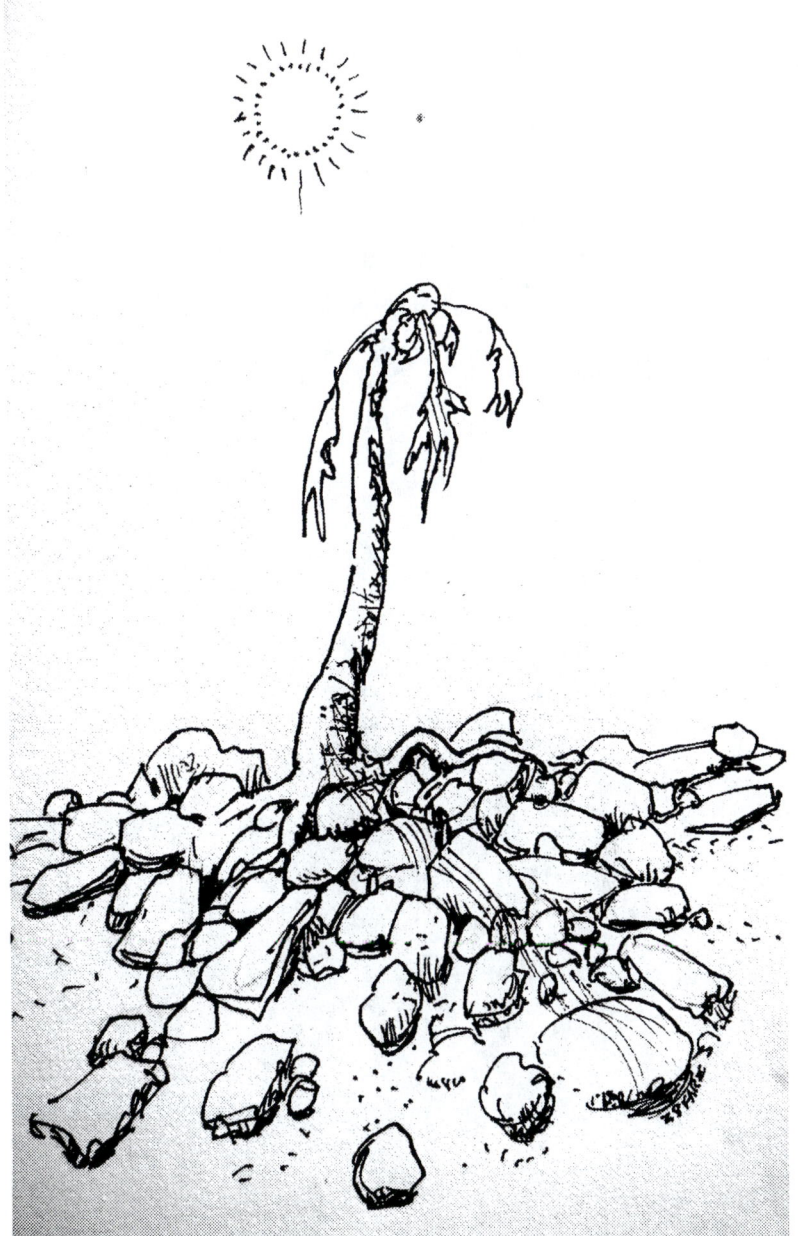

However, when He talks about the third type of ground, it is no longer a sapling but a full-grown tree without fruit in the thorny ground.

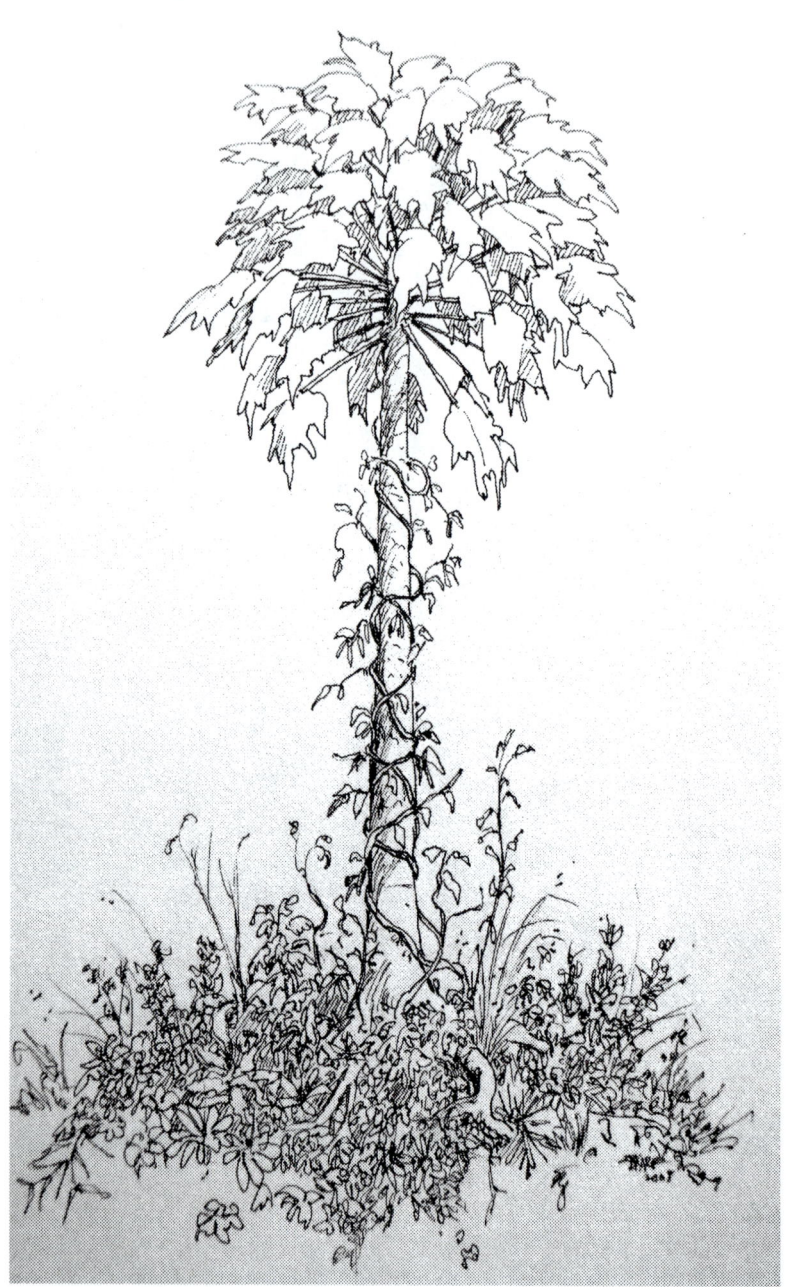

Then we see the tree continue on its growth cycle to the point of bearing fruit in the good ground.

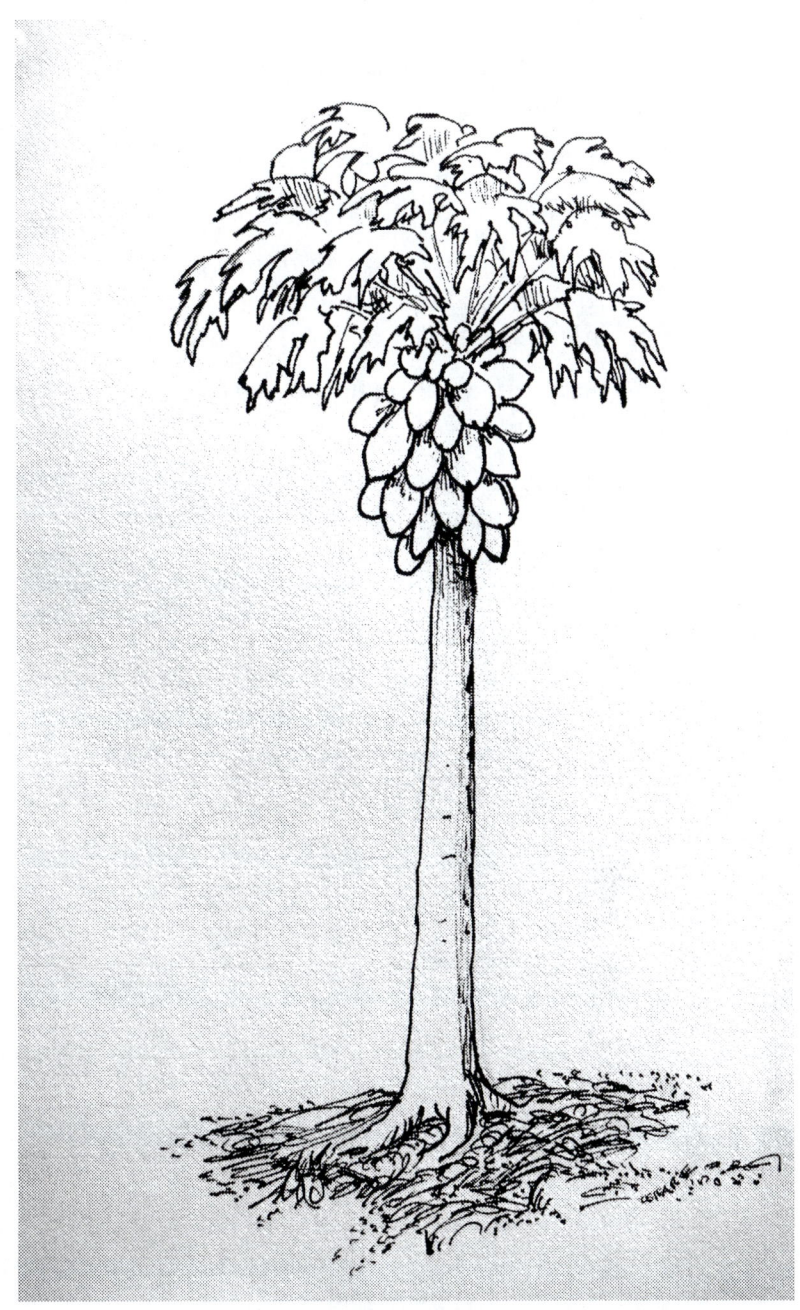

We can dispute what the Lord is trying to show us in this parable, but if this is not the case, then why does He always speak this parable in this sequence? Why not let the thorny ground be first in the chain of events, afterward the wayside ground second, and so on?

There are four spiritual steps to growth in Christ.

(2 Timothy 3:16, 17)

16. All scripture is given by inspiration of God, and is profitable for doctrine, for reproof, for correction, for instruction in righteousness:

17. That the man of God may be perfect, thoroughly furnished unto all good works.

Notice the four spiritual steps of growth: 1. Doctrine; 2. Reproof; 3. Correction; and 4. Instruction in righteousness. In addition, how these steps bring us to the place where we become a perfect men, thoroughly furnished unto all good works.

Observe that this parable is pointing out those four steps, and if we can know these truths and understand them, we can utilize these truths to help us grow up in Christ.

(Understand people of God that just as there are four spiritual steps of growth in Christ, there are four spiritual steps of declining or going further away from God.

People think that if you give a person enough of the Word, that Word will not return to God void. That sooner or later that individual will turn to the Lord and get saved . . .

(Isaiah 55:11) So shall my word be that goeth forth out of my mouth: it shall not return unto me void, but it shall accomplish that which I please, and it shall prosper in the thing whereto I sent it.

. . . Now this is true if that individual will not fight Gods Word. If he or she will allow the Word to perform what God sent it forth to do; and that is to bring him or her to God. However, if that persons refuses to heed to Gods Word; if he or she refuses to repent and allow that Word to work in his or her heart. That same Word will not return to God void, it will accomplish that which God has sent it forth to do, and that is to cause that person to go further from God and not towards God.

(Isaiah 28:12-13)

12. To whom he said, This is the rest wherewith ye may cause the weary to rest; and this is the refreshing: <u>yet they would not hear.</u>

13. But the word of the LORD was unto them precept upon precept, precept upon precept; line upon line, line upon line; here a little, and there a little; that they might go and <u>fall backward,</u> and <u>be broken,</u> and <u>snared,</u> and <u>taken.</u>,)

AS THE SEED OF GOD'S WORD GROWS, THE BATTLE FOR THAT WORD INTENSIFIES!

Notice also that as that seed grows from a seed all the way into a fruit-bearing tree, the battle for that Word intensifies. In the first type of ground, (the wayside ground), since the Word is still in seed form, it is not so much of a concern to the enemy, Satan, so he comes alone to catch that seed that was sown in someone's heart.

(Matthew 13:19) When any one heareth the word of the kingdom, and understandeth it not, then cometh the wicked <u>one,</u> and catcheth away that which was sown in his heart. This is he which received seed by the way side.

However, notice how, as the seed grows from a seed into a small sapling, the battle intensifies.

(Matthew 13:20, 21)

20. But he that received the seed into stony places, the same is he that heareth the word, and anon with joy receiveth it;

21. Yet hath he not root in himself, but dureth for a while: for when tribulation <u>or</u> persecution ariseth because of the word, by and by he is offended.

From these scriptures, we see that the one who does not want us to bear fruit, begins to panic when he sees growth in the second type of ground. Therefore, instead of sending one thing against the Word, he sends two: *tribulation* and *persecution.*

Though the scriptures specifies *tribulation or persecution*, the implication here is *"and", tribulation "and" persecution.* Because the word *or* in the original writing in this verse is also the word that means *"and."* Plus, the fact that as we see the Word growing from a seed, to a full ground tree, the battle intensifies. Therefore, it would stand to reason that if the battle rages from "one," in the first type of ground, "the wayside ground," (*Satan cometh immediately.*) And it climbs to "three," in the third type of ground, "the thorny ground," (1. *The cares of this world,* 2. *The deceitfulness of riches,* 3. *The lusts of other things.*) Then it stands to reason that it would have to be "two," (*Tribulation and Persecution*), in the second type of ground.

Notice the definition of the word *or,* according to the original writing. The word *or* is the Greek word, ἤ ē *ay;* a primary particle of distinction between two connected terms; disjunctive, *or;* comparative, *than:—* <u>and</u>, but (either), (n-) either, except it be, (n-) or (else), rather, save, than, that, what, yea.

As we continue in the study of this parable, we see that in the thorny ground, the seed has grown into a fully mature tree getting ready to bear fruit. Observe how this tree is full-grown and at the verge of producing or already producing fruit.

(Luke 8:14) And that which fell among thorns are they, which, when they have heard, go forth, and are choked with

cares and riches and pleasures of this life, and bring no fruit to perfection.

Notice that the words, *"Fruit to perfection,"* (Bring no fruit to perfection,) in Luke 8:14 is the Greek word τελεσφορέω tĕlĕsphŏrĕō, *tel-es-for-eh´-o;* and this word means to *be a bearer to completion* (maturity), i.e. to *ripen fruit* (fig.):— bring fruit to perfection.

We can see that the implications here are that this was a full-grown tree ready to produce or ripen its fruit, but instead cast them forth before their time.

Also, notice how much more the battle has intensified. We do not see just one thing coming against it, nor do we see two things battling for the Word. On the contrary, now we see three fixations that have united in an all-out effort to choke the Word and keep it from bearing fruit: 1. The cares of this world; 2. The deceitfulness of riches; and 3. The lust of other things.

(Mark 4:18, 19)

18. And these are they which are sown among thorns; such as hear the word,

19. And the cares of this world, and the deceitfulness of riches, and the lusts of other things entering in, choke the word, and it becometh unfruitful.

We need to understand that this parable is a teaching on spiritual growth and the importance of guarding that seed of God's Word, so that Word can be allowed to grow to the place of becoming a full-grown tree with fruit.

There are so many revelations hidden in this parable, that time and space would not allow us to teach them all. Nevertheless, I pray that this chapter will open your understanding and give you enough truth, so that you can rightly divide this parable and get all the truths that are hidden therein.

The further along we come to understanding this parable, the more we know why certain events happen throughout the different stages of growth. We are then better prepared to meet them head on and to use that knowledge to help us grow in Christ, while also helping those who do not have this knowledge grow as well. As we receive greater understanding of this parable, we can utilize that knowledge to beat the enemy at his own game.

Understand that in the first stage of growth, the reason why Satan could catch that seed sown in that person's heart, was that person's inability to understand the Word. Therefore, as ministers of the gospel, we need to endeavor to teach the Word in as simple a manner as possible, so that the person hearing can easily understand it. This gives them a fighting chance at not allowing the enemy to catch the seed that is sown in his or her heart. Understanding this also motivates us to want to work with that individual, until he or she fully comprehends the truth.

Thought it seem that in this first stage of growth, I am laying the responsibility on the ministers who are ministering the Word, instead of on the individual in whom the seed has being sowed; I am! For the reason that, if this parable is about spiritual growth, then the person in whom the Word has been sowed, in the wayside ground, is, (Spiritually speaking), a baby Christian. Therefore, just as a baby in the natural is unable to dress itself or feed itself, neither can a newborn Christian do for itself, they need the support and guidance of a spiritual parent.

If the wayside ground is the first stage of growth in our Christian life, and it runs parallel with the first stage of growth as explain in 2 Timothy 3:16; *All scripture is given by inspiration of God, and is profitable for doctrine, . . .* then that would mean that doctrine is what we give to baby Christians. Nevertheless, can we prove this with scriptures? Yes, in Isaiah 28:9 we read where it says:

(Isaiah 28:9) Whom shall he teach knowledge? and whom

shall he make to understand doctrine? them that are weaned from the milk, and drawn from the breasts.

Those, in whom the seed is sowed, in the wayside ground, represent spiritual babies in Christ. Therefore, they need those that are mature in the Lord to nurture and carry them so they can grow up in Christ. What's more, the best way to nurture them is to give them the understanding of God's Word and the best way to carry them is to pray for and with them.

(Matthew 13:20, 21)

20. But he that received the seed into stony places, the same is he that heareth the word, and anon with joy receiveth it;

21. Yet hath he not root in himself, but dureth for a while: for when tribulation or persecution ariseth because of the word, by and by he is offended.

Observe that in the second stage of growth it speaks of the small sapling on top of rocks. Even though the scriptures say, "*And because they had no root*"; giving us the impression that there are no roots there. However, we know from having learned about planting seeds that the roots always come out first. The roots go down while the plant shoots up. So there are roots, they are just not in the dirt; the rocks serve as a barrier to keep the roots from going into the ground.

Plants will always find a way to spring upwards, as long as their roots are in the ground. This is why, if we have a crack in the sidewalk and there is a plant underneath it, it will eventually make its way through that crack and grow; if left alone, it will break the sidewalk and continue on its growth cycle.

Therefore, the problem here in this second type of ground is not that the plant has no roots, but rather that the rocks are keeping the roots from going into the ground.

Follow carefully so you can understand what is transpiring here, so you will have the knowledge needed to not allow the enemy to stumble or trip you, thereby causing you to drop the Word. As well as not allowing the enemy to cause you to abandon the Word.

Be aware that once that seed has entered your heart and begun its germinating process, the Devil cannot take it. He does not have the power to take that Word from you. Therefore, what he does is send you the tribulation and persecution in an effort to get you to drop or abandon that Word.

It is like this. Say you are a football player. As you catch the ball that has been thrown to you, you look up and see all these big tough players from the opposite team running toward you. They do not want you. They are not after you. They want that ball. They want to take that ball from you. Now, you have a choice, to run with that ball and hold onto it for dear life, or you can throw the ball away, because if you do not have the ball, they will leave you alone. This is what most Christians do at this stage of their growth cycle, not understanding that all along, God is in complete control of the situation.

Just as those players from the other team will motivate you to hold on to the ball and run, to make the touch down. So will the understanding of this truth, motivate and inspire you, to not allow the enemy of your soul, to trip you up or cause you to abandon the Word!

Notice the definition of the word *offended* found in Mark 4:17. σκανδαλίζω skandalizō, *skan-dal-id´-zo* ("scandalize"); to *entrap*, i.e. *trip* up (fig. *stumble* [tran.] or *entice* to sin, apostasy or displeasure):— (make to) offend.

(Mark 4:17) And have no root in themselves, and so endure but for a time: afterward, when affliction or persecution ariseth for the word's sake, immediately they are <u>*offended.*</u>

Note that one of the definitions is *apostasy*. One of Webster's definitions for the word *apostasy* is "abandonment of a previous loyalty." If the Devil cannot take the Word from you, he will do everything in his power to get you to cast the Word away, to abandon it or try to trip you up, to make you stumble and drop or lose the Word.

However, it does not have to be this way, if you understand that even the Devil is subject to God. Even when the Devil thinks he is doing his own thing; God is in control over that situation as well. Observe that while the Devil is trying to get you to drop or abandon the Word, God is actually using the Devil to push that Word deeper, past the rocks so that the roots can be pushed down into the ground and that small tree can continue to grow. Look at the definition of the words *affliction* and *persecution,* as found in the original writings.

Affliction: θλίψις thlipsis, *thlip´-sis;* pressure (lit. or fig.):— afflicted (-tion), anguish, burdened, persecution, tribulation, trouble.

The word *pressure* according to Webster's is the word that means, 1. The burden of physical or mental distress. 2. The application of force to something by something else in direct contact with it. *Compression*; 3.A. the action of force against an opposing force. B. the force or thrust exerted over a surface divided by its area.

The word *burdened* according to Webster's means, 1. Something that is carried, a load. . . the bearing of a load. . .

Persecution: διωγμός diōgmŏs, *dee-ogue-mos´; persecution:*— persecution

Persecution according to the American College Standard Reference Dictionary, (Copyright 1959 by Spencer Press, Inc. Published in New York by Random House, Inc.,) means 1. the act of persecuting. 2. State of being persecuted.

The word *persecute* according to the American College Standard Reference Dictionary, (Copyright 1959 by

Spencer Press, Inc. Published in New York by Random House, Inc.,) is to oppress with injury or punishment. The word *oppress* means 1. to lie heavily upon (the mind, a person, etc.). 2. to burden with cruel or unjust impositions or restraints. 3. To weigh down. 4. To press against or down . . .

As we can see, the words *affliction* and *persecution* mean to put pressure, to weigh down or burden, to oppress or press down.

What is really happening here, is, that while the enemy is trying to get you to get rid of or lose the Word, God is in fact using him to push that Word deeper into your heart, to establish the root system in the ground past the rocks. If you do not know this, you will get offended and abandon the Word, or allow the afflictions and persecution to trip you up or make you stumble and cause you to drop that Word. However, if you know what is actually happening here and you know the end result of God's plan for your life, you will hold on to that Word with all your might, until it fulfills that which God has sent it forth to do.

As God uses us to bring people to Christ and we understand these truths, we can be an encouragement to those individuals. When we see these things happening to them, we encourage them to hold on and not give up.

WAKE UP CHURCH!

(Mark 4:18, 19)

18. And these are they which are sown among thorns; such as hear the word,

19. And the cares of this world, and the deceitfulness of riches, and the lusts of other things entering in, choke the word, and it becometh unfruitful.

Now we come to the last and final stage of growth before an individual produces fruit. The truths behind this stage of growth are so vast and so profound that only God can teach them to us with time alone. Therefore, because of this, many individuals and churches as a whole are caught in the fiery whirlwind of this vicious cycle.

It all begins so sincerely. There is a genuine desire to do things for others, your family, church members, and people from other countries who cannot do for themselves; in other words, what the scriptures calls, *"The cares of this world."* The only problem is that all these things you want to do for others require money. This in turn opens the door to, *"The deceitfulness of riches"*: "If I only had more money, I could give to the church so they could build the new building we need so much;" "If I only had more money, I could send to that missionary in Africa".

You have a sincere desire to do those things that you feel are pleasing to God, but you do not have the money to do them. Consequently, you believe God to provide you with the money, (Which is easy to do with all the "believe it" and "claim it" sermons being preached nowadays). Therefore, you start a business to make more money, all the time justifying it with words like, "God is calling me into the ministry, and I want to become financially independent so I can devote all my time to the ministry." The only problem is that when all that money does start coming in, so does *"The lust of other things"*!

So many of God's people have started out with a sincere heart to do the Lord's will, but now their lives are wrapped around their big houses, their expensive cars, trips, and other luxuries of this world.

In the third stage of growth, "The thorny ground," the thorns do not all grow at the same time. If they did, you would be aware that something was not right, when, *"The cares of this world," "The deceitfulness of riches,"* and *"The lust of other things,"* suddenly pops up and surrounds you. However, because they come in a progression of events, they deceive you into falling prey to their tactics.

It is so unfortunate that one can climb so high in God in the third stage of growth, coming so close to what God is looking for in that person, and still fall so hard.

It is difficult to help a person at this stage of growth, because they know so much of the Word of God that you cannot teach them anything. In addition, most people who might help would not know what to do. Because a person at this stage of growth, is so well educated in the scriptures, that he or she can use them to justify his or her actions, proving to others how right he or she is, even if he or she is wrong in the eyes of God.

IT IS NOT ABOUT US, BUT ALL ABOUT THE SEED, (WORD)!

As we begin to see the revelation behind the parable of the sower, we begin to understand the importance and the worth of the Word of God in our hearts.

The enemy of our soul could care less about us or our ministry; what he wants to do is to keep the Word from growing and producing fruit. However, we must ask ourselves the question, "Why would the Devil fight us so much to keep that Word from growing to full term?" There is something that the Devil does not want us to produce — the fruit? Yes, the fruit, but he is after more than that: the seed in the fruit! Because the seed is, what the sower needs to bring more people into the kingdom of God. And, if he can keep us from bearing fruit, he stops the supply of seeds that the sower needs, in order for other souls to be born into the kingdom of God.

As we continue in this book, we will learn what the fruit is, and upon knowing that, how to utilize the fruit to bring souls to Christ.

CHAPTER TEN

THE FRUIT

³Hearken; Behold, there went out a sower to sow: ⁴And it came to pass, as he sowed, some fell by the way side, and the fowls of the air came and devoured it up. ⁵And some fell on stony ground, where it had not much earth; and immediately it sprang up, because it had no depth of earth: ⁶But when the sun was up, it was scorched; and because it had no root, it withered away. ⁷And some fell among thorns, and the thorns grew up, and choked it, and it yielded no fruit. ⁸And other fell on good ground, and did yield fruit that sprang up and increased; and brought forth, some thirty, and some sixty, and some an hundred... ¹I am the true vine, and my Father is the husbandman. ²Every branch in me that beareth not fruit he taketh away: and every branch that beareth fruit, he purgeth it, that it may bring forth more fruit. ³Now ye are clean through the word which I have spoken unto you. ⁴Abide in me, and I in you. As the branch cannot bear fruit of itself, except it abide in the vine; no more can ye, except ye abide in me. ⁵I am the vine, ye are the branches: He that abideth in me, and I in him, the same bringeth forth much fruit: for without me ye can do nothing. ⁸Herein is my Father glorified, that ye bear much fruit; so shall ye be my disciples (Mark 4:3-8; John 15:1-5, 8).

As a person seeks to please God by way of His Word, it does not take long for that individual to realize that the bearing of fruit is of grave importance in the life of a Christian. We can understand through various teachings in the scriptures that a professing child of God must bear fruit! The author would even have to say that without any fruit in the life of a person, confessing to be a Christian, who has been around long enough to have produced fruit, by all probability, that individual will not enter the kingdom of God. Furthermore, when you take a look at many so-called Christians of this day, we can see that many fall short of bringing into fruition the bearing of fruit. Why is that? The author believes that the reason for this is that many Christians do not really know what the fruit is. Reason being, because they have not been taught what the fruit in fact is.

In this next revelation, we will learn what the fruit is and how to use the fruit to win souls for Christ.

GOD DESIRED FRUIT FROM HIS PEOPLE IN THE PAST AND HE IS STILL SEEKING FRUIT FROM HIS PEOPLE NOW!

[33]Hear another parable: There was a certain householder, which planted a vineyard, and hedged it round about, and digged a winepress in it, and built a tower, and let it out to husbandmen, and went into a far country: [34]And when the time of the fruit drew near, he sent his servants to the husbandmen, that they might receive the fruits of it. [35]And the husbandmen took his servants, and beat one, and killed another, and stoned another. [36]Again, he sent other servants more than the first: and they did unto them likewise. [37]But last of all he sent unto them his son, saying, They will reverence my son. [38]But when the husbandmen saw the son, they said among themselves, This is the heir; come, let us kill him, and let us seize on his inheritance. [39]And they caught him, and cast him out of the vineyard, and slew him. [40]When the lord therefore of the vineyard cometh, what will he do unto those husbandmen? [41]They say unto him, He will miserably destroy those wicked men, and will let out his vineyard unto other husbandmen, which shall render him the fruits in their seasons. [42]Jesus saith unto them, Did ye never read in the scriptures, The stone which the builders rejected,

154

the same is become the head of the corner: this is the Lord's doing, and it is marvelous in our eyes? [43]Therefore say I unto you, The kingdom of God shall be taken from you, and given to a nation bringing forth the fruits thereof (Matthew 21:33-43).

WHAT IS THE FRUIT?

Many Religious teachings teach us that the fruit we are supposed to bear is a person that we win to the Lord. In other words, if I, Luis, tell Mary about Jesus Christ and Mary accepts Christ as her Lord and Savior, this makes Mary my fruit. Because I won her to the Lord, she is now the fruit that I have brought forth. Though this may sound good, and has been widely accepted as truth among religious circles, this does not make the slightest bit of sense whatsoever.

Let us look at what has actually transpired here.

For Mary to have been born into the kingdom of God, I would have had to have a seed first, (the seed of the Word of God), to sow into the ground of Mary's heart. Now, if Mary is my fruit, then where did I get the seed to sow into her heart, prior to Mary becoming my fruit? If Mary is my fruit, as is commonly taught, then the seed would be in her, because the seed is always found in the fruit. HOWEVER, would I not need to have had a seed first to sow into Mary's heart, before she even came into the picture? How could she, if she is my fruit, come into existence before the seed that was needed to sow into her heart?

Nature teaches us that before we can grow something, we must first have a seed to sow, and that seed needs to come out of another fruit before we can sow it. Therefore, Mary cannot be my fruit. I must first bear fruit before Mary is even in the equation, and then I can use the seed of that fruit to sow into Mary's heart in order to win her to the Lord.

So then, what is the fruit? A careful study of the scriptures...

(Matthew 12:33, 34)

33. Either make the tree good, and his fruit good; or else make the tree corrupt, and his fruit corrupt: for the tree is known by his fruit.

34. O generation of vipers, how can ye, being evil, speak good things? for out of the abundance of the heart the mouth speaketh.

...implies, (especially if we stay in the context of what our Lord is saying going from verse 33 to verse 34), that the fruit, whether good or corrupt, is the words that proceed out of our mouth.

Furthermore, when we look at the next scripture and others like it...

(Proverbs 18:21) Death and life are in the power of the tongue: and they that love it shall eat the fruit thereof.

...we have a tendency to believe that our fruit, whether good or corrupt, is in fact the words that proceed out of our mouths.

So then, is our fruit the words that proceed out of our mouths, or is it something else?

Now bear in mind that the fruit is the culmination of all that God is looking for in our lives. Therefore, when we look at other scriptures like:

(2 Timothy 3:16) That the man of God may be perfect, thoroughly furnished unto all <u>good works</u>.

and:

(Titus 3:14) And let ours also learn to maintain <u>good works</u> for necessary uses, that they be not unfruitful.

plus:

(Ephesians 2:10) For we are his workmanship, created in Christ Jesus unto <u>good works</u>, which God hath before ordained that we should walk in them

...we get the impression that the end result of what God is looking for in a Christian is "good works".

The bearing of fruit is the culminating result of our growth in Christ, so if good works are the ultimate action that the Lord looks for in a person, then it is safe to say that our good works would be our fruit.

Now we seem to have a problem, and the problem is that many scriptures appear to point to the fact that the words that proceed out of our mouths, are our fruit, while still other scriptures indicate that our good works are our fruit. So then, which of the two are our fruit, our "words", or our "works"?

Well, the truth is that they are both our fruit, our "words", as well as our "works". What we need to remember is that fruits are made up of two properties, the flesh that surrounds the seed and the seed in the middle of the fruit.

Therefore, it is the same with our spiritual fruit; our words represent the seed in the fruit, while our works represent the flesh that surrounds the seed. Moreover, this truth is the same whether a person is a Christian or not. If the individual is a Christian, then the Word of God that proceeds out of his or her mouth represents the seed, and the good works that he or she produces represent the flesh.

(1 Peter 2:12) Having your conversation honest among the Gentiles: that, whereas they speak against you as evildoers, they may by your good works, which they shall behold, glorify God in the day of visitation.

(Colossians 1:10) That ye might walk worthy of the Lord unto all pleasing, being fruitful in every good work, and increasing in the knowledge of God;

However, if the person is a non-believer, then the seed is represented by the corrupt words that come out of his or her mouth, and the evil works that he or she produces represent the flesh.

(Matthew 12:34) O generation of vipers, how can ye, being evil, speak good things? for out of the abundance of the heart the mouth speaketh.

(Colossians 1:21) And you, that were sometime alienated and enemies in your mind by wicked works, yet now hath he reconciled.

Many ministers believe and teach that the souls that we win to the Lord are our fruit. However, those that we win for the Lord are won as a direct result of our fruit, but they are not our fruit. Those that come to know Christ, come, because of a direct result of the "Word of God that proceeds out of our mouths" and our "good works." However, because they are very closely related to our fruit, many ministers believe and preach that they are our fruit, when in fact they are the direct result of our fruit.

God's people must understand that the fruit is our good works coupled with the Word of God that proceeds out of our mouths.

Other ministers preach and teach that the "Fruit of the Spirit", is our fruit. However, the fruit of the Spirit is just that, "THE FRUIT OF THE SPIRIT". When you are baptized with the Holy Ghost, and you acquire more of the Spirit of God as you grow, (which we will discussed later in this book), there will be more of the fruit of the Spirit amalgamated together with your fruit. Therefore, because of this, when you perform a good work and speak the Word of God to accompany that good work, you will perform it with more of the fruit of the Spirit; more love, more kindness, more patience, more joy and so forth and so forth.

A person can perform a good deed and speak the Word of God, (endeavoring to sow the seed into the heart of that person to whom the good deed was done), but they may not have love or be showing love in the process . . .

(1 Corinthians 13:1-3)

1. Though I speak with the tongues of men and of angels, and have not charity, I am become as sounding brass, or a tinkling cymbal.

2. And though I have the gift of prophecy, and understand all mysteries, and all knowledge; and though I have all faith, so that I could remove mountains, and have not charity, I am nothing.

3. And though I bestow all my goods to feed the poor, and though I give my body to be burned, and have not charity, it profiteth me nothing.

. . . This is why we need the empowering of the Holy Ghost to have the love, joy, peace, longsuffering, gentleness, goodness, faith, Meekness, and temperance, to go along with our fruit.

If someone is in need of you to feed or shelter him or her, are you doing it with kindness, (goodness), or joy? Are you performing that good deed coupled with the love of God, or are you proud, rough or harsh?

Question: "What are our good works?"

159

Answer: Anything that we do that proceeds out of CHARITY, is motivated by CHARITY, will produce acts of CHARITY or whose end result is CHARITY!

With the knowledge revealed in this lesson, "What is the fruit", let us study how it is that we as Christians should utilize our fruit to win souls for the kingdom of God.

Note: Do not confuse what we are going to teach in the following paragraphs, with those that go out to the byways and the highways to compel them to come in. That is something that the Lord has told us to do and we must do. However, if you understand the fruit and how to use it to win souls for God, you will have a better edge in your efforts to win people to the Lord when you go out to the highways and byways.

Also, do not think that this is to replace the preaching of the gospel in the churches or tent meetings. Utilizing your fruit to lead someone to Christ will only have a higher impact on an individual coming to the Lord in a church or a tent meeting, if they have already tasted of your fruit and it was desirable in their spiritual mouth.

Most people when they are trying to win someone for the Lord first start by talking to them about the Lord. Telling them of how He died on the cross for their sins and how God loves them and so forth. In other words, they are trying to sow the seed of the Word of God in the ground of that person's heart. This may seem like the proper way to do it, and is more or less, what is taught, but let us take a closer look at this process.

Consider this same approach in the natural realm.

As an example, let us say you are in your house doing what you normally do, and somebody who you do not even know and may never have seen in the past is out in your backyard digging a hole, because he is going to plant a seed on your property. How would you respond? You would be mad that this person had the nerve to come onto your property and do whatever he feels like doing. You would run outside and ask, "Hey, what do you think you are doing?" Now if that person were to say, "Well, I am going to plant this seed that will grow into a tree that will bear these delicious fruit," and if he were to give you the fruit to taste, you would probably slap the fruit out of his hand and demand that he leave your property immediately. You would not be interested in tasting the fruit or having the seed planted in your yard, simply because of the approach that this individual made. You would not want to hear what he has to say, nor would you listen.

What was the problem here? He tried to plant the seed before you had a chance to taste the fruit!

Now let us look at another example but with a different approach.

Let us say you are in somebody's house and he has a bowl of fruit on the table. You grab one of the pieces of fruit and proceed to eat it. To your amazement, the fruit is juicy and very tasty in your mouth. Because it really satisfies your taste buds, you ask the owner, "Where did you buy this fruit?" The owner tells you, "Oh, you cannot buy it. It came off a tree that I planted in my back yard." You would most likely ask him, "Can I have the seed of this fruit so I can plant it in the ground of my property?"

What is the difference here? The difference is that you had an opportunity to taste the fruit, and it was something you had to have for your own!

IT IS THE FRUIT THAT PEOPLE SEE, TASTE AND HEAR THAT CAUSES THEM TO WANT WHAT YOU HAVE

Many Christians in their endeavors to bring a person to the Lord are not aware that the Lord has designed a way for us to win souls by using our fruit, the flesh and the seed. Additionally, even fewer know what the fruit is. For the reason that they have not been taught what the fruit in fact is! Furthermore, many people cannot bring someone to the Lord, either because they do not have the words to shed light on someone's darkness or, if they do have the words, their deeds are so corrupt, (the flesh around the seed), that most people would say, "If he is a Christian, then leave me the way I am, because I am a better person then him."

Many Christians lose precious opportunities to lead others to Christ because of the lack of knowledge surrounding God's Word. Understanding this principle that God has ordained in His Word should teach us that we need to speak and act like the sons of God we are professing to be.

Let us look at a good example that the Lord left us in His Word to see the fruition of using our fruit, (seed and flesh), to bring people to the Lord.

(Matthew 5:16) Let your light so shine before men, that they may see your good works, and glorify your Father which is in Heaven.

Before we begin looking at this revelation to understand this truth, we need to understand that the light mentioned in verse 16 refers to the Word of God that proceeds out of our mouths. (We will see this more clearly in the next chapter.) This is also represented by the seed in the fruit. Remember also that the good works represent the flesh surrounding the seed of the fruit. Therefore, what the Lord is saying to us in this verse is to allow people to understand, (see), our good works.

If you perform good works before men and they do not understand the reason behind them, they may be suspicious of your intentions or question your motives. They may think that you are just a good person and nothing more.

Therefore, if someone is in need of your help, whether to feed his or her hunger, or clothe his or her nakedness or bring him or her in from the cold, to shelter them and you perform a good work, by helping them in one of the above areas. You just let that individual taste of the meat portion of your fruit.

However, if you never let your light shine, by allowing the Word of God to proceed out of your mouth, thereby letting him or her understand why you did what you did. That individual will not understand the reason behind your actions. Therefore, that individual will not glorify our father, who is in Heaven, (which means to come to God on their day of visitation), simply because you fail to sow the seed of the Word of God in his or her heart.

On the other hand, you could let your light shine by saying something like, "The reason for why I am helping you is because of the love of God that is shed abroad in my heart", or because that at one time you were also in need and someone showed you the love of God. Therefore, it is His love that compels you to help others. The point is that we need to accompany our good works with the Word of God to be affective in sowing the Word of God into the ground of the heart of someone that has tasted or our good works.

In addition, this is a perfect opportunity to sow the Word in that person's heart, because that individual has already tasted of the flesh of your fruit, (your good works). Moreover, if it tasted good to him or her, they may be ready to have the seed of that fruit planted in his or her heart. Additionally, if your fruit was very appealing to them, they may even ask you if they can have the seed to plant in the ground of his or her heart. In other words, they may want to accept Christ right then and there.

Remember that it is human nature for a person to try something before deciding to purchase it. People use these principles in the marketplace every day. This is why you may see an orange cut up in pieces on display in a store, so that people can try them. If they are good, then people will buy the oranges.

The same principles apply in our efforts to win someone for the Lord. We allow a person to taste of our fruit, (our good works), and that compels that person to want what we have. (Study chapter eleven carefully to further see how this works, so as to understand in more detail how it is that we use our fruit to win souls for Christ).

FRUIT MEET FOR REPENTANCE VERSUS FRUIT PRODUCED AS A RESULT OF THE TREE HAVING GROWN INTO A FULL-GROWN TREE

What is the difference between the fruit that we bear, because of the Word of God having grown into a full-grown tree, and the fruit that we are supposed to bring forth as a result of us having repented, (*Bring forth therefore fruits meet for repentance (Matthew 3:8.))*?

The fruit that we bear because of that tree growing into a full-grown tree is the fruit that we studied in this chapter. The fruit that we bring forth because we have repented is the same fruit, (our good words coupled with good works). However, the difference is that the fruit we bring forth when we repent are actions that we, within our own power and efforts, endeavor to produce because we believe His Word and are trying to do as He says. This is the proof that we believe His Word, (Jesus), and are trying to do as He says. *And why call ye me, Lord, Lord, and do not the things which I say? (Luke 6:46).* One is produced by our efforts because we believe His Word and are trying to show God that we believe His Word, by trying to do as He says. The other comes along naturally because of having grown into that Word.

For example, someone may treat me badly or unkindly. Now, it would be human nature to want to treat that person the same way. However, because I have repented and know that Jesus said to love your enemy; I endeavor to turn the other cheek. Instead of treating him badly, I force myself to love that person and do good toward him. In my heart I may want to treat him the same; however, I refrain from doing so because I know that God would not be pleased with my actions. That is an action, (fruit), that I am forcing myself to bring forth, Because of believing what His Word says.

On the other hand, if I have grown up into Christ and have taken on the nature of that Word, when that individual treats me unkindly, my very nature is to treat him well. I do not have to force myself to be good to that person, it will naturally flow forth from me, because of the nature of Christ that I have taken on.

One action is brought about because I believe His Word, and the other is brought about because I have grown up into the Word: same fruit, but brought about differently.

This is why we see such scriptures as . . .

(John 15:9) As the Father hath loved me, so have I loved you: continue ye in my love.

Here we see Him telling us to continue in His love. In other word, to love others as He has loved us; to love one another. However, notice that the next verse says . . .

(John 15:10) If ye keep my commandments, ye shall abide in my love; even as I have kept my Father's commandments, and abide in his love.

. . . but what is His commandments? Verse 12 of that same chapter tells us!

(John 15:12) This is my commandment, That ye love one another, as I have loved you.

But why is he telling us to do the same thing twice? Because, one is an act that we perform as a result that we believe His Word, and want to please Him, (Fruit meet for

165

repentance), (*If ye keep my commandments . . . This is my commandment, That ye love one another . . .*). The other comes about because of having grown into the Word, (*. . . Ye shall abide in my love*).

In the next chapter, we will learn that the light and the seed in the fruit are one and the same. We will also learn what it is that we need to do in order to bear much fruit

CHAPTER ELEVEN

THE LIGHT

[14]Ye are the light of the world. A city that is set on an hill cannot be hid. [15]Neither do men light a candle, and put it under a bushel, but on a candlestick; and it giveth light unto all that are in the house. [16]Let your light so shine before men, that they may see your good works, and glorify your Father which is in Heaven (Matthew 5:14-16).

It is unfortunate that most Christians do not know what the light in fact is. Especially considering that it is the light that we are supposed to use in order to win souls for Christ.

When Jesus said, "Ye are the light of the world", and, "Let your light so shine," He was letting us know that He has illuminated us and placed the control switch of that light in our hands. We are the ones who determine whether that light is *on* or *off.*

What's more, if a person does not know what the light is, how will he know if the light is, in fact, *on* or *off?* Even though once the Lord has illuminated a person that light can never be turned off, we can, however, by our actions obstruct that light by putting a bushel over it or placing it under a bed without knowing it.

WHAT IS THE LIGHT?

(God in His infinite wisdom and knowledge has spoken His Word in such a manner that even a child can understand it. However, by the same token He has inspired it so, that it is written in a way that if the Spirit of God does not give the interpretation, it cannot be understood. It is like trying to break a code that cannot be broken. Therefore, the secret to understanding His Word is to recognize that it is, in fact, God's Word, and that we are nothing more than ministers of that Word and we, without His leading, are helpless to understand it.

We must show Him that we hunger for His Word more than even the very food that we eat. Moreover, that we desire His Word more then all the earthly treasures of this world combined, thereby touching the heart of God in a manner that will move Him to make His Word known to us. Because it is His desire to reveal His Word to His children, by opening their spiritual eyes to the understanding of His Word).

In order to see the revelation behind what the light is, we need to understand that many times when God teaches us about a truth, He gives us clues that will guide us into the very heart of that truth.

On the subject of the light, the Lord has done just that. The hint here is Matthew 5, verse 15: *"Neither do men light a candle, and put it under a bushel, but on a candlestick; and it giveth light unto all that are in the house"*.

When we find a verse that says the same thing or something very similar to the same thing, we can be fairly sure that it is speaking of the same subject. This is the Spirit's way of directing our understanding to bring us to the truth that God wants us to see, (in this case, what the light is). Therefore, by studying carefully those clue scriptures and the ones associated with them, we can find the answers to what we are looking for.

Now, if we look at Mark 4:21 and Luke 8:16, we notice that these two verses say pretty much the same statement as Matthew 5:15. Therefore, it is the author's belief that our journey to understanding what the light is should begin here.

(Mark 4:21) And he said unto them, Is a candle brought to be put under a bushel, or under a bed? and not to be set on a candlestick?	(Luke 8:16) No man, when he hath lighted a candle, covereth it with a vessel, or putteth it under a bed but setteth it on a candlestick, that they which enter in may see the light.

As we look at the two sets of scriptures above, we can see that Mark 4:21 and Luke 8:16, are both recounting basically the same remark that the Lord said in Matthew 5:15, consequently these verses and the ones associated with them should be leading us toward understanding what the light is.

After the Lord told them that He had illuminated them, as a man would light a candle, He went on to tell them that no one lights a candle to place it where that candle would be of no use; a candle is lit to serve a purpose. Up to this point, the Lord had told them neither what that purpose was nor what the light is. He simply told them that He had illuminated them and to be careful so as not to obstruct the brightness of that light.

(Mark 4:22-24)	(Luke 8:17, 18)
22. For there is nothing hid, which shall not be manifested; neither was any thing kept secret, but that it should come abroad.	17. For nothing is secret, that shall not be made manifest; neither any thing hid, that shall not be known And come abroad.
23. If any man have ears to hear, let him hear.	18. take heed therefore how Ye hear;. . .
24. And he said unto them, Take heed what ye hear:	

In these two sets of scriptures, the Lord does tell them what one of the purposes of the light is and also indirectly, what the light is. Furthermore, He goes on to do more than that, because He still must teach them how to use that light to bring men to the place where they glorify God. He must also teach them what they need to do in order to acquire more light, so that light can shine brighter, thereby illuminating more. Therefore, if the light is in fact the substance that we use to lead souls to the Lord, then the greater the degree of light shining, the more souls we can lead to the Lord.

Let us now together dissect these scriptures to see these revelations hidden within.

As we said earlier, we can tell that in verse 21 and verse 16 above, the Lord is telling His followers that He has illuminated them. He has not illuminated them to hide that light or to place some kind of covering over that light, but for that light to be seen. He goes on to tell them in verse 22 and verse 17 above, that He has a purpose for that light and that purpose we can see is to manifest those things that are hidden and bring to light those things that are kept secret in the heart of man.

(Revealing the hidden and secret things that are in the heart of man is only one purpose of that light, but we will stay on this subject for now, because these few verses are where we learn and understand what the light is. Later in this chapter, we will see what those hidden and secret things are that need to be exposed and how revealing those things cause a person to come to the Lord and glorify our Father, which is in Heaven.

We will also see that another purpose of that light is to shine upon our good works. This is also a design plan of God as well, so that souls can come to the Father, after having seen our good works.

The shining of our light upon our good works is another way the Lord tells us and shows us how to utilize both the seed and the flesh of our fruit to bring souls into the kingdom of God).

When the Lord finishes telling them that they are the light and not to cover it, because that covering would not allow the light to accomplish its purpose; notice that in verse 24, He goes on to say, "Take heed "*what*" you hear", and in verse 18, "Take heed therefore, "*how*" you hear".

If God in His infinite wisdom and knowledge is teaching us what the light is, then why does it sound as if He has gone off somewhere into left field? If He is showing us what the light is, then what does, "*what*", we hear and, "*how*", we hear have anything to do with understanding what the light is? Verse 24 and verse 18 of the scriptures above do not seem to follow the context of what the Lord is saying — or do they? Once we have learned what the light is, we will see that it does follow the context of what He is saying to a T.

So then, what is the light? Furthermore, what does, "*how*", we hear and, "*what*", we hear have to do with the light?

THE LIGHT IS THE WORD OF GOD THAT PROCEEDS OUT OF OUR MOUTHS!

The light is the Word of God that illuminates our understanding, so we can have the knowledge needed to enlighten our path, thereby seeing our way clearly to journey to the kingdom of God.

(Psalms 119:105, 130)

105. Thy word is a lamp unto my feet, and a light unto my path.

130. The entrance of thy words giveth light; it giveth understanding unto the simple.

171

(Proverbs 6:23) For the commandment is a lamp; and the law is light; and reproofs of instruction are the way of life:

(John 1:1, 4, 14)

1. In the beginning was the Word, and the Word was with God, and the Word was God.

4. In him was life; and the life was the light of men.

14. And the Word was made flesh, and dwelt among us . . .

(John 8:12) Then spake Jesus again unto them, saying, I am the light of the world: he that followeth me shall not walk in darkness, but shall have the light of life.

(Isaiah 42:6, 7)

6. I the LORD have called thee in righteousness, and will hold thine hand, and will keep thee, and give thee for a covenant of the people, for a light of the Gentiles;

7. To open the blind eyes, to bring out the prisoners from the prison, and them that sit in darkness out of the prison house.

Therefore, the light, (Word), must proceed out of our mouths, to shed light upon those that are in darkness.

(Isaiah 8:20) To the law and to the testimony: if they speak not according to this word, it is because there is no light in them.

(Proverbs 4:18) But the path of the just is as the shining light, that shineth more and more unto the perfect day.

Now let me explain this, while explaining how, "*what*", we hear and, "*how*", we hear, can keep us from allowing that light to shine, as well as how, "*what*", we hear and, "*how*", we hear allows us to radiate more light.

The light is the Word of God that proceeds out of our mouths. Therefore, the Lord wants us to be careful about, "*what*", we hear and, "*how*", we hear, because everything that goes into our ears has a direct pipeline into our hearts, and everything that is in our hearts will eventually come out of our mouths.

……………………………………………………..

(In a future lesson we will learn that when an individual loves Gods Word so much, that he or she makes whatever effort possible to get that Word; being very careful "what", and "how", they hear, thereby, proving to God that they want, need and love His Word more then anything else that they could receive. These actions will move the hand of God to give that person more understanding of the mysteries, (truths), of the Word of God.

(Matthew 13:10-13)

10. And the disciples came, and said unto him, Why speakest thou unto them in parables?

11. He answered and said unto them, Because it is given unto you to know the mysteries of the kingdom of heaven, but to them it is not given.

12. For whosoever hath, to him shall be given, and he shall have more abundance: but whosoever hath not, from him shall be taken away even that he hath.

13. Therefore speak I to them in parables: because they seeing see not; and hearing they hear not, neither do they understand.

(Mark 4:24, 25)

24. And he said unto them, Take heed <u>what</u> ye hear: with what measure ye mete, it shall be measured to you: and unto you that hear shall more be given.

25. For he that hath, to him shall be given: and he that hath not, from him shall be taken even that which he hath.

(Luke 8:9, 10 and 18)

9. And his disciples asked him, saying, What might this parable be?

10. And he said, Unto you it is given to know the mysteries of the kingdom of God: but to others in parables; that seeing they might not see, and hearing they might not understand.

18. Take heed therefore how ye hear: for whosoever hath, to him shall be given; and whosoever hath not, from him shall be taken even that which he seemeth to have.

Many modern day ministers are only receiving the parable understanding of the Word of God and not the mysteries, (truths), behind the Word. Reason being, that they have not come to the place where they love Gods Word with everything that is in them. Their desire is to know the Word only to have something to minister to Gods people, not because they love Gods Word and want to teach Gods people His Word so that Word can have the same effect on their congregation as it has on them. God minister should minister the Word because of their love for His Word, and because of what that Word, (the Son of God), means to them.

These books, "Mysteries of the kingdom revealed" have been many years in the making, and the only reason for them being published is, because of what these truths have done in the authors life. How these truths have built such a love for the Word of God that the author cannot keep them to himself, but must share them with all who love and will hear the Word of God; *"freely ye have received, freely give"*. The author is neither a writer nor a scholar. Neither has the author attended any religious school of higher learning. These truths have been made known to the author simply because of his love and desire for the Word of God that has cause him to be careful what he hear and how he hears; *"Study to shew thyself approved unto God, a workman that needeth not to be ashamed, rightly dividing the word of truth"*. The author is nothing more then a servant of the most high God who loves God and His Word, and who's desire is to love and know God and His Word more then life itself. The author however, realizes that there are truths in the Word of God that are not known, therefore, not being

174

ministered; truths that His people desperately need. Truths that will cause the people of God to become the vessels of honor that God desires for them to be. Therefore, the author is stepping up to the plate and doing what he feels needs to be done by the grace of God, to minister His Word to as many believers as possible).

....

Let us look closely at the next two verses.

(Mark 4:14, 15)

14. The sower soweth the word.

15. And these are they by the way side, where the word is sown; but when they have <u>heard</u>, Satan cometh immediately, and taketh away the word that was sown in their <u>heart</u>.

Notice that a portion of the verse we just read says, *"But when they have heard."* Now, it does not take a rocket scientist to know that for us to have "heard" something, it would have had to go into our ears, why then is it that when Satan comes to take away that Word, he has to go to the person's heart to get it? Why does he not go to his ears to take the Word? Would that not be where the Word should be? No! He goes to the heart to get it because he knows that whatever goes into our ears goes directly into our hearts.

This is why Jesus cautions them to take heed, *"what"* and *"how"* they hear. Because He knows that the light is the words that proceed out of their mouths and if they are not careful as to, *"what"* or *"how"* they hear, then the wrong words will go into their hearts, producing the wrong words to come out of their mouths. Therefore, because of not hearing the right things, that light will not be affective in fulfilling its purpose, because, *"Out of the abundance of the heart the mouth speaketh."*

(Matthew 15:16-19)

175

16. And Jesus said, Are ye also yet without understanding?

17. Do not ye yet understand, that whatsoever entereth in at the mouth goeth into the belly, and is cast out into the draught?

18. But those things which proceed out of the mouth come forth from the heart; and they defile the man.

19. For out of the heart proceed evil thoughts, murders, adulteries, fornications, thefts, false witness, blasphemies:

Jesus let His followers know that whatever goes into the mouth of a person does not defile that person. However, the things that come out of a person's mouth defile him because they come out of the heart. Nevertheless, how did those things get into the heart in the first place? By way of the ears

Whatever is in the heart of a person will proceed out of that person's mouth. Therefore, if you are not careful of what goes into your ears; if you are filling your ears with the junk you see on television or hear over the radio; if you are listening to gossip, you are filling your heart with the wrong things.

(Also, bear in mind that what you behold with your eyes is nothing more than words in picture form. You are putting words into your heart by way of your eyes, through such things as pornographic movies or books, violence in movies, and the like. No wonder the hearts of men are filled with so much garbage and wickedness, being expressed in the words that come out of their mouths).

If you are not careful of what goes into your heart, you will become what you have allowed to go in there. Therefore, a person's words are the evidence of what that person is in his heart. But how do those things get into the heart of a person in the first place? It happens the same way that it happens if we are trying to make a Christian out of someone. We sow the Word of God in his heart through his ears. As that Word enters his ears, it goes directly into his heart. Once in his heart, it germinates and grows into a tree that will bear fruit. The fruit is there in the form of words and deeds

Let us look at the next series of scriptures to see the fruition of listening to the Word of God, to know what to say so that the hidden or secret things in the heart of a person can be brought to the light, thereby making them manifest. Also in these scriptures, we will see the Lord telling us again what the light is; that it is the Word of God that comes out of our mouths.

(Luke 12:1-3)

1. In the mean time, when there were gathered together an innumerable multitude of people, insomuch that they trod one upon another, he began to say unto his disciples first of all, Beware ye of the leaven of the Pharisees, which is hypocrisy.

2. For there is nothing covered, that shall not be revealed; neither hid, that shall not be known.

3. Therefore whatsoever ye have spoken in darkness shall be heard in the light; and that which ye have spoken in the ear in closets shall be proclaimed upon the housetops.

In Luke 12:1, we see the Lord warning His disciples to, *"Beware of the leaven of the Pharisees which is hypocrisy."* Keep in mind that hypocrisy is something hid in the heart of a person. It is not something that an individual can see, nor did the Pharisees walk around with a sign on their backs that read, "I'm a hypocrite." So how then are the disciples supposed to beware of hypocrisy in the Pharisees if they are not able to see it; hypocrisy among other things, are things that people have hidden and covered in their hearts where no one will know their secrets?

Notice that in verse 3, He says, *"Therefore whatsoever ye have spoken in darkness shall be heard in the light; and that which ye have spoken in the ear in closets shall be proclaimed upon the housetops."* He says this after telling them, *"There is nothing covered, that shall not be revealed; neither hid, that shall not be known."* Once again, we see that clue verse, the Spirit thus signifying that this story is associated with the light. And, if it says that, *"There is nothing covered, that shall not be revealed; neither hid, that shall not be known."* Then it is obvious that what He is telling them in the next verse, verse 3, must be the format for how to reveal those things that are covered and make known those things that are hidden. Since this must happen to expose the hypocrisy in the heart of the Pharisees.

If verse 3 above, is the way that we expose the things that are covered or hidden, then verse 3 must be indirectly telling us what the light is, because it is the light that reveals those things. And if the light is actually the words that come out of our mouths, then verse 3 must somehow be telling us how to get that information into our ears, (because remember, He warns us to be careful *"what"*, and *"how"*, we hear). So that information can be in our heart and will come out of our mouths, to shed light on those hidden and secret things — and in this case, the hypocrisy in the Pharisees!

It does not give us a clear picture the way it is written in Luke 12:1-3, but if we look at Matthew 10:26 and 27, we can understand what the Lord is actually saying in verse 3 of Luke 12.

Notice that Jesus, speaking about the same situation, tells them in Matthew 10:26 and 27, *"For there is nothing covered, that shall not be revealed; and hid, that shall not be known."* Then He proceeds to tell them, *"What I tell you in darkness, that speak ye in light: and what ye hear in the ear, that preach ye upon the housetops."*

By comparing Luke 12:1-3 and Matthew 10:26, 27, we can understand that what the Lord was telling them in Luke 12:1-3 was this: in the authors own words, "You need to be wary of the leaven of the Pharisees which is hypocrisy. However, because I know that you cannot look into the heart of a person and see those things that are hidden or kept covered, I will tell you in your ear, in the darkness of your prayer closet. Then you proclaim them openly; in doing so, you will be manifesting those hidden and secret things in the heart of man."

What we have seen here is the fruition of being very careful as to, "*what*", we hear and, "*how*" we hear, to make sure that it is the Word of God. Then those Words will proceed out of our mouths, acting as a light to reveal those things that are covered and making known that which is hidden in the heart of a person.

Because our words are the light that is supposed to expose those hidden and secret things in the heart of a man, we only know what to say as we hear the voice of God talking to us. If we do not listen for His voice because we are too busy, listening to garbage, then those things in the heart of man will never be revealed and that individual may never come to the Lord. The greatest way for us to listen to the voice of God as He speaks to us, is through the study of His Word, because God will never speak to you in your prayer closet about something that does not align with His written Word.

We said that the light is the Word of God that proceeds out of our mouths. Which is why we need to be careful, "what" and, "how" we hear, because what comes out of our mouths is determined by what is in our hearts, and what is in our hearts is governed by what we hear. Moreover, we said that one of the purposes of that light is to reveal those things that are hidden or bring to light those things that are kept secret in the heart of a person.

HOW IS IT THAT THE LIGHT WORKS AT BRINGING A SOUL TO GOD?

Keep in mind that prophecy is anything that is the Word of God. Prophecy is not limited to someone standing up in church and giving a prophecy, nor is it limited to someone saying, "Thus saith the Lord." Prophecy comprises anything that is the Word of God, whether it is preaching or teaching the Word. It also could be the revelation of God's Word or speaking knowledge or doctrine of the Word of God.

(I Corinthians 14:6) Now, brethren, if I come unto you speaking with tongues, what shall I profit you, except I shall speak to you either by revelation, or by knowledge, or by prophesying, or by doctrine?

Keeping this in mind, as well as the fact that the light is the Word of God that proceeds out of our mouths, this would make the light, "Prophecy." Remembering also that one purpose of the light is for the revealing and exposing of the hidden and secret things in the heart of a man, look closely at the next verse.

(I Corinthians 14:23-25)

23. If therefore the whole church be come together into one place, and all speak with tongues, and there come in those that are unlearned, or unbelievers, will they not say that ye are mad?

24. But if all prophesy, and there come in one that believeth not, or one unlearned, he is convinced of all, he is judged of all:

25. And thus are the secrets of his heart Made manifest; and so falling down on his face he will worship God, and report that God is in you of a truth.

The light is not to humiliate or judge a person, but to get that individual to recognize that God knows and see all things and that He knows what is in a man's heart, even if no one else does. God knows it and will one day call that person into account for all that he thinks, says, and does. Thereby placing the fear of God in him; that fear in turn causing him to repent and turn to God for forgiveness and salvation. The

Word of God is able to accomplish this by whatever means it comes: preaching, teaching, or Bible study.

What we have seen in the above verses is that when we hear the voice of God and speak forth that Word, that prophetic Word becomes the light that reveals the secret things that are hidden in the heart of a person, thus causing that person to turn to the Lord.

God has ordained and designed the words that come out of our mouths as the means by which people come to know God. Our words set in motion the process by which people come to know God. The Word of God that proceeds out of our mouths is the light.

It is very important, and this fact cannot be stressed enough, that God's people fill themselves with His Word so they will have the right words to shed light on someone lost in darkness.

Many of God's people believe that there is nothing wrong with what they listen to, thinking that it cannot hurt or affect them. They believe that it is just a natural occurrence that will go through them and nothing else. However, they do not realize that what they are doing is filling their ears with words that will germinate in their hearts, and produce trees that will bear fruit that will eventually proceed out of their mouths and produce effects in the speaker of those words as well as the hearer of those words. Therefore, our very words could be the substance that will keep a soul from receiving eternal life by simply saying the wrong thing or by not saying the right things.

Many ministers will say, "If you have nothing good to say, then don't say anything at all," or, "We should be seen and not heard; Let people see the love of Christ in us." However, though this is true to some degree. There is also much untruth to this, which originates with the enemy of our souls that wants to keep a shade over our light and keep people in darkness. Christians need to be heard to bring people to the Lord. It is the seed that the Lord uses to sow into the heart of a person. If you have nothing good to say, shut off the television and spend more time in the Word of God to fill your heart with His Word, then you will have things to say. Additionally, as you fill your heart with the Word of God, that Word will fill up your heart with itself and push out all the other junk that has been placed there which is not of God. It is like filling a glass of milk with clear water. As you pour more water in, eventually the fluid in the glass will turn from milky white to crystal clear, as the clear water pushes out the milk.

The Word of God that proceeds out of our mouths is the light; whether the Spirit of God uses it to reveal those things that are kept secret or hidden in the heart of man, or whether He uses it to guide a person out of darkness. It is still His Word and it is still the light, and we have an obligation to fill our heart with it so that we can speak it.

We have tried to show that the light is the Word of God that proceeds out of our mouths. Furthermore, that the Word of God that proceeds out of our mouths is also the seed in the fruit that we are supposed to bear. We have also tried to show that our good works are the meat portion of the fruit surrounding the seed, and that the two properties are used together to win souls for the Lord. In the next few paragraphs, we will see the fruition of this, as we explain it, thereby proving that the Lord is saying the same thing in verse 15 of Matthew, chapter 5.

(Matthew 5:15) Let your light so shine before men, that they may see your good works, and glorify your Father which is in Heaven.

When you perform a good work, (the performing of that good work being the way that you allow someone or a group of people to taste of the meat of your fruit), you also need to shed light on those good works by accompanying it with the Word of God. This way, that person or group of people can then see, (understand), your good work. To perform a good work and never shed light on it, by not ministering the Word of God, will only make you a good person and nothing else. However, letting your light shine on your good works is the culmination of sowing that seed into the ground of a heart that has already seen and felt the love of God flow forth from you through the meat portion of your fruit. Your good works have cultivated that ground so that the seed of God's Word can be sowed, grow and flourish. This brings to pass the fulfilling of the scripture that says, *"And glorify our father which is in Heaven."*

Though this may sound like new revelation, it is actually, what the body of Christ has been practicing for as long as we can remember. We send missionaries into a country; we feed them and clothe them; we build houses and relationships. Those are our good works. We then shed light on those good works by ministering the gospel of Jesus Christ to them. It is the same procedure, but on a personal scale, one on one. Notice that I Peter 2:12 says the same thing, but words it differently.

(I Peter 2:12) Having your conversation honest among the Gentiles: that, whereas they speak against you as evildoers, they may by your good works, which they shall behold, glorify God in the day of visitation.

Note the definition of the word *conversation* according to the original writing.

Conversation; ἀναστροφή anastrŏphē, *an-as-trof-ay´; behavior:—* conversation.

In other words, *"Conversation"*, is the word that means how we act, as it relates to what we say. Therefore, what Peter is saying is, "That when our words and actions are right, our words will act as a light to illuminate our good works, so that on their day of visitation, those who behold, (see), them, will glorify, (accept Jesus Christ as their Lord and Savior), our father God".

Jesus said, *"Behold, I stand at the door and knock. If anyone hears my voice and opens the door, I will come in to him and dine with him, and he with me."* He does not stand at the door forever; if someone does not open, He will go to another door. However, if that person has seen, (understood), the good works of a child of God, by the light having been shed upon it, (the word of God accompanying that good work). That individual, on his day of visitation, will allow Jesus in, because he will remember the good deed that that child of God performed as well as the words that were spoken to him.

Up to this point, we have seen what the light and the fruit are, (chapter 10 and 11). Furthermore, we have learned how to utilize them to win souls for the Lord. In the next chapter, we will learn how the Word of God in our hearts will, as it proceeds out of our mouths, produce the actions of good works in our lives, thus giving us the culmination of the fruit in our lives.

CHAPTER TWELVE

WORDS THAT PRODUCE ACTIONS

³³Either make the tree good, and his fruit good; or else make the tree corrupt, and his fruit corrupt: for the tree is known by his fruit. ³⁴O generation of vipers, how can ye, being evil, speak good things? for out of the abundance of the heart the mouth speaketh. ³⁵A good man out of the good treasure of the heart bringeth forth good things: and an evil man out of the evil treasure bringeth forth evil things. ³⁶But I say unto you, That every idle word that men shall speak, they shall give account thereof in the day of judgment. ³⁷For by thy words thou shalt be justified, and by thy words thou shalt be condemned (Matthew 12:33-37).

It is with no doubt that when our Lord said this statement; He did so because of the evil things that they were saying about Him. Even though all that He said and did, (His fruit), was good; His fruit, (His words and His actions), were the evident token that He was all good; yet they spoke of Him as if He were evil.

All people are trees, (metaphorically speaking), and those trees will either produce good or evil fruit. The fruit being the evidence that proves whether that tree is good or evil. Every tree that God did not plant will one day be rooted up and cast into the fire.

(Matthew 15:13) But he answered and said, Every plant, which my heavenly Father hath not planted, shall be rooted up.

(John 15:4-6)

4. Abide in me, and I in you. As the branch cannot bear fruit of itself, except it abide in the vine; no more can ye, except ye abide in me.

5. I am the vine, ye are the branches: He that abideth in me, and I in him, the same bringeth forth much fruit: for without me ye can do nothing.

6. If a man abide not in me, he is cast forth as a branch, and is withered; and men gather them, and cast them into the fire, and they are burned.

The substantiation that determines if a tree was planted by God, is whether that tree came from the seed of God's Word. If that is the case, then that tree will produce good fruit. The fruit is the proof of whether a tree was planted by God or man. However, many people, (ministers and those who listen to them), do not realize that they have a major role in moving the hand of God in sowing the seed of the Word of God into someone's heart.

As ministers, if we are not careful to make sure that it is the Word of God that is in our hearts when we minister, it may not be His Word that we are sowing. (Remember, it is God that does the work, but He does it through His ministers).

As a hearer of those who minister the word, we need to make sure that what we are hearing is the Word of God. If not, we will be allowing the wrong seeds to be sown into our hearts. Then when that tree does produce fruit, it will not be the fruit that is indicative of being from the Word of God.

(Proverbs 14:7) Go from the presence of a foolish man, when thou perceivest not in him the lips of knowledge.

UNDERSTANDING WHAT IT TAKES TO BE A TREE THAT PRODUCES GOOD FRUIT

In the verses at the beginning of this chapter, (Matthew 12:33-37), I believe that the Lord is showing His disciples and us as well what we need to understand and do in order to make sure that we are a good tree.

186

Notice that He says, *"Either make the tree good and his fruit good or else make the tree corrupt, and his fruit corrupt; for the tree is known by his fruit."* This statement, along with what He says afterwards, lets us know that the choice is up to us as to whether we will do one or the other.

As we read this statement, we are not the ones that have criticized Him, so what benefit can we receive from this statement, other than knowing that those in His day spoke evil of Him and we must be careful to not make the same mistake? The greatest benefit we can gather from this statement is to see the mystery hidden in it and utilize it to make our tree good, not evil.

Observe that in this statement, the insinuation is for us to be careful what proceeds out of our mouths, because those words will one day either condemn us or justify us.

However, a careful study of the scriptures shows that when we are finally judged, we do not see the Lord judging us because of our words, nor telling us, "I know your words," or, "Because you said this or that, you are condemned." What it does say is, "I know your works."

(Revelation 2:1, 2, 8, 9, 12, 13, 18, 19)

1. Unto the angel of the church of Ephesus write; ...

2. I know thy works,

8. And unto the angel of the church in Smyrna write;...

9. I know thy works,

12. And to the angel of the church in Pergamos write;...

13. I know thy works,

18. And unto the angel of the church in Thyatira write;...

19. I know thy works,

We find that it is by our actions, (works), and not our words, that we will one day either be condemned or justify.

(Matthew 25:31-46)

31. When the Son of man shall come in his glory, and all the holy angels with him, then shall he sit upon the throne of his glory:

32. And before him shall be gathered all nations: and he shall separate them one from another, as a shepherd divideth his sheep from the goats:

33. And he shall set the sheep on his right hand, but the goats on the left.

34. Then shall the King say unto them on his right hand, Come, ye blessed of my Father, inherit the kingdom prepared for you from the foundation of the world:

35. For I was an hungered, and ye gave me meat: I was thirsty, and ye gave me drink: I was a stranger, and ye took me in:

36. Naked, and ye clothed me: I was sick, and ye visited me: I was in prison, and ye came unto me.

37. Then shall the righteous answer him, saying, Lord, when saw we thee an hungered, and fed thee? or thirsty, and gave thee drink?

38. When saw we thee a stranger, and took thee in? or naked, and clothed thee?

39. Or when saw we thee sick, or in prison, and came unto thee?

40. And the King shall answer and say unto them, Verily I say unto you, Inasmuch as ye have done it unto one of the least of these my brethren, ye have done unto me.

41. Then shall he say also unto them on the left hand, Depart from me, ye cursed, into everlasting fire, prepared for the Devil and his angels:

42. For I was hungered, and ye gave me no meat: I was thirsty, and ye gave me no drink:

43. I was a stranger, and ye took me not in: naked, and ye clothed me not: sick, and in prison, and ye visited me not.

44. Then shall they also answer him, saying, Lord, when saw we thee an hungered, or athirst, or a stranger, or naked, or sick, or in prison, and did not minister unto thee?

45. Then shall he answer them, saying, Verily I say unto you, Inasmuch as ye did it not to one of the least of these, ye did it not to me.

46. And these shall go away into everlasting punishment: but the righteous into life eternal.

Upon reading these passages of scriptures, we can understand that we will one day be judged by the things that we do and not by the things that we say.

Why then did the Lord say in His statement, that by our words, we will be condemned and by our words, we will be justified? Why did He not say that by our works, we will be condemned and by our works, we will be justify? This does not seem to make sense. It does, however, if you understand the principle of actions produced by words. Notice carefully the next set of scriptures.

(James 3:1-6)

1. My brethren, be not many masters, knowing that we shall receive the greater condemnation.

2. For in many things we offend all. If any man offend not in word, the same is a perfect man, and able also to bridle the whole body.

3. Behold, we put bits in the horses' mouths, that they may obey us; and we turn about their whole body.

4. Behold also the ships, which though they be so great, and are driven of fierce winds, yet are they turned about with a very small helm, whithersoever the governor listeth.

5. Even so the tongue is a little member, and boasteth great things. Behold, how great a matter a little fire kindleth!

6. And the tongue is a fire, a world of iniquity: so is the tongue among our members, <u>that it defileth the whole body</u>, and setteth on fire the course of nature; and it is set on fire of Hell.

Follow carefully to understand what the scriptures are trying to teach us.

In this set of scriptures, the Lord is showing us that with a small bit in a horse's mouth, we can direct that horse in the direction that we want it to go. We can accomplish the same objective with a ship. Even in a raging storm we can turn a massive ship either to the right or the left with a very small helm.

In like manner, our tongue will create the direction for the rest of our body. If in our heart are adulterous thoughts, then those words will come out of our mouths and our tongues will act as a bit that will lead the rest of our body to commit an adulterous act.

Whatever is in the heart of a person will eventually proceed out of a person's mouth, thereby producing the actions of those words in deed form, whether those deeds are good or evil.

(Matthew 15:16-20)

16. And Jesus said, Are ye also yet without understanding?

17. Do not ye yet understand, that whatsoever entereth in at the mouth goeth into the belly, and is cast out into the draught?

18. But those things which proceed out of the mouth come forth from the heart; <u>and they defile the man</u>.

19. For out of the heart proceed evil thoughts, murders, adulteries, fornications, thefts, false witness, blasphemies:

20. <u>These are the things which defile a man</u>: But to eat with unwashen hands defileth not a man.

What are the things that defile a man? Evil thought; murders, adulteries, fornication, thefts, false witness, blasphemies and the like! Now if they only come out in words, how can just speaking words defile a person? Why is it that the words that come out of our mouths defiles us? Because they create in action form, (evil works), those things that defile him. Those things that will cause that man, one day when he is judge, to be condemned. Which is why we must be very careful what we say and even more careful what we allow to enter into our heart by way of what we hear. Understanding also that what we see is nothing more than words in picture form, we are hearing words by way of our eyes. For this reason, we must also be careful what we look at.

(Proverbs 4:23, 24)

23. Keep thy heart with all diligence; for out of it are the issues of life.

24. Put away from thee a froward mouth, and perverse lips put far from thee.

Words are very powerful; they have the power to create life or destroy it.

(Proverbs 18:21) Death and life are in the power of the tongue: and they that love it shall eat the fruit thereof.

When words come out of our mouths, they create the actions that will, when we stand before God, cause us to be either condemned or justified.

The reason Jesus said that by our words, we will be condemned and by our words, we will be justified. Moreover, the reason that in the scriptures we see no one being judged by their words, but rather by their actions, is, because our works, (our actions), are the evidence of what has been coming out of our mouths all along. When we stand before God on the day of judgment, the works that our bodies have produced, (our actions), will tell the story of what has been coming out of our mouths.

For example, if you see a body builder with massive muscles, (the muscles represents our works). You do not have to see him lifting weights, (him lifting weights, represents us speaking words), to know that this is how he spends a large part of his time; his muscles are the evident token that he spends a lot of time lifting weights. In like manner, on judgment day our works will be the evident token of what has been coming out of our mouths all along. Thus, by our words, we will be condemned, and by our words, we will be justified.

Jesus said that by our words, we will be justified and by our words, we will be condemned. James 3:6 says, "*And the tongue is a fire, a world of iniquity: so is the tongue among our members, that it defileth the whole body*". Notice that it is the tongue that "defileth the whole body". Remember also that Jesus said, in Matthew 15:20, "*But those things which proceed out of the mouth come forth from the heart; and they defile the man*". As we have things that are in our heart that are not pleasing to God, those things will proceed out of our mouths, and because those words have the power to create in action form, what we speak, we produce in works what we speak, thereby defiling us.

Let us recap what we have learned so far.

1. God gave us His Word so that we can have the knowledge needed to know Him, serve Him, and live for Him. He first gave us His Word in spoken form. Which is why we see the scriptures say, "And the Word of the Lord came to Ezekiel", as well as, "And the Word of the Lord came to Isaiah". We also see the scriptures say, "And they heard the voice of the Lord God walking in the garden in the cool of the day" (Genesis 3:8).

God knew that His creation needed an even more personal relationship with Him, so He made a body for His Word, (*Wherefore when he cometh into the world, he saith, Sacrifice and offering thou wouldest not, but a body hast thou prepared me*). Thereby His Word could live among us,

(*And the Word was made flesh, and dwelt among us, (and we beheld his glory, the glory as of the only begotten of the Father,) full of grace and truth*). In this manner, we not only heard His Word, but also saw and handle His Word. His Word became a living, breathing, walking and talking organism among us. His Word became one of us.

However, that Word still needed to be giving to the rest of the world. Thus, God in His infinite wisdom and knowledge further gave us His Word in written form. Though the living Word is sitting at the right hand of the Father on high, God has giving to every man His Word in written form, in what we call The Bible.

The name of that book is not important, but the information, the truths, the revelations, that still speak to us from that book, is coming from the same God that uttered His first Word from the foundations of the earth. That written Word has the same power to save, heal, and deliver as He did when He was in spoken form, as well as in living form. That precious written Word is still saying, "I am a lamp unto your feet and a light unto your path". Because that Word is still showing us the way to come to the Father. He is still teaching us the truths that we need to know to come to the Father. Furthermore, by the Spirit that emanates from the Word, we receive the life and power to live for the Father. This is why He is still saying, in the form of the written Word, "I am the way, the truth and the life, and no man comes to the father but by me".

2. God made a contract, (covenant), with us to carry out the fulfilling of our salvation. And He makes this covenant in three stages: (1.) Putting His fear in us; (2.) Giving us His law, so that we will understand His requirements for living right so we can do them, thereby having the proof that we believe in His Son, (Word); (3.) Writing His law in our hearts, (which we will learn how and why later in this book).

3. The fear of the Lord in us motivates us to search, study, and acquire His Word, (the Lord Jesus Christ), so we can know how to walk before Him. This produces a love in us for His Word that will lead us to desire more of His Word.

4. Salvation is based on a person believing that Jesus Christ is the son of God, but the evidence that a person believes in Jesus is apparent when that individual does as He Jesus, (the Word), says thereby causing that individual to turn from doing evil to doing good.

5. As we saturate our hearts with His Word, that Word will flush out all the other ungodly things in our hearts, things we were born with and also those we have put there by what we have heard and looked upon, and now have grown into a tree that has been producing corrupt fruit.

6. We must watch over the seed of God's Word sown into our hearts to keep from losing it, so it can grow into a fruit-bearing tree. As we wait for the fruition of the growth of that Word, we put a watch over what we hear, what we say, and what we do. In this manner we keep the wrong things from going into our hearts while also being very careful what proceeds out of our mouth, knowing that our tongue works as a bit that will produce in action form, (in our bodies), the things that we speak.

7. As that Word grows in our hearts, the fruit of it comes out in word form, that produces the action form of good works in our bodies that now serve to fulfill the scriptures that say, "Brother So-and-so believes in Jesus Christ and his belief is counted to him for righteousness."

(James 2:17-24)

17. Even so faith, if it hath not works, is dead, being alone.

18. Yea, a man may say, Thou hast faith, and I have works: shew me thy faith without thy works, and I will shew thee my faith by my works.

19. Thou believest that there is one God; thou doest well: the Devils also believe, and tremble.

20. But wilt thou know, O vain man, that faith without works is dead?

21. Was not Abraham our father justified by works, when he had offered Isaac his son upon the altar?

22. Seest thou how faith wrought with his works, and by works was faith made perfect?

23. And the scripture was fulfilled which saith, Abraham believed God, and it was imputed unto him for righteousness: and he was called the Friend of God.

24. Ye see then how that by works a man is justified, and not by faith only.

Understand that faith is an action word, and the actions produced by your faith are the evidence that you have faith.

Notice the definition of the word *faith*, according to the original writings is:

Faith: πίστις pistis, *pis´-tis; persuasion,* i.e. *credence;* mor. *conviction* (of *relig.* truth, or the truthfulness of God or a relig. teacher), espec. *reliance* upon Christ for salvation; abstr. *constancy* in such profession; by extension, the system of religious (Gospel) *truth* itself:— assurance, belief, believe, faith, fidelity.

Understand that the primary meaning of the word *faith* is "persuasion."

According to Random House Webster's Unabridged Dictionary, (Second Edition, Copyright 1997, by Random House Inc. New York, NY,) the word *persuasion* is defined as: 1. the act of persuading or seeking to persuade. 2. The power of persuading . . . 3. The state or fact of being persuaded or convinced. 4. A deep conviction or belief.

Random House Webster's Unabridged Dictionary, (Second Edition, Copyright 1997, by Random House Inc. New York, NY,) also defines the word persuade as: to prevail on (a person) to do something as by advising or urging.

If you cannot prevail on a person to do something then there is no persuasion. Therefore, we can see in these definitions that if there is no action on the part of the hearer, then there is no persuasion, (faith).

To illustrate, imagine you are in an auditorium and the person in charge runs in yelling, "Fire, Fire! Everybody get out of the building!" Now, you may not see flames, feel heat, or even see or smell smoke, but if you believe that person, what will you do? You will get out of the building to safety. Your belief caused you to do something and that something was to get out of the building.

In the same manner, if you believe in Jesus Christ, (the Word of God), your belief in Christ, if you really believe in Him, should cause you to do something. And that something would be to do as He tells you in His Word, your actions being the evidence that you believe in Him, thereby meriting you obtaining eternal life. You do not the something of doing as He says, because you are working for your salvation, but rather because you believe in Him and this grants you salvation.

We cannot work for our salvation. It is a free gift to those that believe in Jesus Christ.

(Ephesians 2:8, 9)

8. For by grace are ye saved through faith; and that not of yourselves: it is the gift of God:

9. Not of works, lest any man should boast.

We must realize, however, that somewhere along in our walk with the Lord, we must produce the fruit, (the fruit being the word and the works — the word producing the good works), as the evidence that we believe in Jesus Christ.

(Ephesians 2:10) For we are his workmanship, created in Christ Jesus unto good works, which God hath before ordained that we should walk in them.

For this reason the scriptures say, "Not of works..." but then goes on to say, "For we are His workmanship, created in Christ Jesus <u>unto</u> good works..."

As we continue on this journey through God's Word, we will learn that we do not have the ability, the means, or the power to be a doer of God's Word. God has to work that in us. However, He has left us tools that we can use to stand righteous before Him until He works the nature of Christ in us. Thereby us having then the ability, power and nature to not only do His Word, but become a living Epistle of His Word.

CHAPTER THIRTEEN

WALK AFTER THE SPIRIT

¹There is therefore now no condemnation to them which are in Christ Jesus, <u>who walk not after the flesh, but after the Spirit.</u> ²For the law of the Spirit of life in Christ Jesus hath made me free from the law of sin and death. ³For what the law could not do, in that it was weak through the flesh, God sending his own Son in the likeness of sinful flesh, and for sin, condemned sin in the flesh: ⁴That the righteousness of the law might be fulfilled in us, <u>who walk not after the flesh, but after the Spirit</u> (Romans 8:1-4).

(Galatians 5:16, 18, 25)

16. This I say then, <u>Walk in the Spirit</u>, and ye shall not fulfill the lust of the flesh.

18. But if ye be <u>led of the Spirit</u>, ye are not under the law.

25. If we live in the Spirit, let us also <u>walk in the Spirit</u>.

If an individual did a careful study of the scriptures, he would soon learn that when the scriptures say, "Walk after the Spirit" and, "Walk in the Spirit," they are in fact saying the same thing.

Walking after the Spirit and walking in the Spirit are not two different statements teaching us that we must do these two different actions. These two statements are in fact telling us that we need to do the same thing; the only difference is that they are worded differently in each verse. Moreover, a careful study of these two statements in their complete context, with reference to the teachings of Paul, in his letters to the Christians of that era, clearly shows that they come together in perfect harmony to give us an indisputable understanding of what it is to walk after the Spirit. Therefore, one must know with certainty what it is to walk after the Spirit if one is to endeavor to walk in the Spirit. Because it is when you walk in the Spirit that you do not fulfill the lust of the flesh.

A person who truly desires to serve God faithfully must know how to walk after the Spirit. He must know what God says, is walking after the Spirit, and not what man says is walking after the Spirit. All of our victory is in walking after the Spirit; for it is in this that, a Christian has power over his flesh and over sin.

Many Bible-believing Christians have fallen by the wayside simply for not knowing how to walk after the Spirit. They fight desires and passions of the flesh, always honestly trying to keep from committing them, but sooner or later they succumb to the allure of them. Even though they hate the very act of what they are doing, they seem to be a helpless prisoner of their own lust. Promising God and themselves that they will never do it again as they fall on their knees crying out to Him for forgiveness, only to go a day, a week, a month or maybe even years free from the control of that sin. Only to one day, find themselves being drawn again by the lust of their flesh. They know that they are heading in that direction and that they need to fight the desire to give in to their lust, but they seem to be completely controlled by some outside force, pulling them into the very act that they hate so much.

Soon the inevitable happens. They give in, they sin, and even in the middle of the very act of their sinning, they ask themselves, "God, what am I doing? How can I be committing this evil again?" They may even be asking for forgiveness during the very act of their transgression, but they know it is too late. The deed has already been committed. Even if they stop now, the damage has already been done. That sin has already been added to their account. And then when it is all over, many times they cry bitterly as they ask themselves, "How could I have done that? How could I have hurt my Lord and Savior that way, especially after I promised Him the last time I would never do that again?"

As they are burning with guilt, they wish they could reverse time so they could start all over and this time not do it, but they know that is not possible. They ask themselves, "Why did I do that again? How could this have happened? I am trying with everything that is in me not to sin, but this thing has control over me. It seems to possess me. But how can this be when I've given my life to God? His Spirit is dwelling in me, or that is what the Bible says. God's Word does not lie, so the problem must be in me. I have been taught that if I walk in the Spirit, I will not fulfill the lust of the flesh and I am doing that. I pray; I read and study the Bible; I attend church; I fast sometimes and give to the church. What can be wrong?"

And as the questions arise, so do the insinuations from the enemy of our souls. He attacks their minds telling them, "Well, you may as well give up. God won't forgive you this time, not after you promised never to do it again. Maybe you were never saved; maybe you are not meant to be saved. God doesn't love you anymore. Just give up." And many times, if it were not for the fear of ending up in Hell, the very guilt of their actions would drive them to commit suicide. And many a weary victim have done just that, though the road to suicide has many faces.

In this journey through this revelation, we will learn how to walk after the Spirit. We will also discover the benefits of walking after the Spirit. Moreover, we will learn that when the scriptures say, "To walk in the Spirit", they are in fact saying, "To walk after the Spirit".

Though this may come as a shock to many in the religious world, especially ministers of the gospel, walking after the Spirit is not praying. It is not reading or studying the Bible, nor is it going to church and giving to the church;

neither is it fasting. All of these actions empower us to walk after the Spirit, but they are not how we walk after the Spirit. Our effort to walk after the Spirit is made so much easier when we do all these other works. They give us the insight, the strength, and the endurance needed, but they are not in fact how we walk after the Spirit. And if you are one of the victims describe above, you will bear witness that when you fell prey to the lure of the flesh, you most likely were doing some if not all of these things, and you still fell!

THE LAW OF SIN AND DEATH IS MADE VOID WHEN WE WALK AFTER THE SPIRIT!

Let us first start by seeing the major benefit of walking after the Spirit. There are many benefits to walking after the Spirit; however, there is one in particular, that is not only beneficial, but the truth of the matter is that if an individual does not have the benefit of this particular one, that person cannot enter the kingdom of God. Because this culminating benefit of walking after the Spirit is the evident token that an individual truly believes in Jesus Christ. And our entitlement to enter into the kingdom of God hinges on our belief in Jesus Christ!

(John 3:16) For God so loved the world, that he gave his only begotten Son, that whosoever believeth in him should not perish, but have everlasting life.

In order to understand this major benefit of walking after the Spirit, we need to know why a person must walk after the Spirit. What is produced by walking after the Spirit?

We read at the beginning of this chapter that *1. There is therefore now no condemnation to them which are in Christ Jesus, <u>who walk not after the flesh, but after the Spirit</u>. 2. <u>For the law of the Spirit of life in Christ Jesus</u> hath made me free from the <u>law of sin and death</u>.* Notice that — staying in the context of the verses that we just read — when a person is <u>walking after the Spirit</u> in verse 1, the scriptures go on to let us know in verse 2, that this is how that person walks <u>in the law of the Spirit of life in Christ Jesus</u>. A person that is in Christ and walking after the Spirit is simultaneously fulfilling the law of the Spirit of life in Christ Jesus. And when a person walks under that law, he is made free from the law of sin and death.

If we are to clearly understand how to walk after the Spirit and what this big benefit is upon which our salvation is hinged, we must now veer off course for just awhile in order to learn what the law of sin and death is.

WHAT IS THE LAW OF SIN AND DEATH?

Romans 7:7 spells out to us what the law of sin and death is.

(Romans 7:7) For when we were in the flesh, the motions of <u>sins</u>, which were by the <u>law</u>, did work in our members to bring forth fruit unto <u>death</u>.

Notice that it says the motions of SINS, which were by the LAW, did work in our members to bring forth fruit unto DEATH — SIN, LAW, DEATH. THE LAW OF SIN AND DEATH is when our flesh produces sins that are brought about by the law, which will eventually bring about death. Follow along carefully to understand this truth more clearly.

How is it that the motions of sins or the results of sins or the outcome of sins can be brought about by the law, which in turn leads to death? Isn't the law holy and just and good?

(Romans 7:11, 12)

11. For sin, taking occasion by the commandment, deceived me, and by it slew me.

12. Wherefore the law is holy, and the commandment holy, and just, and good.

Yes! The law is holy and just and good, but the problem is that we are carnal. Our very nature is enmity towards God and all that is of God, especially His Law!

(Romans 8:7) Because the carnal mind is enmity against God: for it is not subject to the law of God, neither indeed can be.

Therefore, because of this problem we get the result of our flesh producing sins brought about by the law which will eventually bring about death.

Notice how this happens. Let us say you are a thief and you are going about your merry way doing what you are — stealing. Furthermore, the law that says, "Thou shalt not steal", comes behind you and tries to pull you in the opposite direction, telling you, "THOU SHALT NOT STEAL." (The law of God has a specific job to do, and that is to work in you its righteousness. *For what the law could not do, in that it was weak through the flesh, God sending his own Son in the likeness of sinful flesh, and for sin, condemned sin in the flesh: That the righteousness of the law might be fulfilled in us. . .).* Now, if you as a thief would turn and go in the opposite direction, never stealing again, then the law that says, "Thou shalt not steal", would have been successful at working in you its righteousness. You would be fulfilling that law. However, because you are carnal and not subject to the law of God, and neither indeed can be, when that law comes upon you to try to conform you to itself, you say, "Oh yeah, you want me to stop stealing? Ha, now I'm going to steal more." Now instead of that law working its righteousness in you, the reverse happened. Because you are carnal and not subject to the law of God, that law became the substance that gave strength to sin. Your flesh is strengthened to sin more.

(I Corinthians 15:56) The sting of death is sin; and the strength of sin is the law.

This was a small demonstration to more clearly illustrate what the law of sin and death is. Additionally, this is from what the law of the Spirit of life in Christ Jesus sets us free. But remember, that only those who walk after the Spirit are fulfilling the law of the Spirit of life in Christ Jesus.

The law of the Spirit of life in Christ Jesus is nothing more, than a person being in Christ and walking after the Spirit! A person who is in Christ but is not walking after the Spirit, will still be under the law of sin and death and will suffer many unnecessary hardships, and maybe even shipwreck.

Now that we have learned what the law of sin and death is, let us study how it is that we walk after the Spirit to bring about this freedom from the law of sin and death!

At the beginning of this chapter, we mentioned that walking in the Spirit, is in fact, walking after the Spirit. Let us study this so we can prove it, while simultaneously learning how to walk after the Spirit. This will result in us seeing the law of sin and death being made void in our lives, as well as the end results of the righteousness of the law being fulfilled in us, which is the chief evident work that is added to our faith as the obvious proof that we believe in Christ Jesus.

(Galatians 5:14-23)

14. For all the law is fulfilled in one word, even in this; Thou shalt love thy neighbor as thyself.

15. But if ye bite and devour one another, take heed that ye be not consumed one of another.

16. This I say then, <u>Walk in the Spirit</u>, and ye shall not fulfill the lust of the flesh.

17. For the flesh lusteth against the Spirit, and the Spirit against the flesh: and these are contrary the one to the other: so that ye cannot do the things that ye would.

18. But if ye be led of the Spirit, ye are not under the law.

19. Now the works of the flesh are manifest, which are these Adultery, fornication, uncleanness, lasciviousness,

20. Idolatry, witchcraft, hatred, variance, emulations, wrath, strife, seditions, heresies,

21. Envyings, murders, drunkenness, revelings, and such like: of the which I tell you before, as I have also told you in time past, that they which do such things shall not inherit the kingdom of God.

22. But the fruit of the Spirit is love, joy, peace, longsuffering, gentleness, goodness, faith,

23. Meekness, temperance: against such there is no law.

In part of Paul's letter to the Galatians we read above, he is telling them, in verse 17, not to put themselves in a position where they will find themselves in a tug-of-war between the Spirit leading in one direction and their flesh pulling in the other. Verse 16 says that in order to avoid this, they need to walk in the Spirit, and that by doing this they would not be fulfilling the lust of the flesh. Notice that fulfilling the lust of the flesh, begins first, with the flesh pulling you in the direction where you will end up committing one of the works of the flesh. This is opposite the direction that the Spirit is trying to lead you.

Also notice that he goes on to say in verse 18, "But if we be led of the Spirit we are not under the law." Why does he say in verse 16, "Walk in the Spirit, and ye shall not fulfill the lust of the flesh," and then, (staying in the context of what he is telling them), in verse 18, why does he say, "If ye be led of the Spirit ye are not under law"? What do you being under the law have to do with you fulfilling the lust of the flesh? Because there seems to be an implication that somehow because the law is over you, that this is the contributing factor that is causing you to go in the direction of the flesh? And if this is the case, how do you, being led of the Spirit, remove the law from being over you? Therefore, is it just saying that the Spirit is leading us, or must there be a conscious effort on our part to follow the Spirit as He leads us? Because if you are being led of the Spirit, then you must be following the Spirit as He leads you. What's more, this seems to somehow remove the law from being over you.

What does the law have to do in all this? It has all the difference in the world to do with this! The law is what keeps you moving in the direction of the flesh! Notice carefully in the next demonstration how all this happens.

Observe first that verse 14 above tells us, *"For all the law is fulfilled in one word, even in this; Thou shalt love thy neighbor as thyself."* Now let us continue with our demonstration. You are a Christian, and your flesh begins to rise up and is trying to draw you in one direction to commit sin, but on the other side is the Spirit trying to lead you in the opposite direction. You want to follow God, but your flesh is pulling you in the other direction. You want to follow God, but you cannot, and you hate that you cannot. You are being drawn in the other direction by your flesh and you are yielding to it. You hate that you are yielding to it because you do not want to go in that direction, but you cannot help it.

(Romans 7:15, 19)

15. For that which I do I allow not: for what I would, that do I not; but what I hate, that do I.

19. For the good that I would I do not: but the evil which I would not, that do I.

206

YOU DO NOT KNOW IT, BUT YOU ARE SMACK DAB IN THE MIDDLE OF THE LAW OF SIN AND DEATH!

Let us allow God in His infinite mercy to pull the scales from our eyes and see the revelation here.

Observe what is happening and understand what role the law plays in all this and how to reverse this process. Notice that after verse 17, of Galatians 5, verse 18 tells us "But if ye be led of the Spirit, ye are not under the law." Why does it say that? It implies that the law is a problem here and needs to be taken out of the way, and that being led of the Spirit will do the job of taking it out of the way. This is exactly what it means. This is what happens and needs to happen.

Remember in our prior demonstration, if you are a thief and the law is upon you, trying to conform you to itself, instead of working in you its righteousness, it did just the opposite. The law was the substance that gave strength to your sin. Well, this is what is happening here. Between you and the Spirit is the law. As the Spirit tries to lead you in His direction, the law, (because of your carnal nature), causes you to go in the opposite direction to fulfill the desires of the flesh. The Spirit draws you and because the law is before you, you are motivated to go in the opposite direction of the Spirit.

The law is lending support to your flesh. You have no power to overcome because the law has strengthened your flesh to sin. How then can you get rid of the law and remove that which gives strength to sin? You must be led by the Spirit! How? You must walk after the Spirit! HOW?

YOU WALK IN LOVE THAT IS HOW!

Remember that verse 14 above says, *"For all the law is fulfilled in one word, even in this; Thou shalt love thy neighbor as thyself."* Why did it start with this verse? It is because this is how we walk after the Spirit; this is how we walk in the Spirit; this is how we are led of the Spirit. When we walk in love, by loving our neighbor as ourselves, we *fulfill all the law*; therefore, the law is done away with.

This is why verse 23 of this same letter says, *"Against such there is no law."* The substance that is not allowing you to turn from following your flesh and follow the Spirit is taken out of the way. Now you will be free from the control of that pulling in the opposite direction. This is why we must walk after the Spirit to have victory over that which gives strength to sin.

Remember what our Lord said in Matthew 5:18; *"For verily I say unto you, Till Heaven and earth pass, one jot or one tittle shall in no wise pass from the law, <u>till all be fulfilled</u>."* He was saying that Heaven and earth would pass away first before the law passes away without it first being fulfilled. When we fulfill all the law in our lives, then against us there is no more law. That which gives strength to sin is removed. And the only way that we can fulfill all the law is to walk in love, to love our neighbor as ourselves!

(Romans 13:8-10)

8. Owe no man any thing, but to love one another: for he that loveth another hath fulfilled the law.

9. For this, Thou shalt not commit adultery, Thou shalt not kill, Thou shalt not steal, Thou shalt not bear false witness, Thou shalt not covet; and if there be any other commandment, it is briefly comprehended in this saying, namely, Thou shalt love thy neighbor as thyself.

10. Love worketh no ill to his neighbor: therefore love is the fulfilling of the law.

This is why Romans 8, verses 3 and 4, says, *"For what the law could not do, in that it was weak through the flesh, God sending his own Son in the likeness of sinful flesh, and for sin, condemned sin in the flesh: that the righteousness of the law might be fulfilled in us, who walk not after the flesh, but after the Spirit."*

When God gave His law, it was for the purpose that people live after that law. Furthermore, this would serve as the proof that they are righteous and thereby be found just before God, and justified to enter into eternal life.

(Deuteronomy 6:25) And it shall be our righteousness, if we observe to do all these commandments before the LORD our God, as he hath commanded us.

Therefore, it was the work of the law to work in us its righteousness; however, because of our nature as we read previously, that was an impossibility. God knew this, which is why He made a new covenant with us. Furthermore, that covenant involves being in Christ Jesus, which must include walking after the Spirit, as the Spirit leads us. Therefore, the awesome benefit of walking after the Spirit is twofold: (1) we rid ourselves of the substance that gives strength to sin, while (2) simultaneously fulfilling the righteousness of the law. Through this we are providing for ourselves the evidence that we need; the works that are added to our faith, needed to fulfill the scripture that says Abraham believed God and it was counted to him for righteousness. However, instead of Abraham's name being there, our name will be placed there. The evidence is there that shows that we believe in Jesus Christ, because the works are now added to our faith. (The works being the righteousness of the law added to our faith.)

(Romans 2:13) For not the hearers of the law are just before God, but the doers of the law shall be justified.

THE SPIRIT WILL ALWAYS LEAD US IN THE DIRECTION THAT WILL PRODUCE ACTIONS OF LOVE!

In Galatians 5:14-23, we can see that the flesh always will draw us in the direction of where we will produce evil works, but the Spirit will always lead us in the direction where we will produce the fruit of the Spirit, and all those attributes of the fruit of the Spirit are associated with charity.

(Galatians 5:18-25)

18. But if ye be led of the Spirit, ye are not under the law.

19. Now the works of the flesh are manifest, which are these Adultery, fornication, uncleanness, lasciviousness,

20. Idolatry, witchcraft, hatred, variance, emulations, wrath, strife, seditions, heresies,

21. Envyings, murders, drunkenness, revelings, and such like: of the which I tell you before, as I have also told you in time past, that they which do such things shall not inherit the kingdom of God.

22. But the fruit of the Spirit is love, joy, peace, longsuffering, gentleness, goodness, faith,

23. Meekness, temperance: against such there is no law.

25. If we live in the Spirit, let us also walk in the Spirit.

We live in the Spirit when we are in Christ, but we walk in the Spirit when we walk after the Spirit, and we walk after the Spirit when WE WALK IN LOVE.

This is why Ephesians chapter 5, verses 1 and 2, says:

(Ephesians 5:1, 2)

1. Be ye therefore followers of God, as dear children;

2. And walk in love, as Christ also hath loved us, and hath given himself for us an offering and a sacrifice to God for a sweet smelling savor.

If we are following God as His dear children, then we are following His Spirit, and His Spirit is the one that is leading us as Galatians 5:18 states, *"If you be led of the Spirit."* If His Spirit is leading us, why would we be led in any other direction than in the direction of love, when we just read that it says, *"And walk in love"*?

It is when a person is fulfilling the righteousness of the law that he is doing those things contained in the law and is the evidence needed to prove that he really believes in Christ. However, we must remember that only those that walk after the Spirit are the ones that will fulfill the righteousness of the law.

(Romans 8:4) That the righteousness of the law might be fulfilled in us, who walk not after the flesh, but after the Spirit.

(Romans 2:13) For not the hearers of the law are just before God, but the doers of the law shall be justified.

This is that person who is just and is justified to enter into the kingdom of God and receive eternal life.

What the Spirit of Christ does is lead us to where we walk in love or come to the place where we walk in love. An individual who loves his neighbor will not commit adultery with his neighbor's spouse. If a person loves his neighbor, he will not steal from him. If a person loves his neighbor, he will not kill his neighbor or hurt him in any way because, "Love worketh no ill to his neighbor."

(Romans 13:10) Love worketh no ill to his neighbor: therefore love is the fulfilling of the law.

As carnal beings, we fight struggles to keep from fulfilling the works of the flesh. These struggles are there because of the spiritual law of God that is trying to conform

211

us to itself, but it cannot because we are carnal. The two clash because of the difference that one is of the spiritual realm and the other is of the carnal realm; they do not mix and can never mix. It is just like trying to mix oil and water — it cannot be done.

Notice the definitions of the word, "after", in the verse, "walk after the Spirit", and the word, "in", "walk in the Spirit."

After: κατά **kata**, *kat-ah´;* a primary particle; (prep.) *down* (in place or time), in varied relations (according to the case [gen., dat. or acc.] with which it is joined):— about, according as (to), after, against, (when they were) × alone, among, and, × apart, (even, like) as (concerning, pertaining to touching), × aside, at, before, beyond, by, to the charge of, [charita-] bly, concerning, + covered, [dai-] ly, down, every, (+ far more) exceeding, × more excellent, for, from ... to, godly, in (-asmuch, divers, every, -to, respect of), ... by, after the manner of, + by any means, beyond (out of) measure, × mightily, more, × natural, of (up-) on (× part), out (of every), over against, (+ your) × own, + particularly, so, through (-oughout, oughout every), thus, (un-) to (-gether, -ward), × uttermost, where (-by), with. In composition it retains many of these applications, and frequently denotes *opposition, distribution,* or *intensity.*

In: ἐν **náe**, *en;* a primary prep. denoting (fixed) *position* (in place, time or state), and (by impl.) *instrumentality* (medially or constructively), i.e. a relation of *rest* . . . ; "*in,*" at, (up-) on, by, etc.:— about, after, against, + almost, × altogether, among, × as, at, before, between, (here-) by (+ all means), for (...sake of), + give self wholly to, (here-) in (-to, wardly), × mightily, (because) of, (up-) on, [open-] ly, × outwardly, one, × quickly, × shortly, [speedi-] ly, × that, × there (-in, -on), through (-out), (un-) to (-ward), under, when, where (-with), while, with (-in). Often used in compounds, with substantially the same import; rarely with verbs of motion, and then not to indicate direction, except (elliptically) by a separate (and different) prep. Notice that the two words, *after*, "Walk *after* the Spirit", and *in*, "walk *in* the Spirit", are very similar in meaning.

WALKING AFTER THE SPIRIT IS NOT GOD'S ULTIMATE GOAL FOR OUR LIVES!

Though walking after the Spirit is the means by which sin has no power over us, because that which gives strength to sin, (the law), is taken out of the way. It is not, however, the last goal that God has designed for our lives for us to come to the place where we never sin again and so that sin will never have dominion over our flesh.

The ultimate goal that God has ordained for us to come to in our lives so that sin will never have control over our flesh is for us to be conformed into the image of His son, Jesus Christ, His Word. Once this has happened in its entirety, then we will live the kind of life where sin no longer rules over us, and sin will cease to exist for us. We have no desire, no impulses, no need, no nature to commit sin, and the very sight of sinful acts, insinuations, gestures, or other sinful actions will be repulsive to us. We will have come to the place where we hate the very sight of sin. No matter how it is committed, whether it is live; on the television; in books, magazines, songs; or on the radio, it will vex our righteous souls, and a holy hatred for sin will rise up in us — a holy hatred for sin, "NOT FOR THE SINNER". We will also feel the pain that God feels because of sin, which will cause us to pray, intercede, and stand in the gap for those who are living in sin, especially God's people.

God has given to us, (His people), things that will aid and enable us to live the kind of life that is pleasing to Him. Those things are, "The Fear of the Lord", and "Walking after the Spirit." However, there is still a struggle to do these things in order to remain in them. You may want something that your neighbor has, but you will not steal it because you love your neighbor. Nevertheless, the desire to have it is still there, so you are still struggling with that desire. However, when we are transformed into the image of Christ, all those struggles cease. This transpires when we are conformed to the image of Christ because we put on Christ, which is why the scriptures say:

(Romans 8:29) For whom he did foreknow, he also did predestinate to be conformed to the image of his Son, that he might be the firstborn among many brethren.

(Galatians 3:27-29)

27. For as many of you as have been baptized into Christ have put on Christ.

28. There is neither Jew nor Greek, there is neither bond nor free, there is neither male nor female: for ye are all one in Christ Jesus.

29. And if ye be Christ's, then are ye Abraham's seed, and heirs according the promise.

This baptism that He is referring to here is the complete three stages of baptism that we go through, Water, Spirit, and Fire, which the scriptures say we must be baptized into, in order to come to this complete stage of growth. (See chapter five and six)

(Philippians 2:5) Let this mind be to in you, which was also in Christ Jesus.

The mind that was in Christ Jesus has now been transplanted into our mind, so that we now think like Jesus, talk like Jesus, and act like Jesus.

God's whole purpose for our lives is that we become like His Son, conformed into the image of His Word. As this happens, we become living Epistles of His Word, that man can see and read. Through us, they are seeing and reading the gospel of Christ, and that gospel is being used by God to draw all men to Him.

In the next chapters, we will learn the steps that are found in the Word of God that we need to go through in order to put us in the process that conforms us into the image of Christ. Understanding this process causes us to make a decision as to how far we really want to go on in God, while also learning of the glory that we can obtain in the life to come.

CHAPTER FOURTEEN

GOD HELPS THOSE THAT HELP THEMSELVES

³Blessed be the God and Father of our Lord Jesus Christ, which according to his abundant mercy hath begotten us again unto a lively hope by the resurrection of Jesus Christ from the dead, ⁴To an inheritance incorruptible, and undefiled, and that fadeth not away, reserved in Heaven for you, ⁵Who are kept by the power of God through faith unto salvation ready to be revealed in the last time (I Peter 1:3-5).

¹⁵So, as much as in me is, I am ready to preach the gospel to you that are at Rome also. ¹⁶For I am not ashamed of the gospel of Christ: for it is the power of God unto salvation to every one that believeth; to the Jew first, and also to the Greek (Romans 1:15, 16).

"God helps those that help themselves." We have heard this phase, oh, how many times? Some even think or say that it is in the Bible. People have used it in movies; some would justify a thief's actions after stealing something by saying, "God helps those that help themselves." Many say it when trying hard to accomplish something as if reminding God that He also has to do His part. However, a careful search of the scriptures will reveal that the Bible does not say it at all. Nevertheless, the reality of this statement is, in fact scriptural.

We know that salvation is a free gift; we cannot work for it, nor can we purchase it with money, gold, or silver. However, if you think that you have salvation simply by coming forward and saying a simple prayer and then going about your merry way, you are as ignorant of God's Word as those that Jesus was referring to when He said,

(Matthew 7:17-27)

17. Even so every good tree bringeth forth good fruit; but a corrupt tree bringeth forth evil fruit.

18. A good tree cannot bring forth evil fruit, neither can a corrupt tree bring forth good fruit.

19. Every tree that bringeth not forth good fruit is hewn down, and cast into the fire.

20. Wherefore by their fruits ye shall know them.

21. <u>Not every one that saith unto me, Lord, Lord, shall enter into the kingdom of Heaven; but he that doeth the will of my Father which is in Heaven.</u>

…How do we know the will of the Father?…

22. Many will say to me in that day, Lord, Lord, have we not prophesied in thy name? and in thy name have cast out devils? and in thy name done many wonderful works?

23. And then will I profess unto them, I never knew you: depart from me, ye that work iniquity.

24. <u>Therefore whosoever heareth these sayings of mine, and doeth them,</u>

…A person doing the sayings of Jesus is doing the will of His Father! This is why God sent Him, to make His will known to us. For this reason, we cannot just say that we believe in Him, but must also show that we believe in Him by doing as He says…

I will liken him unto a wise man, which built his house upon a rock:

25. And the rain descended, and the floods came, and the winds blew, and beat upon that house; and it fell not: for it was founded upon a rock.

217

26. And every one that heareth these sayings of mine, and doeth them not, shall be likened unto a foolish man, which built his house upon the sand:

27. And the rain descended, and the floods came, and the winds blew, and beat upon that house; and it fell: and great was the fall of it.

A careful study of the above scriptures, from Matthew chapter 7, verses 17 through 27, along with what the scriptures teach in Luke chapter 6, verses 43 through 49, allows us to understand that the house falling or not falling is not referring to whether an individual remain faithful to God during the trials of life. Rather, to when he or she stands before God on the day of judgment, and they are either justified or condemned.

Even though salvation is a free gift to all those who believe in Jesus Christ and we cannot work for it nor can we purchase it, there are numerous scriptures that let us know that there are things we must do that will serve as proof of our belief in Jesus Christ, thereby validating our place in Heaven. We cannot overlook the many scriptures that let us know that there are things that must be evident in our lives that are indicative that we are believers. Here are scriptures that confirm this.

(James 2:20, 24)

20. But wilt thou know, O vain man, that faith without works is dead?

24. Ye see then how that by works a man is justified, and not by faith only.

(Titus 1:16; 3:8)

1:16. They profess that they know God; but in works They deny him, being abominable, and disobedient, and unto every good work reprobate.

3:8. This is a faithful saying, and these things I will that thou affirm constantly, that they which have believed in God might be careful to maintain good works. These things are good and profitable unto men.

...Observe that the scripture does not say, "That they which have believed in Jesus Christ might be careful to maintain good works", but rather, "That they which have believed in God might be careful to maintain good works". However, is not our faith suppose to be in Jesus Christ, (Let not your heart be troubled: ye believe in God, believe also in me), to merit us salvation. Most everybody believes in God, or in some god, (the devils also believe, and tremble), but why then does it say, "That they which have believed in God might be careful to maintain good works". Because God and His Word, (Jesus), are one, the two cannot be separated. Furthermore, if you say that you believe in God, but do not do as the Word says then you are separating the two; believing in one, but not doing as He tells you through the other, His Word. Therefore, you must have proof that you believe in God, and the proof is there when you do as He says through His Word. Jesus Christ is the Word of God that was made flesh. When you do as the Word tells you to do, you are indicating that you believe in God, as well as in Jesus Christ...

(Matthew 7:21) Not every one that saith unto me, Lord, Lord, shall enter into the kingdom of Heaven; but he that doeth the will of my Father which is in Heaven.

(Luke 6:46) And why call ye me, Lord, Lord, and do not the things which I say?

(Romans 2:6-10)

6. Who will render to every man according to his deeds:

7. To them who by patient continuance in well doing seek for glory and honor and immortality, eternal life:

8. But unto them that are contentious, and do not obey the truth, but obey unrighteousness, indignation and wrath,

9. Tribulation and anguish, upon every soul of man that doeth evil, of the Jew first, and also of the Gentile;

10. But glory, honor, and peace, to every man that worketh good, to the Jew first, and also to the Gentile:

(John 15:1, 2)

1. I am the true vine, and my Father is the husbandman.

2. Every branch in me that beareth not fruit he taketh away

If this is true, then why are there scriptures that say such things as the following?

(Ephesians 2:8, 9)

8. For by grace are ye saved through faith; and that not of yourselves: it is the gift of God:

9. Not of works, lest any man should boast.

(Romans 4:3-5)

3. For what saith the scripture? Abraham believed God, and it was counted unto him for righteousness.

4. Now to him that worketh is the reward not reckoned of grace, but of debt.

5. But to him that worketh not, but believeth on him that justifieth the ungodly, his faith is counted for righteousness.

Why do they seem to contradict each other?

How do we justify them?

What are they telling us?

They are not contradicting each other. Salvation is a free gift to those who believe in Jesus Christ, but there must be evidence in the life of a person that says that he or she believes in Jesus Christ. The good fruit that we endeavor to bear is the proof that the person does truly believe in Him. (See latter part of chapter twelve, the section on faith.)

(Acts 26:20) But shewed first unto them of Damascus, and at Jerusalem, and throughout all the coasts of Judaea, and then to the Gentiles, that they should repent and turn to God, and do works meet for repentance.

(Matthew 3:7, 8)

7. But when he saw many of the Pharisees and Sadducees come to his baptism, he said unto them, O generation of vipers, who hath warned you to flee from the wrath to come?

8. Bring forth therefore fruits meet for repentance:

These scriptures are letting us know that we must make an effort to show God that we mean business with Him, that we really believe His Word, by trying to do His Word in order to please Him. This conscious effort on our part is the indicator to God that we really believe His Word, (Jesus, His Son). Furthermore, this effort moves the hand of God in our favor to bring us to that place to which we cannot bring ourselves, and produces in us the fruit that God is looking for as the proof that we believe in His Son. The scriptures refer to this as, "God gives the increase."

This is where the truth that God helps those that help themselves comes into play.

HOW IS IT THAT WE ARE KEPT BY THE POWER OF GOD, THROUGH FAITH, UNTO SALVATION?

Notice that I Peter 1:5, at the beginning of this chapter states, *"Who are kept by the power of God through faith unto salvation."*

For us to understand how it is that God keeps us through faith unto salvation, we must first know what the power of God is that He uses to keep us. Comprehending what this is will help us in understanding how it keeps us and

221

if there is anything on our part that we must do in order to be kept.

First, we must realize that God is all powerful; His power is as vast as the universe itself. God, however, does not utilize all of His power to keep us through faith unto salvation. He only utilizes a portion of His power to keep us. For example, God has the power to make us into robot-like humans, who would heed His every command, doing everything He says so we can do right and go to Heaven. However, God did not ordain it this way; He does not utilize His power in that manner.

THE POWER THAT GOD UTILIZES TO KEEP US IS THE GOSPEL OF JESUS CHRIST!

(Romans 1:16) For I am not ashamed of the gospel of Christ: for it is the <u>power of God</u> unto salvation to every one that believeth;

Observe the three key words here: Power, Salvation, and Believeth. Furthermore, observe the three key words in I Peter 1:5: Power, Faith, and Salvation.

WE ARE KEPT BY THE POWER OF GOD, (THE GOSPEL OF JESUS CHRIST), THAT BRINGS US UNTO SALVATION, THROUGH OR AS A RESULT OF OUR FAITH OR BELIEF IN JESUS CHRIST, WHO IS THE WORD OF GOD!

We are kept by the power of God, (the Gospel of Jesus Christ), that brings us unto salvation, through or as a result, of our faith or belief in Jesus Christ, who is the Word of God.

222

But how is it that the Gospel of Jesus Christ, (the power of God), keeps us? We can see the answer to this in the next verse.

(Romans 1:17) For therein is the righteousness of God revealed from faith to faith: as it is written, The just shall live by faith.

However, we must understand Romans 1:17, if we are to know how to be kept by the power of God. Knowing this will also help us understand that there is a part that we must perform, so we can be kept by the power of God. Thereby, bringing into play the truth that God helps those that help themselves.

Verse 17, of Romans chapter 1 says, "For therein is the righteousness of God revealed." What does this mean? Why do we need to see the righteousness of God in the Gospel of Jesus Christ, to know how to come unto salvation? Isn't believing all we have to do and that is it? No!

All people are ignorant of God's righteousness unless they understand the Gospel of Jesus Christ. Moreover, without this knowledge all people are lost, (unsaved).

(Romans 10:1-4)

1. Brethren, my heart's desire and prayer to God for Israel is that they might be saved.

2. For I bear them record that they have a zeal of God, but not according to knowledge.

3. For they being ignorant of God's righteousness, and going About to establish their own righteousness, have not submitted themselves unto the righteousness of God.

4. For Christ is the end of the law for righteousness to every one that believeth.

The gospel of Christ establishes the righteousness of God. So as we understand the gospel, His righteousness is being revealed to us, and as this happens we act upon it, thereby submitting ourselves to it.

When we receive faith through hearing, ("*So then faith cometh by hearing, and hearing by the word of God*"), but predominantly through *understanding* the Word, ("*For I bear them record that they have a zeal of God, but not according to knowledge*"), we act upon it; this in turn brings us closer to salvation. And as we receive more understanding of the Word, our faith grows from that level of faith to the next level of faith, so that we can walk in that next level of understanding of that Word.

Jesus Christ is the righteousness of God. His actions, His Words, His lifestyle, and His teachings that He showed while on earth revealed to us the righteousness of God. His suffering and dying on the cross and shedding His blood for our sins are all part of the righteousness of God. When we believe in Him and the work that He accomplished on the cross, when we accept Him as our Lord and Savior and ask Him to forgive our sins, we enter into that process where the seed is planted in our hearts. We enter, as it were, into a race, but we must finish the race; we must continue to grow from that seed to a fruit-bearing tree, the fruit being the substantiation that serves to show God that "Yes, I did and do believe in your Son." When God looks and that tree is growing, even if it is growing slowly, whether there is fruit or not, everything is according to His plan. If that individual were to die prematurely, in that state, even if there is no fruit. (The fruit from the tree, not the fruit as proof that this individual has repented, as describe in chapter 10, page 164, lines 7-32 and page 165, lines 1-18). That individual would still receive eternal life. However, if God keeps coming to that tree and it has stopped growing and there continues to be no growth and no fruit, after a while God will call for that tree to be cut down. Because the continual growth, the continual running in this race as it were, is the evidence that that person truly believed and truly believes in Jesus Christ.

(Luke 13:6-9)

6. He spake also this parable; A certain man had a fig tree planted in his vineyard; and he came and sought fruit thereon, and found none.

7. Then said he unto the dresser of his vineyard, Behold, these three years I come seeking fruit on this fig tree, and find none: cut it down; why cumbereth it the ground?

8. And he answering said unto him, Lord, let it alone this year also, till I shall dig about it, and dung it:

9. And if it bear fruit, well: and if not, then after that thou shalt cut it down.

UNDERSTANDING HOW THE RIGHTEOUSNESS OF GOD IS REVEALED TO US

In order for us to understand what the righteousness of God is that needs to be revealed to us. Moreover, how it is revealed to us and tie it in with how, "We are kept by the gospel of Jesus Christ unto salvation," so that we can see the role that we play in being kept by the power of God, (God helps those that help themselves), we must go to II Corinthians 3:18.

(II Corinthians 3:18) But we all, with open face beholding as in a glass the glory of the Lord, are changed into the same image from glory to glory, even as by the Spirit of the Lord.

First, let us dissect this verse so we can learn what it is telling us.

If we were to do a careful study of this verse, we would soon learn that the five words, "B*eholding as in a glass*", in the original writings, are in fact one word, κατοπτρίζομαι katŏptrizŏmai, *kat-op-trid´-zom-ahee;* to *mirror oneself,* i.e. to *see reflected* (fig.):— behold as in a glass.

For us to be changed into the same image of the Lord, this verse is telling us that we must, "Behold as in a glass the glory of the Lord." But why then is the meaning of "Beholding as in a glass," to "mirror oneself, to see reflected"; if we are supposed to be looking at the glory of the Lord? We are not supposed to be seeing ourselves; we are supposed to be looking at the image of the Lord.

When a person looks at a mirror and sees a reflection, what that individual is seeing is his or her own image, not someone else's. In spite of this, the verse says, "Beholding as in a glass the glory of the Lord." Are we then seeing ourselves, or are we beholding the glory of the Lord?

Yes, to both questions!

What the scriptures are letting us know in this verse is that the mirror of God's Word is the only mirror that allows us to see two images at the same time: ours and the Lord's. We need to understand that we have to see both images, because that is how we see our unrighteousness — when we also see His righteousness. We see our flaws when we see His flawlessness.

It is like this: say you walk into a department store and try on a new suit, while you stand in front of a huge mirror. Now you may be dirty and in need of a shave, your hair may be long and shaggy, your fingernails may be long and not manicured, you may be overweight and out of shape. Nevertheless, to yourself you look good because you are trying on a new suit. On the other hand, let us say that while you are trying on that new suit, your twin brother stands next to you trying on the same suit. However, he is clean shaven, his hair is neatly cut and combed, his fingernails are well manicured, and he has a good build. As a result of that, because he is standing next to you and now you are able to see both you and your brother at the same time, you begin to realize that you do not look as good as you thought you did, because now you have someone with whom to compare yourself. This person is someone, whose qualities, brings out your lack of quality; someone whose beauty, brings out your ugliness; and in the case of Jesus Christ, (the Word of God), someone whose holiness, brings out your lack of holiness; whose righteousness reveals your unrighteousness.

HOW ENDEAVORING TO BE A DOER OF HIS WORD SETS IN MOTION THE PROCESS THAT WILL ULTIMATELY CHANGE US INTO HIS IMAGE

So then, how is it that upon seeing the righteousness and holiness of Jesus Christ, a person is changed into His image? Since His image is holy and righteous, does that mean that just because we read, hear, study, and believe His Word that — zap — we are instantly made holy and righteous, and now are kept by the power of God in this state unto salvation? No, we are changed into His image as we make an effort to do as His Word tells us to do.

(Luke 6:46) And why call ye me, Lord, Lord, and do not the things which I say?

(James 1:22) But be ye doers of the word, and not hearers only, deceiving your own selves.

However, this in itself does not change us into His image. This sets in motion the course of action that by the hand of God ultimately produces the change in us. Notice how this happens.

(James 1:22-24)

22. But be ye doers of the word, and not hearers only, deceiving your own selves.

23. For if any be a hearer of the word, and not a doer, he is like unto a man beholding his natural face in a glass:

24. For he beholdeth himself, and goeth his way, and straightway forgetteth what manner of man he was

When a person is a hearer of the Word of God and does not do what the Word tells him to do, he is like unto a man that looks into the mirror of Gods Word and sees how he is not like Christ. Nevertheless, he forgets how unlike Christ he is; therefore, he does not make an effort to try to be like Him.

On the other hand, a person who is a doer of the Word is that person who looks into the mirror of God's Word and sees how miserably short he comes to being like Christ. Therefore, as a result, he tries to do the Word so that he can be more like the Word that has been revealed to him.

Now, we could stop here and say that that is all it takes to be made into His image, but there are too many scriptures that show us that there are things we must go through in order to become more like Christ. Subsequently, if we do not learn those things, when we do go through them, we will not understand them and will wonder, "What is this strange thing that is happening to me? Why am I going through this?"

(Romans 8:28, 29)

28. And we know that all things work together for good to them that love God, to them who are the called according to his purpose.

29. For whom he did foreknow, he also did predestinate to be conformed to the image of his Son, that he might be the firstborn among many brethren.

(II Corinthians 4:8-11)

8. We are troubled on every side, yet not distressed; we are perplexed, but not in despair;

9. Persecuted, but not forsaken; cast down, but not destroyed;

10. Always bearing about in the body the dying of the Lord Jesus, that the life also of Jesus might be made manifest in our body.

11. For we which live are always delivered unto death for Jesus' sake, that the life also of Jesus might be made manifest in our mortal flesh.

(I Peter 4:12, 13)

12. Beloved, think it not strange concerning the fiery trial which is to try you, as though some strange thing happened unto you:

13. But rejoice, inasmuch as ye are partakers of Christ's sufferings; that, when his glory shall be revealed, ye may be glad also with exceeding joy.

This allows us to understand that just because we try to do the Word, this in and of itself does not change us. As we said earlier, this brings us to the place where God puts us in the molding process that ultimately transforms us into the image of Christ, like a caterpillar is changed into a butterfly. Let us follow this chain of events to see how it works and how to use this knowledge to better understand and better serve God.

As people endeavor to do the Word, at this point in their lives, they soon learn that all they can do is try to do the Word. Many will quickly learn that they do not have the ability or the power to do the Word; although they know they must try because God's Word commands us to do so. At this phase in their walk with the Lord, many will throw in the towel, because they will think that they are hopeless or that God's Word does not work. Others will just surrender to the lures of the flesh and accept some kind of church with teachings that will justify their lifestyle, while others will say something like, "Well, God knows I'm only human," or, "I can't help it — the Devil made me do it," and never even try.

Still others could be doing the Word outwardly, but be breaking it in their minds; for example, they may not be committing adultery with someone physically, but they might be lusting after others in their hearts. They may not even feel any guilt because they are not openly doing it or hurting anyone.

As an individual endeavors to be a doer of the Word, however, and fails miserably, it does not mean that the failure has to end in sin, because God in His infinite mercy and goodness, knowing that we will walk this road, has left us powerful principles in His Word. Furthermore, if we know these principles and apply them, they will keep us from sinning against Him while we go through this chain of events, which ultimately brings us to the place where we are transformed into the image of His Son.

The truths of, "The Fear of the Lord," which we studied in chapters two and three, and "Walking after the Spirit," which we studied in chapter thirteen, are truths that are given to us to help us remain holy and righteous before God, even though we may be struggling to be doers of His Word.

HOW THE WHEELS OF GOD'S MERCY AND GRACE TURN AS THEY MOLD US INTO THE IMAGE OF HIS SON, JESUS CHRIST

An individual has to endeavor to be a doer of the Word of God even if he fails, because this is all part of the chain of events that God has designed. This effort on the part of that individual and his or her failing only leads, or should lead them, (if he or she truly means business with God), to realize that without God, he or she cannot do it, (the second link in the chain of events). This in turn, leads him or her to pray and cry out to God for help and strength to be victorious in his or her walk with the Lord, (the third link in the chain of events). Moreover, this then proves to God that this individual is serious about his or her walk with the Lord and that he or she means business with God, thereby moving the hand of God to put this person in the molding process that ultimately transforms them into the image of Christ, (the fourth link in the chain of events). <u>*Never* underestimate the power of your tears and your prayers before God that proceed out of a sincere, broken, and contrite heart!</u>

As individuals, we cannot do the Word, but we must try, because the doing of the Word is the evidence that we believe in Jesus Christ. Moreover, with the truths that God has given us in His Word, we can be successful in performing it. Although we may struggle, we will be able to do it. For example, if you have a problem with stealing and you want to take something that does not belong to you, "The fear of the Lord", (because you do not want to have to face God's wrath on Judgment Day), will keep you from stealing. Nevertheless, you will still struggle with the temptation of taking what does not belong to you. You will do the Word of not stealing, but in the process, you will fight an internal battle with it.

Moreover, you "Walk after the Spirit", when you walk in love. Therefore, if you are tempted to have an affair with your neighbor's wife, you will not do it if you are walking in love, because, *"Love worketh no ill to his neighbor."* When you walk in love, you will not do anything that will bring pain or hurt to your neighbor. Although you may fight a battle with wanting to have an affair with your neighbor's wife, the action of, "Walking after the Spirit", will keep you from breaking that commandment. In other words, you will be doing the Word, but failing miserably because of the internal battles that you have to go through in order to be faithful to do the Word.

God has left us these precious truths in His Word so that we can be doers of the Word, even though we will fight major struggles to perform them. This is how we endeavor to do His Word and fail, but without that failure having to end up in sin. This is why the ultimate place where God wants to bring us is where we take on the image of Christ. "The Fear of the Lord" and "Walking after the Spirit," and I am sure there are other truths in His Word that He still desires to reveal to us, are truths that we are to utilize until we take on His image. Once that happens, then the performing of His Word becomes our way of life and it will become impossible for us to not do His Word. When we take on the image of Christ, we become like Him. We talk like Him, we act like Him, and we love like Him, because we have put on Christ. *"Let this mind be in you which was also in Christ Jesus" (Philippians 2:5).* When the mind that was in Christ Jesus has been transplanted into our minds, we are identical to Him in word and in deed.

Let us follow carefully to see how all this takes place, culminating in us being transformed into the image of Christ. Furthermore, what we are learning is indirectly revealing to us what we are supposed to do in order to be kept by the power of God unto salvation. (God helps those that help themselves)!

The image of Christ that an individual takes on is directly related to the degree of light that that individual radiates, so if we can learn how we radiate light, we can understand what is involved in taking on the image of Christ. This results in our understanding the process we go through that conforms us into the image of Christ.

If the light is also the Word of God that proceeds out of our mouths, then somehow this piece of the puzzle will fit in place with the other pieces that we have already seen and discussed in the previous chapters.

Note:

Understand carefully, people of God, that God will put an individual through this molding process, whether he knows it or not, whether he understands it or not, and whether he likes it or not. Because God will give everybody the same opportunity to climb as high in Christ as possible, so that in eternity no one will be able to stand before God and say that He was unfair in not allowing him or her the opportunity to acquire a better resurrection. Consequently, you should learn these truths so that when you do go through this process, you will know why and where God is trying to bring you. This way you will have a good attitude and give Him the praise and glory while you are going through the process, instead of murmuring and complaining.

In the next chapter, we will learn what is needed for a person to radiate light, spiritual light in this life to be a light to those that are in darkness and literal light in the life to come in Heaven. We will also learn how to radiate a greater degree of spiritual light in this life so God can use us as a mighty beacon, versus Him using us as a small flashlight to guide someone to the kingdom of God. We will then understand how we will radiate a greater degree of literal light in the life to come, so that the glory with which we radiate literal light for all eternity in the next life can be as bright as the sun versus the moon or the stars.

(I Corinthians 15:40-42)

40. There are also celestial bodies, and bodies terrestrial: but the glory of the celestial is one, and the glory of the terrestrial is another.

41. There is one glory of the sun, and another glory of the moon, and another glory of the stars: for one star differeth from another star in glory.

42. So also is the resurrection of the dead . . .

As we understand the process that we must go through in order to radiate light, as well as radiating a greater degree of light, we will also be learning the process that we need to go through, so that we can be transformed into the image of Jesus Christ.

CHAPTER FIFTEEN

RADIATING LIGHT

¹Do we begin again to commend ourselves? or need we, as some others, Epistles of commendation to you, or letters of commendation from you? ²Ye are our Epistle written in our hearts, known and read of all men: ³Forasmuch as ye are manifestly declared to be the Epistle of Christ ministered by us, written not with ink, but with the Spirit of the living God; not in tables of stone, but in fleshy tables of the heart (II Corinthians 3:1-3).

In the days of the early church, because there were, false ministers then as there are today; if someone came from another region and was unknown to the congregation, he would not be given an open door to minister in the assembly. The reason for this was that he might bring in a false doctrine and deceive the saints or bring in confusion. The way that it was determined if the person was of God or not was by a letter of introduction from other pastors or ministers who already knew the traveling minister, who would introduce him to the congregation by way of the letter. With this letter, the congregation could safely allow that person to come and give a word of edification or exhortation.

In the three verses that we read above, we see Paul asking the church at Corinth, "Do I need to introduce myself to you, or do you need a letter from someone introducing me to you, or do I need a letter of introduction from you introducing me to someone else?" Notice that he goes on to say, "Ye are our Epistle written in our hearts, known and read of all men."

What Paul was saying to them was, "You yourselves are my letter of introduction. Whoever sees you and understands your lifestyle; whoever knows you will know me, because I have taught you to the point that you have become what I am. You know who I am because you have become like me. That which is written in my heart has been transcribed into your hearts, and when someone sees you and reads your lifes, they are seeing what is also in my heart, and now know who I am."

"I have ministered the Word to you to the point that, that which I am; that which I believe; that which I preach is what you have become. Now, what I have ministered to you are the writings of Christ, so you really have not become like me, but like the one that I have become and that is Christ. When people now see you, they see me; when people read your lifestyle, they are reading mine. Actually, they are not seeing you or me — they are seeing and reading the Lord Jesus Christ, whom I have taken on and then passed on to you." This is why Paul says, *"Wherefore I beseech you, be ye followers of me"*, as well as, *"Be ye followers of me, even as I also am of Christ"* (I Corinthians 4:16; 11:4).

When a person believes something to the point that he lives what he speaks, and when a person practices what he preaches, his very lifestyle will cause people to want what he has in order to become like him. For the reason that, your words will convict them and teach them how they should live, while your actions set the example for them to follow, to show them how to live. This is how you fulfill the scripture that says:

(Matthew 5:19) Whosoever therefore shall break one of these least commandments, and shall teach men so, he shall be called the least in the kingdom of Heaven: but whosoever shall do and teach them, the same shall be called great in the kingdom of Heaven.

This is how your righteousness exceeds the righteousness of the Scribes and Pharisees.

(Matthew 5:20) For I say unto you, That except your righteousness shall exceed the righteousness of the scribes and Pharisees, ye shall in no case enter into the kingdom of Heaven.

Notice the righteousness of the Scribes and Pharisees as described in chapter 23 of Matthew, verses 1 through 3:

(Matthew 23:1-3)

1. Then spake Jesus to the multitude, and to his disciples,

2. Saying, The scribes and the Pharisees sit in Moses' seat:

3. All therefore whatsoever they bid you observe, that observe and do; but do not ye after their works: <u>for they say, and do not</u>.

It was the obligation or the job of the Scribes and the Pharisees to teach the law and to teach the people how to live according to God's Word, but they needed to do this with their words as well as their actions. Unfortunately, they preached it, but they surely did not practice it.

It is not good enough to just speak the Word, nor is it good enough to just live the Word; we must practice what we preach, we must do and teach, (here we see our fruit again). *". . . But whosoever shall do and teach them, the same shall be called great in the kingdom of Heaven. (Matthew 5:19)"*

Paul understood this, and the next two verses verify this:

(I Corinthians 4:16, 17)

16. Wherefore I beseech you, be ye followers of me.

17. For this cause have I sent unto you Timotheus, who is my beloved son, and faithful in the Lord, who shall bring you into remembrance of my ways which be in Christ, as I teach every where in every church.

His ways in Christ, being how he lived as it related to what he said or taught, was how God empowered him to be an able minister of the New Testament — "speaking and living the Word of God."

(II Corinthians 3:2-6)

2. Ye are our Epistle written in our hearts, known and read of all men:

3. Forasmuch as ye are manifestly declared to be the Epistle of Christ ministered by us, written not with ink, but with the Spirit of the living God; not in tables of stone, but in fleshy tables of the heart.

4. And such trust have we through Christ to God-ward:

5. Not that we are sufficient of ourselves to think any thing as of ourselves; but our sufficiency is of God;

6. Who also hath made us able ministers of the new testament; not of the letter, but of the spirit: for the letter killeth, but the spirit giveth life

When a person believes something regarding the Word of God so strongly that that belief compels him and empowers him to live what he believes in such a way that he cannot live any other way, that is the indication that God has inscribed that portion of His Word upon that person's heart. Consequently, you have taken on the nature or image of that portion of God's Word. You become, as it were, that Word. You live that Word; you cannot break that portion of the Word that has been inscribed upon your heart.

(Romans 2:13-15)

13. For not the hearers of the law are just before God, but the doers of the law shall be justified.

14. For when the Gentiles, which have not the law, do by nature the things contained in the law, these, having not the law, are a law unto themselves:

15. Which shew the work of the law written in their hearts...

WHAT IS NEEDED FOR US TO RADIATE LIGHT?

We must take note of what else God said and receive understanding of what the Spirit is trying to get us to see.

(II Corinthians 3:7-11)

7. But if the ministration of death, written and engraven in stones, was glorious, so that the children of Israel could not steadfastly behold the face of Moses for the glory of his countenance; which glory was to be done away:

8. How shall not the ministration of the spirit be rather glorious?

9. For if the ministration of condemnation be glory, much more doth the ministration of righteousness exceed in glory.

10. For even that which was made glorious had no glory in this respect, by reason of the glory that excelleth.

11. For if that which is done away was glorious, much more that which remaineth is glorious.

Paul was telling them that if Moses was entitled to radiate light, because he was a minister of the Testament, (the old covenant), the letter of the Testament, how much more would he, Paul, be entitled to radiate light, because he is a minister of the New Testament, (the new covenant), the Spirit of the Testament, not the letter. Not only is he entitled to radiate light, but the light that he would radiate will be greater than the light Moses radiated, because he, (Paul), is a minister of the Spirit of the Testament that produces righteousness, whereas the ministering that Moses did through the law produced death. Thereby his, (Paul's), light will radiate for all eternity.

Moreover, notice what he says in the next verse.

(II Corinthians 3:12) Seeing then that we have such hope, we use great plainness of speech:

Why does he say this? What significance does verse 12 have to do with what he has been saying so far?

Notice the definition of the word *plainness* of speech according to the original writings. παῤῥησία parrhēsia, *par-rhay-see´-ah; all* out-*spokenness, i.e. frankness, bluntness, publicity; by impl. assurance:*— bold (× -ly, -ness, -ness of speech), confidence, × freely, × openly, × plainly (-ness).

Observe that this word means to not keep silent, to be bold and have an "all out-spokenness." In modern conversation, it means not to be afraid of what people think, just speak what you know is true.

Why does he say this after saying, "Seeing that we have such hope?" Because Paul's hope was to one day radiate literal light, just like Moses radiated literal light, but for this to happen, he had to be a minister of the Testament. That is what entitles or qualifies a person to radiate light. And you cannot be a minister of the Testament if you, "NEVER OPEN YOUR MOUTH TO SPEAK FORTH GOD'S WORD!" The gospel has to come out of your mouth for you to be a minister of the New Testament, thereby entitling you to radiate light. This is why he refused to keep silent; this is why he had an "all out-spokenness" — to bring about the realization of his hope.

Furthermore, you must not only be a minister of the New Testament, you must be an *ABLE* minister of the New Testament, and this only happens when God can use you to inscribe His Word upon the hearts of those to whom you minister. Additionally, this will never happen if that Word is not first inscribed in your heart. (This is why Paul said, *"Ye are our Epistle written* (first) *in our heart."*) It has to be written in your heart first in order for God to use you to pass that on to someone else. You cannot give what you do not have!

That Word inscribed in your heart causes you to live the lifestyle, (both in word and in deed), that inspires others to follow you and ultimately take on that same lifestyle, as God also inscribes that Word in their hearts. God can only use you to write His Word upon the hearts of those that hear you when you have the lifestyle; when you practice what you preach; when you live what you say, when you walk the talk.

(Philippians 2:15, 16)

15. That ye may be blameless and harmless, the sons of God, without rebuke, in the midst of a crooked and perverse nation, among whom ye shine as lights in the world;

16. Holding forth the word of life...

The Word of life that we are supposed to hold forth, like the Statue of Liberty holding forth her light in the darkness, is our lifestyle of the Word of God that we live before people. This is how we shine as lights in the world, as spoken by the scriptures: *"Be ye therefore followers,* [an imitator or a mimicker], *of God, as dear children"* *(Ephesians 5:1).*

As you live the Word of God in *word* and in *deed,* that lifestyle becomes a beacon that guides people down the path towards God. It is the fruit you bear that people see, taste, and then desire for themselves, which leads to that seed being sown into their hearts, resulting in them becoming an offspring of yourself, while you are an offspring of the Lord Jesus Christ.

Remember, as an able minister, God can only use you to inscribe onto the hearts of others, only that portion which has been first inscribed on your heart. Therefore, as a result of this, you are now entitled to radiate with that degree of light, because the measure of light that you radiate is in direct proportion to the degree of Word that you can effectively minister.

This should make us want to know how to have the Word of God written upon our hearts so that we can be effective in ministering that Word. Furthermore, that would mean that we should be able to find in the scriptures the revelation of how God inscribes His Word upon our hearts, and what, if anything, we need to do in order to have that Word written upon our hearts.

If we can find this truth in the scriptures, it should also reveal to us how we take on the image of Christ or the process that we must go through to take on His image. Because of the fact that the degree of light we radiate now and in the life to come is directly related to the degree of able ministering that we have done. Moreover, the degree of able ministering that we do is directly related to the degree of the Epistle of Christ that has been written in our hearts. Additionally, we cannot have a portion of the Epistle of Christ written in our hearts and not have taken on that portion of the nature or image of Christ Jesus, who is the Word of God.

HOW GOD USES THE LIGHT THAT WE RADIATE TO BRING PEOPLE OUT OF DARKNESS

In the next few paragraphs, we will see how God uses that light that we are already spiritually radiating in this life to shine on someone that is in darkness so they can see clearly and come out of darkness. Through this, we will also come to understand the process that we must endure in order to take on more of the image of Christ.

Because Paul said, "Seeing that we have such hope," that must mean that he was not radiating light, but hoped to one day. However, we know that we do radiate light now, a light in the spiritual realm that is not seen, because this is how God brings people out of darkness and into His glorious light.

(II Corinthians 4:3-6)

3. But if our gospel be hid, it is hid to them that are lost:

242

4. In whom the god of this world hath blinded the minds of them which believe not, lest the light of the glorious gospel of Christ, who is the image of God, should shine unto them.

5. For we preach not ourselves, but Christ Jesus the Lord; and ourselves your servants for Jesus' sake.

6. For God, who commanded the light to shine out of darkness, hath shined in our hearts, to give the light of the knowledge of the glory of God in the face of Jesus Christ.

Notice that, in the above verses, if a person is lost without Christ, he is so because the god of this world, (the Devil), has blinded the minds of those that believe not. The reason why a person cannot see is because he is in darkness. Moreover, this can be verified by going into the original writings.

The word *blinded* in the original is the Greek word: τυφλόω tuphlŏō, *toof-loá´-o;* from *5185;* to *make blind,* i.e. (fig.) to *obscure:*— blind.

Notice that this word comes from the Greek word… τυφλός tuphlŏs, *toof-los´; opaque* (as if *smoky*), i.e. (by anal.) *blind* (phys. or ment.):— blind.

The word *obscure,* according to Webster's dictionary, is the word that means "lacking or inadequately supplied with light: dark, dusty. To make dark, dim, or indistinct: to conceal or hide by or as if by covering." The word *opaque* as defined by Webster's is the word that means "exhibiting opacity: not pervious to radiant energy and especially light: hard to understand or explain." The word *opacity* means "the quality or state of a body that makes it impervious to rays of light."

As we see from these definitions and the verses that we read, we can understand that the reason for a person being lost is because the light that he needs to see his way clearly to the kingdom of God has not shone on him; he has been kept in darkness.

(As we study further along these teachings, we will see that the scriptures tell us that, many times, the reason for this is our failure as the people of God to let our lights shine. We are supposed to shine that light, but we do not, because we either do not have sufficient light to shine on them or because we have placed some kind of covering over that light, resulting in us not letting our *light shine before man that they may see our good works and glorify our Father who is in Heaven.* This is why we need our fruit, the seed and the flesh around the seed — the "seed" being the Word of God that we speak, the "flesh" being our good works, our "fruit" being our Godly lifestyle in word and in deed that we exhibit before man so that people can follow us as we follow Christ).

Notice that the scriptures go on to say, *"lest the light of the glorious gospel of Christ, who is the image of God, should shine unto them."* Paul then continues, saying, *"For we preach not ourselves, but Christ Jesus the Lord; and ourselves your servants for Jesus' sake."*

What he says here lets us know that the preaching of the gospel of Jesus Christ is how that light is in fact shone on those who are lost, while we endeavor to serve them, (*"and ourselves your servants"*), with our good works, culminating with the fulfillment of the scriptures that say:

(Matthew 5:16) Let your light so shine before men, that they may see your good works, and glorify your Father which is in Heaven.

All this is the recycling work of God in our lives, that is then passed on to others; better yet, it is the continued circle of life, as one seed is planted and another tree comes as a result of that seed, and so on, and so on.

This is why the next verse says, *"For God, who commanded the light to shine out of darkness, hath shined in our hearts, to give the light of the knowledge of the glory of God in the face of Jesus Christ."* God did not shine His light in our hearts to leave it at that, but for us to also give that light to others so that they can also see their way clearly into the kingdom of God. For this reason, we need to be living Epistles of the Word of God, so that others can know how to find God, come to God, and live for God.

This is why it is very important that we know and understand what it takes for us to be transformed in the image of Christ, (the process that we go through in order to take on the image of Christ). So that we allow God to take us through this process, thereby bringing us to the place where we radiate more light.

In the next verses, Paul teaches them, (and us as well), what this process is, and what this process will ultimately do to them, and the place to which it will bring them. They, (as well as us today), needed to know this so that they, (as well as us), do not get discouraged and decide to throw in the towel, because the process is not in itself a joyful one. In fact, this process will produce sorrow, pain, and anguish. Furthermore, if we are unable to see the end result of where this process will bring us to, we will believe that it is not worth it. Moreover, if we do not understand what we are going through, when we do go through the process, we will think that it is not of God, and we will rebuke the enemy and fight tooth and nail to get out of the process.

UNDERSTANDING THE PROCESS

(II Corinthians 4:7)

7. But we have this treasure in earthen vessels, that the excellency of the power may be of God, and not of us.

What treasure is Paul talking about that we have in our earthly earthen vessels? He just finished saying, *"For God, who commanded the light to shine out of darkness, hath shined in our hearts, to give the light of the knowledge of the*

245

glory of God in the face of Jesus Christ." Therefore, this treasure that we have is the ability to give or radiate light. Notice that he continues saying, *"that the excellency of the power may be of God, and not of us."* What does he mean by that? Notice the definition of the word *excellency* according to the original writings.

Excellency: ὑπερβολή hupěrbŏlē, *hoop-er-bol-ay';* from *5235;* a *throwing beyond* others, i.e. (fig.) *supereminence;* adv. *pre-eminently:*— abundance, (far more) exceeding, excellency, more excellent, beyond (out of) measure.

The word *excellency* comes from the Greek word ὑπερβάλλω hupěrballō, *hoop-er-bal'-lo;* to *throw beyond* the usual mark, i.e. (fig.) to *surpass* (only act. part. *supereminent*):— exceeding, excel, pass.

Observe what the word is telling us: our ability to radiate light is a treasure that we have in earthen vessels because it is God who throws that light beyond us to others. In other words, we are not radiating light; rather, God reflects the light off of us to others. We are a mirror for the light of the gospel of Jesus Christ to bounce off of us onto others. We become the mirror of God's Word that people look at and see their unrighteousness as they see the righteousness of Christ in us.

Why is that? Why is it that God reflects that light off of us and would rather not have us radiate with the light? Because in our earthly state, if we radiated with our own light without the nature of Jesus Christ, we would take the glory for ourselves, as if we are gods. It is bad enough that we try to be lords over people now without radiating literal light. Can you imagine how puffed up we would be with pride if we radiated with our own glory?

As a result of this, God will bring us through the process that conforms us into the image of Christ. Then, with His image and nature, we will always give Him the glory and not risk the chance that someday, in this life or the next; we may rise up with pride like Satan did.

Follow along carefully as the scriptures take us on this journey through the revelation of being conformed into the image of Christ.

After verse 7, Paul continues speaking in the next few verses.

(II Corinthians 4:8-11)

8. We are troubled on every side, yet not distressed; we are perplexed, but not in despair;

9. Persecuted, but not forsaken; cast down, but not destroyed;

10. Always bearing about in the body the dying of the Lord Jesus, that the life also of Jesus might be made manifest in our body.

11. For we which live are always delivered unto death for Jesus' sake, that the life also of Jesus might be made manifest in our mortal flesh.

GOING FROM REFLECTING
THE LIGHT OF GOD TO RADIATING WITH
THE LIGHT OF GOD!

Why does Paul begin to paint a somber picture of what they are going to go through; have already gone through; or are going through? He was talking about the light and their ability to either radiate or not radiate light. The subject of them going through trouble or persecution was not part of the conversation. Why, then, did he bring it up? He brought it up because he is showing them the things that they must go through in order to become more like Jesus Christ; he is showing them what it takes to take on more of the life of the Word of God!

247

The more like Him they are, the more they will be a living Epistle of the Word of God, culminating in them becoming an able minister of the New Testament, thereby enabling them to radiate literal light, (spiritual in this life, but literal in the life to come). Observe what he says after that:

(II Corinthians 4:12-14)

12. So then death worketh in us, but life in you.

13. We having the same spirit of faith, according as it is written, I believed, and therefore have I spoken; we also believe, and therefore speak;

14. Knowing that he which raised up the Lord Jesus shall raise up us also by Jesus, and shall present us with you.

What leads him to say what he said in these verses, and what is he telling the Corinthian church? He wants them to understand that they must go through troubling times, so much so that those trials and persecutions can be so hard on our human bodies that they slowly rob us of our physical life. In other words, this conforming process slowly kills us, or works death in us. However, as a result of these trying times, the nature of Jesus Christ is more evident in our lives. Indeed, this is what others need to see to work life in them, spiritual life.

A person that is without Christ is dead even while he lives. It is only when we are in Christ that we truly have life.

What Paul is telling them, is that this death process has to work in him for him to take on the life of Jesus Christ, so then, that life of Christ in him will work life in them, when he, as an able minister, ministers the Epistle of Christ with the Spirit of the living God.

Why does he continue with what he said in verses 13 and 14? Because he has the same spirit of faith as the one he is quoting, King David, who said:

(Psalms 116:10) I believed, therefore have I spoken: I was greatly afflicted:

Notice that King David knew that when he spoke what he believed, it cause him to be greatly afflicted. Well, Paul also knew that when he opened his mouth to speak the truth of God's Word, it resulted in him been afflicted, but he refused to stop because he knew that those afflictions would only produce more of the nature of Christ in him. Moreover, if the afflictions brought him death, he had an assurance that the same God, who raised Jesus up, would also raise him up. As well as anyone else who chooses to walk that straight and narrow road.

(II Corinthians 4:16-18)

16. For which cause we faint not; but though our outward man perish, yet the inward man is renewed day by day.

17. For our light affliction, which is but for a moment, worketh for us a far more exceeding and eternal weight of glory;

18. While we look not at the things which are seen, but at the things which are not seen: for the things which are seen are temporal; but the things which are not seen are eternal.

It is obvious that none of these things moves Paul. He does not murmur or complain; he does not choose to get out of the process, because he is looking at the eternal result of what this process will do to him.

He knows that these things are going to slowly rob him of his physical life, but in the process, his new man, the one that is made after the image of Christ, is renewed day by day. Furthermore, when we, also see the place that the afflictions of this life will bring us to, in eternity, we like Paul will say, "They are not worthy to be compared to the glory that we will receive".

Observe that he says, *"For our light affliction, which is but for a moment, worketh for us a far more exceeding and eternal weight of glory."*

Notice where all these afflictions are going to bring Paul, and us as fellow Saints, if we allow God to also bring us through this process.

The word *exceeding* is a Greek word that comes from two words, one of which is the Greek word; εἰς ĕis, *ice;* a primary prep.; <u>*to* or *into* (indicating the point reached or entered), of place, time, or (fig.) purpose (result, etc.)</u> . . .

Observe carefully, that this first word, (εἰς ĕis, *ice;*), that the word exceeding comes from means, "TO OR INTO; INDICATING THE POINT REACHED OR ENTERED, OF PLACE , TIME OR PURPOSE, (RESULT)".

The other Greek word from which this word *exceeding* comes from is ὑπερβολή hupĕrbŏlē, *hoop-er-bol-ay´;* a *throwing beyond* others, i.e. (fig.) *supereminence;* adv. *pre-eminently:*— abundance, (far more) exceeding, excellency, more excellent, beyond (out of) measure.

Observe that the second word from which *exceeding* comes from is the same word *Excellency*, which we studied in verse 7, *"That the <u>excellency</u> of the power may be of God and not of us."*

Look closely at what has transpired, now as a result of us allowing God to bring us through this conforming process, that transforms us into the image of Christ. These light afflictions, (*light* in the sense that — compared to the glory that they produce for all eternity — they seem insignificant), bring us, "to" or "into", the place where the excellency of the power is now also of us.

In other words, we who have come to this place in Christ are no longer a reflection of the light of God; we now radiate literally with the light of God, (in the next life). Those light afflictions, which were but for a moment, have worked for us a far more exceeding, (the place where we now have come "to" or "into", where we now "throw, (the light), beyond others)," and this is for all eternity. Upon seeing these truths, how could we not allow God to work in us His will? How could we not give Him the praise and glory, instead of murmuring and complaining?

Observe also the word *eternal*; αἰώνιος aiōniŏs, *ahee-o´-nee-os; perpetual* (also used of past time, or past and future as well):— eternal, for ever, everlasting, world (began).

Not only will the glory that we will have, radiate literally, and not only will it shine brighter, if we allow God to work in us more of the image of Christ, but this glory will radiate for all eternity.

(I Corinthians 15:40-42)

40. There are also celestial bodies, and bodies terrestrial: but the glory of the celestial is one, and the glory of the terrestrial is another.

41. There is one glory of the sun, and another glory of the moon, and another glory of the stars: for one star differeth from another star in glory.

42. So also is the resurrection of the dead...

It would behoove us, Saints, to learn God's Word, so we can see what the Spirit of the Lord is trying to show us. This way, as we go through the things in life, that God wants us to go through; we will humble ourselves beneath the mighty hand of God and allow Him to take us to the place that He has ordained for us to go, while we give Him the praise, the honor, and the glory.

(I Peter 1:6, 7)

6. Wherein ye greatly rejoice, though now for a season, if need be, ye are in heaviness through manifold temptations:

7. That the trial of your faith, being much more precious than of gold that perisheth, though it be tried with fire, might be found unto praise and honour and glory at the appearing of Jesus Christ:

In the next chapter, we will learn why it seems that Christ has to continue suffering in our bodies, (*"Always bearing about in the body the dying of the Lord Jesus"*), for us to be conformed into His image. This way, we will be able to understand in a greater way the reason for this and how this brings about the writing of His Word upon our hearts, or rather, the writing of His Word upon the hearts of those who allow God to put them in this conforming process. Moreover, this has to happen, (writing His Word upon our hearts), because this is how we take on the nature of the Word, Jesus the Son of God.

CHAPTER SIXTEEN

THE MINISTRY OF JESUS,
OUR HIGH PRIEST

¹Now of the things which we have spoken this is the sum: We have such an high priest, who is set on the right hand of the throne of the Majesty in the heavens; ²A minister of the sanctuary, and of the true tabernacle, which the Lord pitched, and not man. ³For every high priest is ordained to offer gifts and sacrifices: wherefore it is of necessity that this man have somewhat also to offer (Hebrews 8:1-3).

⁶But now hath he obtained a more excellent ministry, by how much also he is the mediator of a better covenant, which was established upon better promises (Hebrews 8:6).

As the people of God, we must understand that there are things Jesus Christ still has to do in order to continue to bring about the will and plan of God for our lives.

Observe, that the writer to the Hebrews, in chapter eight of Hebrews, in verse one, (after having made known certain things to the readers,) he summarizes what he had been trying to get them to see, saying, *"Now of the things which we have spoken this is the sum."* Notice the conclusion that he comes to, *"We have such an high priest, who is set on the right hand of the throne of the Majesty in the heavens; A minister of the sanctuary, and of the true tabernacle, which the Lord pitched, and not man. For every high priest is ordained to offer gifts and sacrifices: wherefore it is of necessity that this man have somewhat also to offer!"*

Take note that he is bringing them to the place where he wants them to understand that if, *"Every high priest was* ordained to offer both gifts and sacrifices," then it stand to reason, that as our new high priest, Jesus also has to offer gifts and sacrifices, because that is the main function of His priestly duties.

In the verses at the beginning of this chapter, we read that Jesus, our high priest, is a minister of the sanctuary and the true tabernacle. Notice the definition of the word *minister* according to the original writings.

"Minister", λειτουργός lĕitŏurgŏs, *li-toorg-os´;* a *public servant*, i.e. a *functionary* in the Temple or Gospel, or (gen.) a *worshipper* (of God) or *benefactor* (of man):— minister (-ed).

Furthermore, notice that the word *ministry* is the Greek word λειτουργία lĕitŏurgia, *li-toorg-ee´-ah;* that means, *public function* (as priest ["liturgy"] or almsgiver):— ministration (-try), service.

We must recognize that as our high priest, Jesus, being, "a public servant," has a ministry or, "a public function," that He has to perform. We must understand what is His ministry, the reason for His ministry, the role that we play in His ministry, and how we fit into the plan of God as a result of His ministry. Upon knowing this, we will see many of the revelations that we have studied fit together to form a beautiful picture of God's Word. However, do not confuse this ministry that He is *now* performing with the ultimate sacrifice that He offered on the cross of Calvary.

We read in Hebrews 8:1: *"We have such an high priest, who is set on the right hand of the throne of the Majesty in the heavens."* Notice that it says, "We *have*," and *"Who is set"*. Observe also that these two words, (have and set), are in the present tense, not in the past tense. When we read also in verse 3, *"It is of necessity that this man have somewhat to offer,"* the word, *"Have"*, is in the present tense as well. Moreover, the scriptures go on to say, *"But now hath he obtained a more excellent ministry,"* the emphasis,

"But now hath he obtained", referring to the present day, and not referring to something He did or had done in the past.

We can see from these verses and the others that follow that Jesus became a high priest, and with that priestly office came certain functions that He took on after His death, burial, and resurrection, not prior to it. This is why, when He came to earth, He took on human form to feel what we feel, so that when He did become the high priest He might be merciful and faithful in His calling.

(Hebrews 2:17) Wherefore in all things it behooved him to be made like unto his brethren, that he might be a merciful and faithful high priest in things pertaining to God, to make reconciliation for the sins of the people.

He was tempted as we are tempted, so that when He became high priest He would be able to help us by aiding us when we are tempted.

(Hebrews 2:18) For in that he himself hath suffered being tempted, he is able to succor them that are tempted.

Notice that He is making intercessions for us. Furthermore, He has to live forever to do this, and He only "lives forever", after His resurrection . . .

(Hebrews 7:25) Wherefore he is able also to save them to the uttermost that come unto God by him, seeing he ever liveth to make intercession for them.

. . . and mostly by offering both gifts and sacrifices in our behalf:

(Hebrews 8:3) For every high priest is ordained to offer gifts and sacrifices: wherefore it is of necessity that this man have somewhat also to offer.

Now if, *"It is of necessity that this man have somewhat also to offer,"* what is it that He has to offer?

It must be, "*Both gifts and sacrifices for sin*", because He has to follow the example that was laid down by the high priest!

(Hebrews 5:1) For every high priest taken from among men is ordained for men in things pertaining to God, that he may offer both gifts and sacrifices for sins:

(Hebrews 8:3) For every high priest is ordained to offer gifts and sacrifices: wherefore it is of necessity that this man have somewhat also to offer.

We read that, "*It behooved him to be made like unto his brethren, that he might be a merciful and faithful high priest in things pertaining to God.*" Furthermore, we just read, "*Every high priest taken from among men is ordained for man in things pertaining to God, that he may offer both gifts and sacrifices for sins.*" If the earthly high priest were ordained for man, IN THINGS PERTAINING TO GOD; and that was done by them offering both gifts and sacrifices for sins. Moreover, if Jesus wanting to be a merciful and faithful high priest, IN THINGS PERTAINING TO GOD, then He must do as they did, BY OFFERING BOTH GIFTS AND SACRIFICES FOR SINS!

These functions, however, are performed after He became a high priest and that transpired after His resurrection, because it is after His resurrection that He lives forever.

(Hebrews 7:24-26)

24. But this man, because he continueth ever, hath an unchangeable priesthood.

25. Wherefore he is able also to save them to the uttermost that come unto God by him, seeing he ever liveth to make intercession for them.

26. For such an high priest became us, who is holy, harmless, undefiled, separate from sinners, and made higher than the heavens;

These functions that the scriptures are referring to, (and that we are studying in order to see this revelation and learn of the ministry of Christ, and thereby understand why there are numerous scriptures that seem to refer that Jesus still has some suffering to go through, and why). Are functions that He, as the high priest, is performing *now*, in the true tabernacle of God. Furthermore, He has to perform His function this way because He has to follow the pattern laid down by the earthly high priest before Him.

(Hebrews 8:3) For every high priest is ordained to offer gifts and sacrifices: wherefore it is of necessity that this man have somewhat also to offer.

The pattern that the Levitical priests followed were given to them from God, so they were in fact following the pattern ordained in Heaven.

(Hebrews 8:5) Who serve unto the example and shadow of heavenly things, as Moses was admonished of God when he was about to make the tabernacle: for, See, saith he, that thou make all things according to the pattern shewed to thee in the mount.

Jesus was not only following their example, but He was also the example for them to follow.

As we said before, because Jesus was following the pattern of the Levitical priest, which required that they offer both gifts and sacrifices for sin, Jesus, in His ministry as high priest, *now*, also has to offer both gifts and sacrifices for sin. Does this mean that His ultimate sacrifice offered on the cross was of no effect? No, of course not! However, we need to understand that Jesus, as the mediator of a better covenant, (which involves writing that covenant upon our hearts,) must perform His function in order to bring about the fruition of Him being the mediator of the better covenant, thereby having that covenant written upon our hearts. Furthermore, for this to happen, something has to transpire, and that something is for Him to offer gifts and sacrifices.

Let us learn how it is that Jesus, performing His public function of offering both gifts and sacrifices, brings about the fruition of Him being the mediator of the better covenants. But first, let us study what the better covenant is.

(Hebrews 8:6-12)

6. But now hath he obtained a more excellent ministry, by how much also he is the mediator of a better covenant, which was established upon better promises.

7. For if that first covenant had been faultless, then should no place have been sought for the second.

8. For finding fault with them, he saith, Behold, the days come, saith the Lord, when I will make a new covenant with the house of Israel and with the house of Judah:

9. Not according to the covenant that I made with their fathers in the day when I took them by the hand to lead them out of the land of Egypt; because they continued not in my covenant, and I regarded them not, saith the Lord.

10. For this is the covenant that I will make with the house of Israel after those days, saith the Lord; I will put my laws into their mind, and write them in their hearts: and I will be to them a God, and they shall be to me a people:

11. And they shall not teach every man his neighbor, and every man his brother, saying, Know the Lord: for all shall know me, from the least to the greatest.

12. For I will be merciful to their unrighteousness, and their sins and their iniquities will I remember no more.

Notice that this better covenant has to do with God putting His law in our minds and writing His law upon our hearts. If we follow the pattern of the Law and the Prophets, we know that this also includes placing His fear in us. This covenant is the same covenant that God made with the nation of Israel when He brought them out of the land of Egypt, except that now His law is put in our minds and written upon our hearts, versus written upon tablets of stone. Furthermore,

His law is written upon our hearts with the Spirit of God, versus written with ink.

(II Corinthians 3:3) Forasmuch as ye are manifestly declared to be the Epistle of Christ ministered by us, written not with ink, but with the Spirit of the living God; not in tables of stone, but in fleshy tables of the heart.

This is very important, because as God writes His law upon our hearts with His Spirit, we take on more of the Spirit of God.

If you take a pen and write on a piece of paper, the ink is transferred from the pen onto the paper. Consequently, in like manner, as God writes His law upon our hearts with His Spirit, His Spirit is also transferred from God via His minister to us. This is why you take on more of the life of God, given that you are taking on more of the Spirit of God.

(II Corinthians 3:6) Who also hath made us able ministers of the new testament; not of the letter, but of the spirit: for the letter killeth, but the spirit giveth life.

(II Corinthians 4:10) Always bearing about in the body the dying of the Lord Jesus, that the life also of Jesus might be made manifest in our body.

(John 6:63) It is the spirit that quickeneth; the flesh profiteth nothing: the words that I speak unto you, they are spirit, and they are life.

However, as ministers of the gospel, God uses us to write His law upon the hearts of those who hear us, and because of that, the Spirit that is used to write His law upon the hearts of those who hear us is coming from us to them. It is God's Spirit, but it is poured out of us onto them.

As this happens, that minister is drained of the life-sustaining Spirit of God that gives him life. For this reason, it is so important that God's minister stay filled with the Spirit of God by staying in prayer and in the study of the Word.

Many a Godly man and woman of God have started out with a passion and zeal for God, and with a spiritual vitality, only to lose it. Because of the pressures of the ministry and the workload, they neglect their personal time with the Lord that keeps them filled with His Spirit, His love, and His power.

Many ministers think that being in revivals, traveling to different churches and preaching night after night, praying for others, and so forth is going to keep them filled with the Spirit of God, so they do not take the time to remain in a personal and intimate relationship with Him.

With His law written upon our hearts, we become, as it were, that law, and cannot break that law.

(Romans 2:14, 15)

14. For when the Gentiles, which have not the law, do by nature the things contained in the law, these, having not the law, are a law unto themselves:

15. Which shew the work of the law written in their hearts . .

.

Observe also, that it is Jesus, who is the mediator of this better covenant. The definition of the word *mediator*, is: μεσίτης mĕsitēs, *mes-ee´-tace; a go-between,* i.e. (simply) an *internunciator,* or (by impl.) a *reconciler (intercessor)*:— mediator.

It is God, who writes His law upon our hearts, but He does this through Jesus; Jesus is the go-between — between us and God — along with ministers as co-laborers with Him in the ministry; Jesus uses them to fulfill His ministry of writing His law upon the hearts of His people.

(II Corinthians 3:3, 6)

3. Forasmuch as ye are manifestly declared to be the Epistle of Christ ministered by us, written not with ink, but with the Spirit of the living God; not in tables of stone, but in fleshy tables of the heart.

6. Who also hath made us able ministers of the new testament; not of the letter, but of the spirit: for the letter killeth, but the spirit giveth life.

The definition of the word *testament*, is: διαθήκη diathēkē, *dee-ath-ay´-kay;* prop. a *disposition*, i.e. (spec.) a *contract* (espec. a devisory *will*):— covenant, testament. Realize that this word, "Testament", is the same word, "Covenant" and is used in the verses of Hebrews chapters 8 and 9.

Given that Jesus is the mediator of the new covenant and in view of the fact that the scripture says, *"But now hath he obtained a more excellent ministry, BY HOW MUCH ALSO He is the mediator of a better covenant,"* there must be a connection between His ministry and His ability to be mediator of that better covenant! Furthermore, since His ministry is that of offering both gifts and sacrifices, then we need to know what those gifts and sacrifices are, how He offers them, and if it involves us, the role that we play in His ministry.

Observe that the verse says, *"But now hath he obtained a more excellent ministry, "BY HOW MUCH ALSO" he is the mediator of a better covenant."* What does this mean? How does His ministry affect or directly relate to His ability to be the mediator? Let us dissect this verse and get the true meaning of what the scripture is telling us.

Notice first that the words, *how* and *much*, in this verse are in fact one word in the original writing, ὅσος hŏsŏs, *hos´-os;* which means: *by redupl. as (much, great, long,* etc.) *as:*— all (that), as (long, many, much) (as), how great (many, much), [in-] asmuch as, so many as, that (ever), the more, those things, what (great, -soever), wheresoever, wherewithsoever, which, × while, who (-soever).

Let us look also at the definition of the word *excellent*; *"But now hath he obtained a more <u>excellent</u>*

ministry." Excellent: διάφορος diaphŏrŏs, *dee-af´-or-os; varying;* also *surpassing:*— differing, divers, more excellent.

Notice that the definitions of this word *excellent* are, *varying, divers,* as well as *differing.* In other words, there are degrees to His ministering: varying, differing or diverse degrees of results. His ministry can vary or differ in results depending on whether the conditions are right or not. Moreover, this leads to varying, differing or divers degrees of results of His ability to be the mediator of the better covenant. In other words, HIS ABILITY TO MEDIATE IS DIRECTLY PROPORTION TO HIS ABILITY TO FULFILL HIS MINISTRY!

To explain His ministry in a manner that the reader can understand — and know the role that we play, so we can submit ourselves to Him, so that both He and we can get the best results, thereby having a greater degree of His Word written upon our hearts; — let us use the example of "Percentages."

The percentage of ministering that Jesus Christ is allowed to perform, determines the percentage that He can mediate of the better covenant. In other words, if He is only able to perform 30 percent of His ministry, then He will be able to write only 30 percent of His covenant upon our hearts! This is the reason why some Christians only produce 30-fold fruit, while others produce 60-fold or 100-fold fruit.

(Mark 4:20) And these are they which are sown on good ground; such as hear the word, and receive it, and bring forth fruit, some thirtyfold, some sixty, and some an hundred.

What determines how well He is able to perform His ministry? Is not this something for which He alone has control? Is He not all powerful, and does He not have all ability? Would He not have the power and desire to perform 100% percent of His ministry? What could stop Him from performing 100 percent of His ministry? WE CAN! Remember, Jesus can only do as much as our level of belief.

Just as we learned in the Bible, about the people that He could not heal because of their unbelief.

You see, the gifts and sacrifices that He offers is Himself. Furthermore, the temple in which He offers those gifts and sacrifices in, is us, — in the temple of our bodies. This is why we find such scriptures as:

(II Corinthians 4:8-11)

8. We are troubled on every side, yet not distressed; we are perplexed, but not in despair;

9. Persecuted, but not forsaken; cast down, but not destroyed;

10. Always bearing about in the body the dying of the Lord Jesus, that the life also of Jesus might be made manifest in our body.

11. For we which live are always delivered unto death for Jesus' sake, that the life also of Jesus might be made manifest in our mortal flesh.

(II Corinthians 1:5, 7)

5. For as the sufferings of Christ abound in us, so our consolation also aboundeth by Christ.

7. And our hope of you is steadfast, knowing, that as ye are partakers of the sufferings, so shall ye be also of the consolation.

(Galatians 2:20) I am crucified with Christ: nevertheless I live; yet not I, but Christ liveth in me: and the life which I now live in the flesh I live by the faith of the Son of God, who loved me, and gave himself for me.

(Colossians 1:24) Who now rejoice in my sufferings for you, and fill up that which is behind of the afflictions of Christ in my flesh for his body's sake, which is the church:

As we begin to comprehend the ministry of Christ, we begin to understand that Christ offers Himself in the temple of our bodies upon the altar of our hearts. Because it is in our bodies that He does this, we feel the pain of what He is going through. He is the one that is, (spiritually speaking), dying in us, (*"Always bearing about in the body the dying of the Lord Jesus"*), but we feel the pain of that death. We feel the sorrow of His suffering. We are the ones who are experiencing the troubles and the anguish of bearing in our bodies the dying of the Lord Jesus.

Jesus Christ, however, is willing to offer Himself in this manner because He knows the outcome or the end result when He fulfills His ministry. The end result is His Word being written upon our hearts and us being transformed that much more into His image.

As the people of God, we need to understand the ministry of our great high priest, which is all part of the molding process. If we do not understand what God is trying to do in our lives when we go through times of testing, trials, and troubles, we will fight Him tooth and nail. We will rebuke the enemy thinking that it is the Devil and do all that we possibly can to get out of the situation. Furthermore, if we cannot get out of the situation, we will murmur and complain and provoke God, just as the nation of Israel did when He brought them out of Egypt.

What's more, what we are actually doing is keeping Jesus from fulfilling His ministry. We are the ones, (because of our ignorance of His Word), who are throwing a monkey wrench into the mechanism of His ministry that keeps Him from fulfilling it 100 percent. This is especially true in a day and hour such as this, when most ministers are preaching that God's people should have the best of everything, that we should always be healthy and never lack for anything, that there is no suffering for Christ's sake.

This is not an easy message to minister because it will require something of the hearers. It will require that we take up our crosses and follow Christ and that we lay down our lives in this life. Additionally, we are living in a day when everyone wants it microwaved and drive-through. Very few want to pay the price of what it takes to become what God has ordained for His people to become.

In the next chapter, we will learn why it is so very important to allow Jesus to fulfill His ministry in us. In addition, we will learn how and why this brings about the culmination of God writing His covenant or testament upon our hearts.

CHAPTER SEVENTEEN

WRITING HIS LAW UPON OUR HEART

¹³For if the blood of bulls and of goats, and the ashes of an heifer sprinkling the unclean, sanctifieth to the purifying of the flesh: ¹⁴How much more shall the blood of Christ, who through the eternal Spirit offered himself without spot to God, purge your conscience from dead works to serve the living God? ¹⁵And for this cause he is the mediator of the new testament, that by means of death, for the redemption of the transgressions that were under the first testament, they which are called might receive the promise of eternal inheritance. ¹⁶For where a testament is, there must also of necessity be the death of the testator. ¹⁷For a testament is of force after men are dead: otherwise it is of no strength at all while the testator liveth. ¹⁸Whereupon neither the first testament was dedicated without blood (Hebrews 9:13-18).

Before we learn why it is so important to allow Jesus to fulfill His ministry in the temple of our bodies, so we can understand how this now bring us to the place where we qualify to have His Word written upon our hearts. I want to first share the benefits of being faithful to God, by allowing His Son to offer Himself as a gift and a sacrifice in the temple of our bodies.

What we are talking about involves suffering. And because we suffer, this suffering takes a toll on our physical bodies, thereby slowly producing physical death. Furthermore, since these troubles and persecutions, trials and tribulations, many times cause pain and, or sorrow, many of us will have the tendency to say, "I'm not sure that I'm ready for this." Our attitude may be, "I'm not sure that I want this," or perhaps even, "I'm not sure that this is worth it!"

However, before we decide this, let us look at the benefits that we will obtain because of having God's Word inscribed upon our hearts.

First, there is the benefit spoken about in the previous chapters. As we take on more of the image of Christ, we become a mightier soul winner in the kingdom of God.

Second, there is the benefit that as we take on more of the image of Christ, we have fewer battles with our flesh, because now those sins no longer have power over us. We have ceased from sin in those areas.

(I Peter 4:1, 2)

1. Forasmuch then as Christ hath suffered for us in the flesh, arm yourselves likewise with the same mind: for he that hath suffered in the flesh hath ceased from sin;

2. That he no longer should live the rest of his time in the flesh to the lusts of men, but to the will of God.

Because we are now wrestling less and less with the flesh, we can concentrate on wrestling in the areas that are more important: the spiritual realm — against principalities, against powers, against the rulers of the darkness of this world, against spiritual wickedness in high places.

(Ephesians 6:12) For we wrestle not against flesh and blood, but against principalities, against powers, against the rulers of the darkness of this world, against spiritual wickedness in high places.

YOU HAVE SOMETHING TO DO WITH DETERMINING THE GLORY WITH WHICH YOU WILL RADIATE FOR ALL ETERNITY!

The greatest benefit of all is becoming more like Christ, where we walk more like Him, talk more like Him, and love more like Him. Therefore, taking on more of His image, produces in us a greater resurrection.

(I Corinthians 15:41, 42)

41. There is one glory of the sun, and another glory of the moon, and another glory of the stars: for one star differeth from another star in glory.

42. So also is the resurrection of the dead. It is sown in corruption; it is raised in incorruption:

Notice that in the two verses we just read regarding the resurrection of the dead, there will be those who will shine with the glory of the stars, while others will shine with the glory of the moon, and still others will shine with the glory of the sun. Moreover, observe that as there are three levels of spiritual fruit production, as we learned in the parable of the sower, (Chapter 9,) thirty fold, sixty fold, and one hundred fold. There are also three degrees of resurrection.

If it is a clear night and there are no clouds in the sky, you will see many stars shining in the heavens, and some will shine brighter than others. However, if there is a full moon out, you are unable to see even the stars, because the light from the moon outshines them. On the other hand, on a clear day when the sun is shining brightly, you will not even see the moon because the sun outshines the moon with more radiance. Not only will some saint's glory outshine others in eternity, but the degree of glory that they obtain will be theirs for all eternity.

A greater understanding of the Word will help you to choose the path that will lead you to a better resurrection.

(Hebrews 11:35)...and others were tortured, not accepting deliverance; that they might obtain a better resurrection:

Why would others allow themselves to endure torture, if they have the faith needed to receive deliverance? Why would they not accept it? Were they crazy, or did they not know how to use their faith? Did they know something that others, including ourselves today, have failed to see? They did! They knew that they could, by faith receive their deliverance, just like the other examples before them in this chapter of Hebrews 11, where they used their faith to overcome the prevailing obstacle. However, they also knew that they could stay under the load of those trials, and allow those situations — no matter how hard and difficult they may have seemed — to mold them into the vessels of honor that would qualify them to receive a greater resurrection: *"That they might obtain a better resurrection"*.

In the resurrection of the dead, the glory that you have acquired in this life is the glory that you will radiate with, for all eternity, not for seventy years or even a thousand years, but for all eternity. For this reason, we need to see the importance of getting it right the first time, since there is no redoing it. For all eternity, you will have to look at others and see what you could have received, but for whatever reason, you missed it!

(II Timothy 2:15) Study to shew thyself approved unto God, a workman that needeth not to be ashamed, rightly dividing the word of truth.

If you still do not think it is worth it, let me share some other truths with you.

(Psalms 2:7-9)

7. I will declare the decree: the LORD hath said unto me, Thou art my Son; this day have I begotten thee.

8. Ask of me, and I shall give thee the heathen for thine inheritance, and the uttermost parts of the earth for thy possession.

9. Thou shalt break them with a rod of iron; thou shalt dash them in pieces like a potter's vessel.

Notice that in these passages of scriptures, God the Father has made His Son the promise to give Him an inheritance. That inheritance is, given to Him the heathen nations and the uttermost parts of the earth. Notice also that He, the Son, will break, (or rule), them with a rod of iron and, "Shalt dash them to pieces like a potter's vessel." However, notice also that in Revelations chapter 2, verses 26 and 27, the Lord Jesus tells us the following:

(Revelations 2:26, 27)

26. And he that overcometh, and keepeth my works unto the end, to him will I give power over the nations:

27. And he shall rule them with a rod of iron; as the vessels of a potter shall they be broken to shivers: even as I received of my Father.

Observe that the same inheritance that the Father gives to the Son, the Son also gives to us, "To us who overcome"!

(Psalms 110:1) The LORD said unto my Lord, Sit thou at my right hand, until I make thine enemies thy footstool.

Here again we see God the Father, giving the Son another very high position of authority, when He tells Jesus Christ to sit with Him on His, the Father's throne. Notice once more how Jesus, the Son, shares this inheritance with those who overcome as well.

(Revelations 3:21) To him that overcometh will I grant to sit with me in my throne, even as I also overcame, and am set down with my Father in his throne.

All through the scriptures, we see where there are peoples, nations, and tribes, as well as angels that are standing around the throne; however, here we see a certain group of people, those who have overcome, that are not standing around the throne. They are, in fact, sitting on the throne, with God the Father and God the Son. "Hallelujah! Glory to God in the highest!" If that does not make you want to forsake this world and run after God and His Word, and endure all that this world throws at you, I do not know what will!

SOME MESSAGES ARE HARD TO MINISTER FOR THEY ARE NOT READILY ACCEPTED, BUT THE TRUTH MUST STILL BE TOLD!

For the longest time, I fought with this message because I knew that God was revealing something to me that I, in all my years in church, had not heard. It seemed that everywhere I turned, ministers were preaching almost the opposite: health, prosperity, and abundant living. Therefore, I fought an internal battle because I could not believe that all these so-called great men and women of God could be wrong and I was right. By the same token, I did not want to be wrong and be preaching something erroneous that would result in running my race in vain. However, I believed what I felt God was showing me in the scriptures and I refused to deny it.

As the battle grew, even my wife would tell me, "Honey, I don't know. Brother So-and-so is saying just the opposite". Nevertheless, I refused to disbelieve and teach otherwise, even if it meant dying and standing before God and finding out that I had been wrong all along. Therefore, I began to cry out to God more earnestly for understanding, asking Him to show me if I was wrong and more or less standing alone. Finally, after one of those prayer sessions, the Lord spoke to me and said, "Go to Hebrews 11."

In Hebrews 11, I found myself reading of all those great men of faith and of all the mighty exploits that they did through faith. I read that through faith they subdued kingdoms, wrought righteousness, stopped the mouths of lions, quenched the violence of fire, escaped the edge of the sword, out of weakness were made strong, obtained promises.

271

"OBTAINED PROMISES?" Wait a minute! The Spirit of God had quickened something to me; I continued to read...*and others were tortured, not accepting deliverance; that they might obtain a better resurrection*...the Lord had showed me something. He spoke to me about those other ministers who seemed to be preaching the opposite of what I was seeing as clearly as these words that you are reading, and said, "They are not wrong. They are just not seeing what I am allowing you to see. (New wine must be put into new bottles, otherwise the old bottles will burst and both the wine and bottles will be lost). They are obtaining their promises now, in this life." Prosperity is a promise, healing is a promise, many of those things that they preach about, that they call blessings are promises, and they are obtaining their promises now in this life. However, at what price? At the price of forfeiting a greater resurrection!

This experience showed me that we all have choices to make, and those choices will have eternal consequence. Moreover, we need the understanding of God's Word to be better equipped to make those decisions.

God in His infinite wisdom and knowledge is giving us the opportunity to make clear and distinct choices that will determine how we will spend the rest of our eternal lives. However, He does this by revealing truths in His Word that are hidden deep in the scriptures.

To illustrate, if God, who is supreme and Lord over all the universe and can give us whatever He wants because there is no other above Him; He has the ultimate say-so. If He was to come to you and say, "So-and-so, (your name), tomorrow I am sending you to earth to fulfill your tour of duty. You will be there for the next eighty years. Now tell me, how do you want to spend those next eighty years?" God is giving you a choice. If you understood His question, you would say, "Well, Lord, I want to be born to a wealthy family. I want to be very beautiful. I want to be very smart and be born in a country that is prosperous. I want to have a good physique. . ."

You would choose those things that you consider appealing to you, because they would be the things that you would live with for the next eighty years. You would not choose something negative like, "Well, Lord, I want to be born a poverty-stricken child with no parents in some third-world country." Would you? No, you would not! Moreover, the decision would be yours. You would not have to feel guilty or embarrassed about it because God Himself, the God of the entire world, was the one who was giving you the choice.

Well, in that same way, God is now, in this life asking us the same question, about how we want to spend eternity. The difference is that He is doing it subtly, through the mysteries that are hidden in the scriptures. However, the difference is that for you to be great in the life to come, you must be the least in this life. For you to have riches in the next life, you must give them away in this life. If you want to gain your life in the life to come, you must lose it in this life. If you want to rule over many in the next life, you must be a servant of all in this life.

MANY MAY THINK THAT SOME SACRIFICES ARE NOT WORTH IT, BUT IN HEAVEN, NO SACRIFICE WILL GO UNREWARDED

There was a man in a dream that found himself in a beautiful room. The room was full of people, and it seemed to be some kind of waiting room. They were all waiting to enter through a massive door that opened into a huge dining room where they all knew that they would sit to dine at the marriage supper of the Lamb.

All the people were anxious. All were pushing, trying to be first into the dining room, wanting to be first so they could find the best seat, the one seat that would be next to the Lord Jesus Himself. All wanted that position of honor and glory to sit and dine with the Master, seated right next to Him.

Just how this man found himself right in front of that huge door, he did not know. He considered that he was just blessed! However, that did not matter. The opportunity to run and beat all the others to the best seat was at his disposal; all he had to do was swing that door wide when it opened and run first to the best seat. (It all seemed like a setting from a Walt Disney World exhibition, when everybody is waiting for the main doors to open and everyone runs to get the best seat.)

"I could do this," he thought. "I have a head start; I have an advantage. As fate would have it, I find myself at the head of the line right in front of the door; no one has a better chance at getting the best seat than I."

Then the moment all were waiting for finally arrived. The door opened, and with a pull, the man swung the door. Instincts told him to fling the door open and run for the seat, make a go for it; but it did not happen that way. As he opened the door, he felt compelled to hold the door open for others. He had been conditioned to hold doors for others, so he could not bring himself to let the door go and allow others to fend for themselves. He wanted to, but he could not. And as the people streamed in, (with the same thought on their minds: to get the best seat), and ran for the seat, he thought to himself, "Lord, I had the opportunity right in my hand, and I let it slip. I was at the front. I would have made it first to the seat, but I lost it. Maybe if I let go of the door now and run, I may still have a chance." However, he still could not bring himself to let go of the door; his nature would not allow him. The more people that rushed in, the more his hopes dwindled and the more he saw his chances fading.

Finally, he resorted to just holding the door for all the others who were also privileged to be invited to this momentous occasion.

His heart sank and sadness overtook him as he thought of how he had the greatest opportunity to sit right next to Jesus Christ at this supper. And he had let it slip through his hands simply because he chose to be a servant and hold the door. He wondered, "Was it worth it?"

As the last person walked hurriedly into the dining room, he also entered with his head lowered and sorrow in his heart, reluctantly walking into the dining room to get whatever seat was left for him. As he walked forward, he lifted his eyes to see what seat was available. There was only one seat left; all the others had been filled. However, to his surprise and amazement, the only seat not occupied was the one right next to the Lord. "But how could this be? It was on everyone's mind to get that seat! What happened," he thought?

While all the guests were rushing in to sit right next to the Lord, all seemed to have forgotten His splendor, His majesty, His glory, and His greatness. The sight of the Lord was so awesome that no one felt worthy enough to sit next to Him. No one felt that they deserved that place of honor of sitting right next to the King of kings and the Lord of lords! No, not even the man! However, he realized that he had no choice but to take that seat, because it was the only one available. He did, although not because he felt worthy, but because it was the only seat available.

Many times, we think that humbling ourselves will weaken us or that we may lose something that we think is of value. However, God's Word stands sure. If we humble ourselves, we can be sure that He in His own way will exalt us.

UNDERSTANDING THE MINISTRY OF JESUS OUR HIGH PRIEST

Why then is it so important for Jesus to fulfill His ministry of offering Himself as a gift and as a sacrifice in our bodies? Why do we have to bear in our bodies the dying of the Lord Jesus?

We have learned that by dying in our bodies, He offers Himself in us as a gift and a sacrifice to God. That is His ministry. Moreover, it becomes a mutual effort, and as a result of that, we suffer with Him. This is how we are crucified with Christ. The toil of all this is that our outward man perishes; however, the benefit is that the inward man is renewed day by day as we put on the Lord Jesus Christ, the Word of God.

We learned that His ability to be a mediator of the new covenant is directly proportional to His ability to fulfill His ministry. For this reason, we must be faithful to allow Him to fulfill His ministry in us without trying to fight Him or without trying to get out from under the load of it.

Not submitting to Him will cause us to lose out with God, because this keeps Him from writing His law upon our hearts. Additionally, if you have a specific calling upon your life that requires that you have more of the nature of Christ, so you can fulfill that calling, then He has to be successful in His efforts at inscribing His Word upon your heart. This means that if you do not allow Him to fulfill His ministry in you the first time around, He will only have to try again later. This is why so many people have to keep going through the same trials over and over again. Therefore, it would behoove us to get it right the first time around.

We learned that if we allow Him to go all the way in fulfilling His ministry in us, we are now qualified to have His Word writing in our hearts, because He can be the mediator of the new covenant and that involves God writing His law upon our heart and putting His law in our minds.

We must understand that His, (Jesus'), ministry of offering Himself as a gift and a sacrifice in us, is for the purpose so that He can, (spiritually speaking), shed His blood and die!

Question number one: "Why does Jesus have to shed His blood and die in us; offering Himself as a gift and a sacrifice?"

Question number two: "What does the shedding of His blood and dying in us do that moves or motivates God to write His law upon our hearts?"

Let us continue as we answer the first question.

(Hebrews 9:9, 13)

9. Which was a figure for the time then present, in which were offered both gifts and sacrifices, that could not make him that did the service perfect, as pertaining to the conscience;

13. For if the blood of bulls and of goats, and the ashes of an heifer sprinkling the unclean, sanctifieth to the purifying of the flesh:

The offering of the blood of bulls and of goats sanctified to the purifying of the flesh, but had no power over the conscience, (the mind). The mind, (heart), has to be changed for there to be a change in the individual. However, notice that with the shedding of the blood of Christ, the blood of Christ will *purge your conscience from dead works to serve the living God.* This is why He has to shed His blood.

(Hebrews 9:14, 15)

14. How much more shall the blood of Christ, who through the eternal Spirit offered himself without spot to God, purge your conscience from dead works to serve the living God?

277

15. And for this cause he is the mediator of the new testament...

The blood of Christ purges our conscience from dead works! However, how is it that it purges our conscience?

When Christ sheds His blood in us, that portion of the Word of God, that God has been wanting to write upon our hearts, is now written in our hearts, causing us to become that portion of the Word of God. The change is produced in us because we become that portion of the Word of God. The change of having taken off our carnal nature, to having put on that portion of the nature of Christ.

(Romans 2:14, 15)

14. for when the Gentiles, which have not the law, do by nature the things contained in the law, these, having not the law, are a law unto themselves:

15. Which shew the work of the law written in their hearts, their conscience also bearing witness, and their thoughts the mean while accusing or else excusing one another;)

However, why does He have to shed His blood in us and why does this cause God to write His Word upon our heart?

For us to understand why He has to shed His blood and how this leads to God writing His Word upon our heart, (Christ being the mediator of the new covenant), we must understand why the scriptures say "who through the eternal Spirit offered Himself," as well as "And for this cause He is the mediator of the new testament."

Notice that the scripture says, "How much more shall..." The word *shall* is a future tense word. It is future in the sense that something still needs to happen in the conscience of many people. Observe also that it says, "Who through the *eternal* Spirit offered Himself without spot." Why does he say, "Through the *eternal* Spirit offered Himself without spot?"

278

The definition of the word *eternal* is αἰώνιος aiōniŏs, *ahee-o´-nee-os; perpetual* (also used of past time, or past and future as well):— eternal, for ever, everlasting, world (began).

The definition of the word *perpetual* according to Webster's dictionary is "continuing forever: everlasting; valid for all time; occurring continually: indefinitely long-continued."

Observe that the word, "perpetual," means continuing forever, occurring continually, also indefinitely long continued. Why is that?

Because this is an ongoing, occurring continually, process as Jesus Christ offers Himself as a gift and sacrifice without spot to God. As long as there is a child of God whose mind is not completely purged, and that individual wants to be changed into the image of Christ, Jesus will continue to fulfill His "MORE EXCELLENT" ministry. That leads to, "HOW MUCH ALSO" He is now the mediator of the better covenant." Thereby purging that mind and producing the change in that person.

(Hebrews 9:14, 15)

14. How much more shall the blood of Christ, who through the eternal Spirit offered himself without spot to God, purge your conscience from dead works to serve the living God?

15. And for this cause he is the mediator of the new testament...

Now what does it mean, *"And for this cause he is the mediator of the new testament . . ."* and how does this help us to understand how this lead us to have the Word of God inscribed upon our hearts?

Notice that the word *cause,* ("And for this *cause*"), is the Greek word, διά dia, *dee-ah´;* that means: διά dia, *dee-ah´;* a primary prep. denoting the *channel* of an act; *through* (in very wide applications, local, causal, or occasional):—

after, always, among, at, to avoid, because of (that), briefly, by, for (cause) ... fore, from, in, by occasion of, of, by reason of, for sake, that, thereby, therefore, × though, through (-out), to, wherefore, with (-in).

The word *cause* is the word that means, "Denoting the channel of an act, (in other words, the means by which something happens); through". Observe the different definitions: "Through, Because of (that), From, By reason of, Wherefore."

Therefore, this verses could be read, "*How much more shall the blood of Christ, who through the eternal Spirit offered himself without spot to God, purge your conscience from dead works to serve the living God?* And through this He is the mediator of the New Testament".

These verses could also be said, "*How much more shall the blood of Christ, who through the eternal Spirit offered himself without spot to God, purge your conscience from dead works to serve the living God?* And because of" or "because of that, He is the mediator of the New Testament."

We could even go on to say these verses in this manner, "*How much more shall the blood of Christ, who through the eternal Spirit offered himself without spot to God, purge your conscience from dead works to serve the living God?* And by reason of this, He is the mediator of the New Testament."

What we are trying to say or establish is that in these verses, the scriptures are saying that as Jesus fulfills His ministry in offering Himself as a gift and a sacrifice, He sheds His blood and dies in us, in the temple of our bodies. (This is not referring to the sacrifice that He made on the cross of Calvary. But rather, (spiritually speaking), a continuation of what He started on Calvary.) It is in doing this and through this that He is the mediator of the New Testament. We have already learned that being the mediator of the New Testament is something that He does as He fulfills His more excellent ministry. By putting the two concepts together, we can see that as we allow Him to fulfill His ministry in our bodies, He sheds His blood and dies. Why?

Let us answer this question while simultaneously answering question number two. "What does the shedding of His blood and dying in us do that moves or motivates God to write His Word upon our hearts?"

Very simply, it allows God to know that the testator has died. You see, Saints, we cannot receive the testament or covenant until the testator dies. Consequently, when God sees the blood, the blood is the evidence that the testator has died, and now that individual qualifies to receive the testament.

(Hebrews 9:14-16)

14. How much more shall the blood of Christ, who through the eternal Spirit offered himself without spot to God, purge your conscience from dead works to serve the living God?

15. And for this cause he is the mediator of the new testament, that by means of death, for the redemption of the transgressions that were under the first testament, they which are called might receive the promise of eternal inheritance.

16. For where a testament is, there must also of necessity be the death of the testator.

It is the same concept that the children of Jacob used when they dipped Joseph's coat of many colors in blood. It was to make Jacob believe that his son Joseph was dead.

(Hebrews 9:17) For a testament is of force after men are dead: otherwise it is of no strength at all while the testator liveth.

The testament is of force only after the testator dies; otherwise, there is no strength in the testament. (Remember that the testament or covenant is the writing of His law upon our hearts and the giving of His law in our minds.) If God writes His law upon our hearts before the testator dies, there is no power in that law to keep us. There is no strength at all in the Word to cause us to become that Word or to take on the nature of that Word.

(Hebrews 9:18) Whereupon neither the first testament was dedicated without blood.

Jesus Christ has to offer Himself in our bodies as a gift and a sacrifice until He sheds His blood and dies. When this happens, God sees the blood, and this serves as the evidence that the testator has died and now qualifies that person to receive the testament. That portion of the testament that has been inscribed upon his heart has the power to cause that change in the heart of that person. That individual now becomes that potion of the Word, thereby taking on that portion of the nature of Christ.

(Mark 4:20) And these are they which are sown on good ground; such as hear the word, and receive it. . .

(And how is it that they receive the Word? By taken Him into their being and allowing the Word, (Jesus), to go through what He has to in order to fulfills His ministry, thereby, bringing into fruition that Word being inscribed upon their, and they being a living epistle of that portion of the Word inscribed upon their heart

. . .and bring forth fruit, some thirtyfold, some sixty, and some an hundred.

Picking up our cross and following Jesus is not an easy road to travel. However, we are never alone, the Son of God is always with us in Spirit form; *I will not leave you comfortless: I will come to you.* This path is a path of pain, sorrow, affliction and tribulation, but the end result is well worth the price. This is why we must always keep our eyes upon Jesus, He let us know that for the joy that was set before Him, He endured the cross, thereby letting us know that for the joy that is also set before us we can also endure our spiritual cross.

(Hebrews 12:2) Looking unto Jesus the author and finisher of our faith; who for the joy that was set before him endured the cross, despising the shame, and is set down at the right hand of the throne of God.

When Jesus said, "If any man will come after Me, let him deny himself and take up his cross and follow Me". Moreover, when He also said, "I go to prepare a place for you and if I go and prepare a place for you, I will come again and receive you unto myself, that where I am there ye may be also. And whither I go ye know and the way ye know." He was thereby, allowing us to understand that He would have to make that journey first by Himself, in so doing, not only leaving us the footprints for us to follow, but also letting us know that He would come back, (in Spirit form,) and retrace all those steps again, with us, in us, and through us.

He let us know that we would be walking down that same crucifying path, that He did, that would bring us to the Father. Which is why He chose to return and abide in us so as to walk down the same path, some times along side us, but many times carrying us, but all the time willing to die in us to bring about the fruition of Gods plan for our lives.

As the people of God, we need to understand what is happening in the spiritual realm. We also need to understand God's Word in order to know this, but this will never happen until we make God's Word the very reason for which we live. When we make God's Word, (His Son), our all and all and we seek for Him as for buried treasure, then He will begin to reveal Himself to us in a manner that we never could have imagined.

I pray that this book will enlighten your eyes and heart to draw closer to God and that the truths in this book will cause a change in your life as they have in mine. May they inspire you to forsake this world and run after God as you have never run before!

Look for more, Mysteries of the kingdom, revealed, in book two.

luiscaquias@yahoo.com